SCOTTISH
FOOTBALL TABLES
1890-2020

EDITOR
Mike Ross

British Library Cataloguing in Publication Data
A catalogue record for this book is available from the British Library

ISBN: 978-1-86223-426-0

Printed in the UK by 4edge Ltd.

FOREWORD

Following the unprecedented effects of the Covid-19 pandemic, the 2019/2020 Scottish football season was suspended during mid-March 2020 when all sporting events were postponed on public health grounds. It soon became clear that it would not be possible to play further games and so, after some procedural wrangling, SPFL members voted for the season to be curtailed. The play-offs were cancelled and final positions (and promotion and relegation) in each division were calculated by points per game. The season was similarly curtailed in the Highland, Lowland and East of Scotland Leagues where the clubs voted for the teams finishing in top spot in the final tables to be Champions. The tables for 2019/2020 show the final league positions and the points per game on which these placings were decided.

This tenth edition of our Scottish Football Tables book contains coverage of the Scottish Football League from its inception in 1890 through to 2013, the Scottish Premier League from its beginnings in 1998 through to 2013 and the Scottish Professional Football League which commenced in 2013, replacing these two earlier Leagues. This book also covers the Highland Football League from 1893 to the present, the Lowland Football League from 2013 to the present and the East of Scotland League from 1923 through to the present.

In addition to final tables for all of these Leagues, this book also contains information about the semi-finals and finals of both the Scottish F.A. Cup (which commenced in 1874) and the Scottish League Cup (which commenced in 1947), to give a fuller understanding of the statistical history of Scottish Football. At the time of going to press, the semi-final and final matches for the 2019/2020 Scottish F.A. Cup had not been played due to the Covid-19 pandemic. The semi-finals are scheduled for late October and early November and the final will now be played on 20th December. Therefore, these results will be included in next year's edition.

Readers wishing to order copies of other titles we publish, including our Football Tables books which cover English League and Non-League football and another covering Welsh tables, can do so by contacting us using the address and telephone information shown on the page opposite, or by ordering direct via our web site – www.soccer-books.co.uk

THE SCOTTISH LEAGUE – AN OUTLINE HISTORY

1890-91 SEASON The League was formed with the 10 Original Founding Clubs in one Division.

1891-92 SEASON The League was enlarged to 12 Clubs in a single Division.

1892-93 SEASON The League was reduced to 10 Clubs in a single Division.

1893-94 SEASON The League was enlarged to 20 Clubs, comprised of First Division of 10 Clubs and a new Second Division also of 10 Clubs.

1900-01 SEASON The League was enlarged to 21 Clubs by increasing First Division to 11 Clubs.

1901-02 SEASON The League was enlarged to 22 Clubs – a First Division of 10 Clubs and a Second Division of 12 Clubs.

1902-03 SEASON The League was enlarged to 24 Clubs – a First Division of 12 Clubs and a Second Division of 12 Clubs.

1903-04 SEASONS The League was enlarged to 26 Clubs – a First Division of 14 Clubs and a Second Division of 12 Clubs.

1905-06 SEASON The League was enlarged to 28 Clubs – a First Division of 16 Clubs and a Second Division of 12 Clubs.

1906-07 SEASON The League was enlarged to 30 Clubs – a First Division of 18 Clubs and a Second Division of 12 Clubs.

1912-13 SEASON The League was enlarged to 32 Clubs – a First Division of 18 Clubs and a Second Division of 14 Clubs.

1913-14 SEASON The League was altered to a First Division of 20 Clubs and a Second Division of 12 Clubs.

1914-15 SEASON The League was enlarged to 34 Clubs in two Divisions – Division 'A' of 20 Clubs and Division 'B' of 14 Clubs.

1915-16 SEASON The League was reduced to 20 Clubs by eliminating the entire Division 'B'.

1917-18 SEASON The League was further reduced to 18 Clubs.

1919-20 SEASON The League was enlarged to 22 Clubs in a single Division

1921-22 SEASON The League was enlarged to 42 Clubs – a First Division of 22 Clubs and a Second Division of 20 Clubs.

1922-23 SEASON The League was reduced to 40 Clubs in two Divisions of 20 Clubs each.

1928-29 SEASON The League commenced with 40 Clubs but two Second Division Clubs resigned during the season.

1929-30 SEASON The League was enlarged back to 40 Clubs in two Divisions of 20 Clubs each.

1932-33 SEASON The League commenced with 40 Clubs but two Second Division Clubs were expelled during November 1932 and these were not replaced for the 1933-34 season.

1939-46 SEASONS The League was suspended for the duration of the Second World War.

1946-47 SEASON The League was reformed with 30 Clubs comprising Division 'A' of 16 Clubs and Division 'B' of 14 Clubs.

1947-48 SEASON The League was enlarged to 32 Clubs by adding two Clubs to Division 'B'.

1955-56 SEASON The League was enlarged to 37 Clubs – Division 'A' of 18 Clubs and Division 'B' of 19 Clubs.

1956-57 SEASON Division 'A' and Division 'B' were redesignated as First and Second Divisions.

1966-67 SEASON The League was enlarged to 38 Clubs by admission of an additional Second Division Club.

1967-68 SEASON The League reduced to 37 Clubs by the resignation of a Second Division club

1974-75 SEASON The League was enlarged to 38 Clubs by admission of an additional Second Division Club.

1975-76 SEASON The League was restructured into a Premier Division of 10 Clubs, a First Division of 14 Clubs and a Second Division of 14 Clubs.

1986-87 SEASON Premier Division was increased to 12 Clubs & the First Division reduced to 12.

1988-89 SEASON The Premier Division reverted to 10 Clubs and the First Division to 14 Clubs.

1991-92 SEASON Premier Division was increased to 12 Clubs & the First Division reduced to 12.

1994-95 SEASON The League was increased to 40 clubs and restructured to comprise Premier, First, Second and Third Divisions each containing 10 Clubs.

1998-99 SEASON A 10 Club Scottish Premier League, backed by the Scottish F.A., was formed. The Scottish Football League now consists of 3 Divisions of 10 Clubs each.

2000-01 SEASON The Scottish Premier League was increased to 12 clubs. Two extra clubs were promoted from the Scottish Football League and two additional clubs joined the Scottish Football League (from the Highland League) to retain 3 Divisions of 10 Clubs.

2013-14 SEASON The Scottish Premier League and Scottish Football League combined to form a new competition, the Scottish Professional Football League. The overall structure of Scottish football remained the same as from 2000 with a 12 club Premier Division above 3 lower Divisions of 10 Clubs each.

A new Lowland Football League was founded with 12 clubs.

2014-15 SEASON The Lowland Football League was expanded to 14 clubs.

2015-16 SEASON The Lowland Football League was expanded to 15 clubs. From this season onwards, a promotion play-off over two legs is held between the champions of the LFL and the Highland Football League. The winners of this tie then face the bottom SPFL club in a two-leg play-off to decide promotion or relegation.

2015-16 SEASON The Lowland Football League was expanded to 16 clubs.

1874 Scottish F.A. Cup
Semi-finals
Queen's Park vs Renton   2-0
Clydesdale vs Blythwood   4-0
Final
First Hampden Park, 21st March 1874
Queen's Park 2   (McKinnon, Leckie)
Clydesdale 0
Attendance 3,000

1875 Scottish F.A. Cup
Semi-finals
Queen's Park vs Clydesdale   0-0, 2-2, 0-0
Renton vs Dumbarton   0-0, 1-0
Final
First Hampden Park, 10th April 1875
Queen's Park 3   (Weir, Highet, McKinnon)
Renton 0
Attendance 7,000

1876 Scottish F.A. Cup
Semi-finals
Queen's Park vs Vale of Leven   3-1
3rd Lanark Rifle Volunteers vs Dumbarton   3-0
Final
Hamilton Crescent, 11th March 1876
Queen's Park 1   (Highet)
3rd Lanark Rifle Volunteers 1   (Drinnan)
Attendance 10,000

Replay
Hamilton Crescent, 18th March 1876
Queen's Park 2   (Highet 2)
3rd Lanark Rifle Volunteers 0
Attendance 8,000

1877 Scottish F.A. Cup
Semi-finals
Vale of Leven vs Ayr Thistle   9-0
Rangers received a bye
Final
First Hampden Park, 17th March 1877
Vale of Leven 1   (Paton)
Rangers 1   (McDougall (og))
Attendance 12,000

Replay
First Hampden Park, 7th April 1877
Vale of Leven 0
Rangers 0
Attendance 14,000

2nd Replay
First Hampden Park, 13th April 1877
Vale of Leven 3   (Baird, Paton, Watt (og))
Rangers 2   (M. McNiel, W. McNiel)
Attendance 15,000

1878 Scottish F.A. Cup
Semi-final
3rd Lanark Rifle Volunteers vs Renton   1-1, 1-0
Vale of Leven received a bye
Final
First Hampden Park, 30th March 1878
Vale of Leven 1   (Hunter (og))
3rd Lanark Rifle Volunteers 0
Attendance 6,000

1879 Scottish F.A. Cup
Semi-finals
Vale of Leven vs Helensburgh   3-0
Rangers received a bye
Final
First Hampden Park, 19th April 1879
Vale of Leven 1   (McFarlane)
Rangers 1   (Struthers)
Attendance 6,000

Vale of Leven were awarded the trophy after Rangers refused to play in the replay on 26th April 1879. Rangers declined to appear after the Scottish F.A. had turned down a protest that they had scored a legitimate second goal in the first game.

1880 Scottish F.A. Cup
Semi-finals
Queen's Park vs Dumbarton   1-0
Thornliebank vs Pollockshields Athletic   2-1
Final
First Cathkin Park, 21st February 1880
Queen's Park 3   (Highet 2, Ker)
Thornliebank 0
Attendance 7,000

1881 Scottish F.A. Cup
Semi-finals
Dumbarton vs Vale of Leven   2-0
Queen's Park received a bye
Final
Kinning Park, 26th March 1881
Queen's Park 2   (Kay 2)
Dumbarton 1   (Brown)
Attendance 20,000

A replay was ordered after a Dumbarton protest about spectators encroaching onto the pitch was upheld.

Replay
Kinning Park, 9th April 1881
Queen's Park 3   (Smith 3)
Dumbarton 1   (Meikleham)
Attendance 10,000

1882 Scottish F.A. Cup

Semi-finals

Queen's Park vs Kilmarnock Athletic	3-2
Dumbarton vs Cartvale	11-2

Final

First Cathkin Park, 18th March 1882

Queen's Park 2   (Harrower 2)
Dumbarton 2   (Brown, Meikleham)

Attendance 12,000

Replay

First Cathkin Park, 1st April 1882

Queen's Park 4   (Richmond, Ker, Harrower, Fraser)
Dumbarton 1   (Miller)

Attendance 14,000

1883 Scottish F.A. Cup

Semi-finals

Dumbarton vs Pollockshields Athletic	5-0
Vale of Leven vs Kilmarnock Athletic	1-1, 2-0

Final

First Hampden Park, 31st March 1883

Dumbarton 2   (Paton, McArthur)
Vale of Leven 2   (Johnstone, McCrae)

Attendance 11,000

Replay

First Hampden Park, 7th April 1883

Dumbarton 2   (R. Brown (I), R. Brown (II))
Vale of Leven 1   (Friel)

Attendance 15,000

1884 Scottish F.A. Cup

Semi-finals

Hibernian vs Queen's Park	1-5
Vale of Leven vs Rangers	3-0

Final

Queen's Park were awarded the Cup. Vale of Leven asked for the Final to be postponed because of the illness of two of their players and the family bereavement of another. The Scottish F.A. decided that this was impossible due to other engagements, such as the international against England. Vale refused to appear for the Final and the trophy was awarded to Queen's Park.

1885 Scottish F.A. Cup

Semi-finals

Renton vs Hibernian	3-2
Vale of Leven vs Cambuslang	0-0, 3-1

Final

Second Hampden Park, 21st February 1885

Renton 0
Vale of Leven 0

Attendance 3,500

Replay

Second Hampden Park, 28th February 1885

Renton 3   (J. McCall, McIntyre 2)
Vale of Leven 1   (Gillies)

Attendance 7,000

1886 Scottish F.A. Cup

Semi-finals

Third Lanark vs Queen's Park	0-3
Hibernian vs Renton	0-2

Final

First Cathkin Park, 13th February 1886

Queen's Park 3   (Hamilton, Christie, Somerville)
Renton 1   (Kelso)

Attendance 7,000

1887 Scottish F.A. Cup

Semi-finals

Hibernian vs Vale of Leven	3-1
Queen's Park vs Dumbarton	1-2

Final

Second Hampden Park, 12th February 1887

Hibernian 2   (Montgomery, Groves)
Dumbarton 1   (Aitken)

Attendance 11,000

1888 Scottish F.A. Cup

Semi-finals

Renton vs Queen's Park	3-1
Abercorn vs Cambuslang	1-1, 1-10

Final

Second Hampden Park, 4th February 1888

Renton 6   (McNee 2, McCallum 2, McCall 2)
Cambuslang 1   (H. Gourlay)

Attendance 11,000

1889 Scottish F.A. Cup

Semi-finals

Third Lanark vs Renton	2-0
Dumbarton vs Celtic	1-4

Final

Second Hampden Park, 2nd February 1889

Third Lanark 3   (Marshall, Oswald Jnr., Hannah)
Celtic 0

Attendance 18,000

The first game was later declared void due to a snow-covered pitch and was ordered to be replayed.

Replay

Second Hampden Park, 9th February 1889

Third Lanark 2   (Marshall, Oswald Jnr.)
Celtic 1   (McCallum)

Attendance 18,000

1890 Scottish F.A. Cup

Semi-finals

| Queen's Park vs Abercorn | 2-0 |
| Vale of Leven vs Third Lanark | 3-0 |

Final

First Ibrox Park, 15th February 1890

Queen's Park 1 (Sellar)
Vale of Leven 1 (McLachlan)

Attendance 10,000

Replay

First Ibrox Park, 22nd February 1890

Queen's Park 2 (Hamilton, Stewart)
Vale of Leven 1 (Bruce)

Attendance 14,000

SCOTTISH LEAGUE 1890-91

Dumbarton	18	13	3	2	61	21	29
Rangers	18	13	3	2	58	25	29
Celtic	18	11	3	4	48	21	21
Cambuslang	18	8	4	6	47	42	20
Third Lanark	18	8	3	7	38	39	15
Heart of Midlothian	18	6	2	10	31	37	14
Abercorn	18	5	2	11	36	47	12
St. Mirren	18	5	1	12	39	62	11
Vale Of Leven	18	5	1	12	27	65	11
Cowlairs	*18*	*3*	*4*	*11*	*24*	*50*	*6*

Celtic, Third Lanark and Cowlairs had 4 points deducted
Renton were expelled from the League after 5 matches when
their record stood as: 5 1 1 3 10 13 3

1891 Scottish F.A. Cup

Semi-finals

| Heart of Midlothian vs Third Lanark | 4-1 |
| Dumbarton vs Abercorn | 3-1 |

Final

Second Hampden Park, 7th February 1891

Heart of Midlothian 1 (Russell)
Dumbarton 0

Attendance 10, 836

SCOTTISH LEAGUE 1891-92

DUMBARTON	**22**	**18**	**1**	**3**	**79**	**28**	**37**
Celtic	22	16	3	3	62	21	35
Heart of Midlothian	22	15	4	3	65	35	34
Leith Athletic	22	12	1	9	51	40	25
Rangers	22	11	2	9	59	46	24
Third Lanark	22	8	5	9	44	47	21
Renton	22	8	5	9	38	44	21
Clyde	22	8	4	10	63	62	20
Abercorn	22	6	5	11	45	59	17
St. Mirren	22	5	5	12	43	60	15
Cambuslang	*22*	*2*	*6*	*14*	*21*	*53*	*10*
Vale of Leven	*22*	*0*	*5*	*17*	*24*	*99*	*5*

1892 Scottish F.A. Cup

Semi-finals

| Celtic vs Rangers | 5-3 |
| Renton vs Queen's Park | 1-1, 0-3 |

Final

First Ibrox Park, 12th March 1892

Celtic 1 (Campbell)
Queen's Park 0

Attendance 40,000

Due to disruption caused by the large crowd, it was decided
that the first game should be classified as a friendly.

The final was replayed with the entrance fee doubled to
reduce the attendance.

Replay

First Ibrox Park, 9th April 1892

Celtic 5 (Campbell 2, McMahon 2, Sillars (og))
Queen's Park 1 (Waddell)

Attendance 20,000

SCOTTISH LEAGUE 1892-93

CELTIC	**18**	**14**	**1**	**3**	**54**	**25**	**29**
Rangers	18	12	4	2	41	27	28
St. Mirren	18	9	2	7	40	39	20
Third Lanark	18	9	1	8	53	39	19
Heart of Midlothian	18	8	2	8	39	41	18
Leith Athletic	18	8	1	9	35	31	17
Dumbarton	18	8	1	9	35	35	17
Renton	18	5	5	8	31	44	15
Abercorn	*18*	*5*	*1*	*12*	*35*	*52*	*11*
Clyde	*18*	*2*	*2*	*14*	*25*	*55*	*6*

1893 Scottish F.A. Cup

Semi-finals

| Queen's Park vs Broxburn Shamrock | 4-2 |
| Celtic vs St. Bernard's | 5-0 |

Final

First Ibrox Park, 25th February 1893

Queen's Park 0
Celtic 1 (Towie)

Attendance 25,000

The first game was played as a friendly due to a frozen pitch.

Replay

First Ibrox Park, 11th March 1893

Queen's Park 2 (Sellar 2)
Celtic 1 (Blessington)

Attendance 22,000

SCOTTISH DIVISION 1 1893-94

CELTIC	18	14	1	3	53	32	29
Heart of Midlothian	18	11	4	3	46	32	26
St. Bernard's	18	11	1	6	53	39	23
Rangers	18	8	4	6	44	30	20
Dumbarton	18	7	5	6	32	35	19
St. Mirren	18	7	3	8	49	47	17
Third Lanark	18	7	3	8	38	44	17
Dundee	18	6	3	9	47	59	15
Leith Athletic	18	4	2	12	36	46	10
Renton	*18*	*1*	*2*	*15*	*23*	*57*	*4*

SCOTTISH DIVISION 2 1893-94

Hibernian	18	13	3	2	83	29	29
Cowlairs	18	13	1	4	72	32	27
Clyde	18	11	2	5	51	36	24
Motherwell	18	11	1	6	61	46	23
Partick Thistle	18	10	0	8	56	58	20
Port Glasgow Athletic	18	9	2	7	52	52	13
Abercorn	18	5	2	11	42	60	12
Greenock Morton	18	4	1	13	36	62	9
Northern	*18*	*3*	*3*	*12*	*29*	*66*	*9*
Thistle	*18*	*2*	*3*	*13*	*31*	*72*	*7*

Port Glasgow Athletic had 7 points deducted

1894 Scottish F.A. Cup

Semi-finals

Rangers vs Queen's Park	1-1, 3-1
Third Lanark vs Celtic	3-5

Final

Second Hampden Park, 17th February 1894

Rangers 3   (H. McCreadie, Barker, McPherson)
Celtic 1   (W. Maley)

Attendance 17,000

SCOTTISH DIVISION 1 1894-95

HEART OF MIDLOTHIAN	18	15	1	2	50	18	31
Celtic	18	11	4	3	50	29	26
Rangers	18	10	2	6	41	26	22
Third Lanark	18	10	1	7	51	39	21
St. Mirren	18	9	1	8	34	34	19
St. Bernards	18	8	1	9	37	40	17
Clyde	18	8	0	10	38	47	16
Dundee	18	6	2	10	28	33	14
Leith Athletic	*18*	*3*	*1*	*14*	*32*	*64*	*7*
Dumbarton	18	3	1	14	27	58	7

SCOTTISH DIVISION 2 1894-95

Hibernian	18	14	2	2	92	28	30
Motherwell	18	10	2	6	56	39	22
Port Glasgow Athletic	18	8	4	6	62	56	20
Renton	18	10	0	8	46	44	20
Greenock Morton	18	9	1	8	59	63	19
Airdrieonians	18	8	2	8	68	45	18
Partick Thistle	18	8	2	8	51	59	18
Abercorn	18	7	3	8	48	66	17
Dundee Wanderers	*18*	*4*	*1*	*13*	*44*	*86*	*9*
Cowlairs	*18*	*2*	*3*	*13*	*37*	*77*	*7*

1895 Scottish F.A. Cup

Semi-finals

Heart of Midlothian vs St. Bernard's	0-0, 0-1
Dundee vs Renton	1-1, 3-3, 0-3

Final

First Ibrox Park, 20th April 1895

St. Bernard's 2   (Cleland 2)
Renton 1   (Duncan)

Attendance 15,000

SCOTTISH DIVISION 1 1895-96

CELTIC	18	15	0	3	64	25	30
Rangers	18	11	4	3	57	39	26
Hibernian	18	11	2	5	58	39	24
Heart of Midlothian	18	11	0	7	68	36	22
Dundee	18	7	2	9	33	42	16
Third Lanark	18	7	1	10	47	51	15
St. Bernards	18	7	1	10	36	53	15
St. Mirren	18	5	3	10	31	51	13
Clyde	18	4	3	11	39	59	11
Dumbarton	*18*	*4*	*0*	*14*	*36*	*74*	*8*

SCOTTISH DIVISION 2 1895-96

Abercorn	18	12	3	3	55	31	27
Leith Athletic	18	11	1	6	55	37	23
Renton	18	9	3	6	40	28	21
Kilmarnock	18	10	1	7	50	45	21
Airdrieonians	18	7	4	7	48	44	18
Partick Thistle	18	8	2	8	46	54	18
Port Glasgow Athletic	18	6	4	8	40	41	16
Motherwell	18	5	3	10	31	52	13
Greenock Morton	18	4	4	10	32	42	12
Linthouse	18	5	1	12	25	48	11

1896 Scottish F.A. Cup

Semi-finals

Heart of Midlothian vs St. Bernard's	1-0
Hibernian vs Renton	2-1

Final

Logie Green, Edinburgh, 14th March 1896

Heart of Midlothian 3   (Walker, King, Mitchell)
Hibernian 1   (O'Neill)

Attendance 17,034

SCOTTISH DIVISION 1 1896-97

HEART OF MIDLOTHIAN	18	13	2	3	47	22	28
Hibernian	18	12	2	4	50	20	26
Rangers	18	11	3	4	64	30	25
Celtic	18	10	4	4	42	18	24
Dundee	18	10	2	6	38	30	22
St. Mirren	18	9	1	8	38	29	19
St. Bernards	18	7	0	11	32	40	14
Third Lanark	18	5	1	12	29	46	11
Clyde	18	4	0	14	27	65	8
Abercorn	*18*	*1*	*1*	*16*	*21*	*88*	*3*

SCOTTISH DIVISION 2 1896-97

Partick Thistle	18	14	3	1	61	28	31
Leith Athletic	18	13	1	4	54	27	27
Kilmarnock	18	10	1	7	42	33	21
Airdrieonians	18	10	1	7	49	39	21
Greenock Morton	18	7	2	9	38	40	16
Linthouse	18	8	2	8	44	53	14
Renton	18	6	2	10	34	40	14
Port Glasgow Athletic	18	4	5	9	38	50	13
Motherwell	18	6	1	11	40	53	13
Dumbarton	*18*	*2*	*2*	*14*	*27*	*64*	*6*

Linthouse had 4 points deducted

1897 Scottish F.A. Cup

Semi-finals

Morton vs Rangers	2-7
Dumbarton vs Kilmarnock	4-3

Final

Second Hampden Park, 20th March 1897

Rangers 5   (Miller 2, Hyslop, McPherson, Smith)
Dumbarton 1   (W. Thomson)

Attendance 15,000

SCOTTISH DIVISION 1 1897-98

CELTIC	18	15	3	0	56	13	33
Rangers	18	13	3	2	71	15	29
Hibernian	18	10	2	6	47	29	22
Heart of Midlothian	18	8	4	6	54	33	20
Third Lanark	18	8	2	8	37	38	18
St. Mirren	18	8	2	8	30	36	18
Dundee	18	5	3	10	29	36	13
Partick Thistle	18	6	1	11	34	64	13
St. Bernard's	18	4	1	13	35	67	9
Clyde	18	1	3	14	21	83	5

SCOTTISH DIVISION 2 1897-98

Kilmarnock	18	14	1	3	64	29	29
Port Glasgow Athletic	18	12	1	5	66	36	25
Greenock Morton	18	9	4	5	47	38	22
Leith Athletic	18	9	2	7	40	39	20
Linthouse	18	6	4	8	38	39	16
Ayr	18	7	2	9	36	42	16
Abercorn	18	6	4	8	33	41	16
Airdrieonians	18	6	2	10	44	56	14
Hamilton Academical	18	5	2	11	26	51	12
Motherwell	18	3	4	11	31	56	10

Renton resigned after 4 matches and their fixtures were taken over by Hamilton Academical. Their individual records were:

Renton	4	0	0	4	2	19	0
Hamilton Academical	14	5	2	7	26	32	12

1898 Scottish F.A. Cup

Semi-finals

Rangers vs Third Lanark	1-1, 2-2, 2-0
Kilmarnock vs Dundee	3-2

Final

Second Hampden Park, 26th March 1898

Rangers 2   (A. Smith, Hamilton)
Kilmarnock 0

Attendance 15,000

SCOTTISH DIVISION 1 1898-99

RANGERS	18	18	0	0	79	18	36
Heart of Midlothian	18	12	2	4	56	30	26
Celtic	18	11	2	5	51	33	24
Hibernian	18	10	3	5	42	43	23
St. Mirren	18	8	4	6	46	32	20
Third Lanark	18	7	3	8	33	38	17
St. Bernard's	18	4	4	10	30	37	12
Clyde	18	4	4	10	23	48	12
Partick Thistle	*18*	*2*	*2*	*14*	*19*	*58*	*6*
Dundee	18	1	2	15	23	65	4

SCOTTISH DIVISION 2 1898-99

Kilmarnock	18	14	4	0	73	24	32
Leith Athletic	18	12	3	3	63	38	27
Port Glasgow Athletic	18	12	1	5	75	51	25
Motherwell	18	7	6	5	41	40	20
Hamilton Academical	18	7	1	10	48	58	15
Airdrieonians	18	6	3	9	36	46	15
Greenock Morton	18	6	1	11	36	42	13
Ayr	18	5	3	10	35	52	13
Linthouse	18	5	1	12	29	62	11
Abercorn	18	4	1	13	42	65	9

1899 Scottish F.A. Cup

Semi-finals

Celtic vs Port Glasgow Athletic	4-2
St. Mirren vs Rangers	1-2

Final

Second Hampden Park, 22nd April 1899

Celtic 2   (McMahon, Hodge)
Rangers 0

Attendance 25,000

SCOTTISH DIVISION 1 1899-1900

RANGERS	18	15	2	1	69	27	32
Celtic	18	9	7	2	46	27	25
Hibernian	18	9	6	3	43	24	24
Heart of Midlothian	18	10	3	5	41	24	23
Kilmarnock	18	6	6	6	30	37	18
Dundee	18	4	7	7	36	39	15
Third Lanark	18	5	5	8	31	38	15
St. Mirren	18	3	6	9	30	46	12
St. Bernard's	*18*	*4*	*4*	*10*	*29*	*47*	*12*
Clyde	*18*	*2*	*0*	*16*	*24*	*70*	*4*

SCOTTISH DIVISION 2 1899-1900

Partick Thistle	18	14	1	3	56	26	29
Greenock Morton	18	14	0	4	66	25	28
Port Glasgow Athletic	18	10	0	8	50	41	20
Motherwell	18	9	1	8	38	36	19
Leith Athletic	18	9	1	8	33	37	19
Abercorn	18	7	2	9	46	39	16
Hamilton Academical	18	7	1	10	33	47	15
Ayr	18	6	2	10	39	48	14
Airdrieonians	18	4	3	11	27	49	11
Linthouse	*18*	*2*	*5*	*11*	*28*	*68*	*9*

1900 Scottish F.A. Cup

Semi-finals

Celtic vs Rangers   2-2, 4-0
Queen's Park vs Heart of Midlothian   2-1

Final

Second Ibrox Park, 14th April 1900

Celtic 4   (McMahon, Divers 2, Bell)
Queen's Park 3   (Christie, W. Stewart, Battles (og))

Attendance 18,000

SCOTTISH DIVISION 1 1900-01

RANGERS	20	17	1	2	60	25	35
Celtic	20	13	3	4	49	28	29
Hibernian	20	9	7	4	29	22	25
Greenock Morton	20	9	3	8	40	40	21
Kilmarnock	20	7	4	9	35	47	18
Third Lanark	20	6	6	8	20	29	18
Dundee	20	6	5	9	36	35	17
Queen's Park	20	7	3	10	33	37	17
St. Mirren	20	5	6	9	33	43	16
Heart of Midlothian	20	5	4	11	22	30	14
Partick Thistle	*20*	*4*	*2*	*14*	*28*	*49*	*10*

SCOTTISH DIVISION 2 1900-01

St. Bernard's	18	11	4	3	42	26	26
Airdrieonians	18	11	1	6	43	32	23
Abercorn	18	9	3	6	37	33	21
Clyde	18	9	2	7	43	35	20
Port Glasgow Athletic	18	10	0	8	45	43	20
Ayr	18	9	0	9	32	34	18
East Stirlingshire	18	7	3	8	34	39	17
Hamilton Academical	18	4	4	10	41	49	12
Leith Athletic	18	5	2	11	22	32	12
Motherwell	18	4	3	11	26	42	11

1901 Scottish F.A. Cup

Semi-finals

Heart of Midlothian vs Hibernian   1-1, 2-1
Celtic vs St. Mirren   1-0

Final

Second Ibrox Park, 6th April 1901

Heart of Midlothian 4   (Walker, Davidson (og),
Thomson, Bell)
Celtic 3   (McOustra 2, McMahon)

Attendance 12,000

SCOTTISH DIVISION 1 1901-02

RANGERS	18	13	2	3	43	29	28
Celtic	18	11	4	3	38	28	26
Heart of Midlothian	18	10	2	6	32	21	22
Third Lanark	18	7	5	6	30	26	19
St. Mirren	18	8	3	7	29	28	19
Hibernian	18	6	4	8	36	23	16
Kilmarnock	18	5	6	7	21	25	16
Queen's Park	18	5	4	9	21	32	14
Dundee	18	4	5	9	15	31	13
Greenock Morton	18	1	5	12	18	40	7

SCOTTISH DIVISION 2 1901-02

Port Glasgow Athletic	22	14	4	4	71	31	32
Partick Thistle	22	13	4	5	55	26	30
Motherwell	22	12	2	8	50	44	26
Airdrieonians	22	10	5	7	41	32	25
Hamilton Academical	22	11	3	8	45	40	25
St. Bernard's	22	10	2	10	30	31	22
Leith Athletic	22	9	3	10	33	38	21
Ayr	22	8	5	9	27	33	21
East Stirlingshire	22	8	3	11	36	45	19
Arthurlie	22	6	5	11	32	42	17
Clyde	22	5	3	14	22	50	13
Abercorn	22	4	5	13	27	57	13

1902 Scottish F.A. Cup

Semi-finals

Hibernian vs Rangers   2-0
Celtic vs St. Mirren   3-2

Final

Celtic Park, 26th April 1902

Hibernian 1   (McGeachan)
Celtic 0

Attendance 15,000

SCOTTISH DIVISION 1 1902-03

HIBERNIAN	22	16	5	1	48	18	37
Dundee	22	13	5	4	31	12	31
Rangers	22	12	5	5	56	30	29
Heart of Midlothian	22	11	6	5	46	27	28
Celtic	22	8	10	4	36	30	26
St. Mirren	22	7	8	7	39	40	22
Third Lanark	22	8	5	9	34	27	21
Partick Thistle	22	6	7	9	34	50	19
Kilmarnock	22	6	4	12	24	43	16
Queen's Park	22	5	5	12	33	48	15
Port Glasgow Athletic	22	3	5	14	26	49	11
Greenock Morton	22	2	5	15	22	55	9

SCOTTISH DIVISION 2 1902-03

Airdrieonians	22	15	5	2	43	19	35
Motherwell	22	12	4	6	44	35	28
Ayr	22	12	3	7	34	24	27
Leith Athletic	22	11	5	6	43	42	27
St. Bernard's	22	12	2	8	45	32	26
Hamilton Academical	22	12	1	9	47	34	25
Falkirk	22	8	7	7	39	37	23
East Stirlingshire	22	9	3	10	46	41	21
Arthurlie	22	5	8	9	33	48	18
Abercorn	22	5	2	15	35	58	12
Raith Rovers	22	3	5	14	34	55	11
Clyde	22	2	7	13	22	40	11

1903 Scottish F.A. Cup

Semi-finals

| Rangers vs Stenhousemuir | 4-1 |
| Dundee vs Heart of Midlothian | 0-0, 0-1 |

Final

Celtic Park, 11th April 1903

Rangers 1   (Stark)
Heart of Midlothian 1   (Walker)

Attendance 35,000

Replay

Celtic Park, 18th April 1903

Rangers 0
Heart of Midlothian 0

Attendance 16,000

2nd Replay

Celtic Park, 25th April 1903

Rangers 2   (Mackie, Hamilton)
Heart of Midlothian 0

Attendance 35,000

SCOTTISH DIVISION 1 1903-04

THIRD LANARK	**26**	**20**	**3**	**3**	**61**	**26**	**43**
Heart of Midlothian	26	18	3	5	63	35	39
Celtic	26	18	2	6	69	28	38
Rangers	26	16	6	4	80	33	38
Dundee	26	13	2	11	54	45	28
St. Mirren	26	11	5	10	45	38	27
Partick Thistle	26	10	7	9	43	40	27
Queen's Park	26	6	9	11	28	47	21
Port Glasgow Athletic	26	8	4	14	33	49	20
Hibernian	26	7	5	14	31	42	19
Greenock Morton	26	7	4	15	31	51	18
Airdrieonians	26	7	4	15	32	62	18
Motherwell	26	6	3	17	26	61	15
Kilmarnock	26	4	5	17	26	65	13

SCOTTISH DIVISION 2 1903-04

Hamilton Academical	22	16	5	1	56	19	37
Clyde	22	12	5	5	51	36	29
Ayr	22	11	6	5	33	30	28
Falkirk	22	11	4	7	50	36	26
Raith Rovers	22	8	5	9	40	38	21
East Stirlingshire	22	8	5	9	35	40	21
Leith Athletic	22	8	4	10	42	40	20
St. Bernard's	22	9	2	11	31	43	20
Albion Rovers	22	8	5	9	47	37	19
Abercorn	22	6	4	12	40	55	16
Arthurlie	22	5	5	12	37	50	15
Ayr Parkhouse	***22***	***3***	***4***	***15***	***23***	***61***	***10***

Albion Rovers had 2 points deducted

1904 Scottish F.A. Cup

Semi-finals

| Celtic vs Third Lanark | 2-1 |
| Rangers vs Morton | 3-0 |

Final

Third Hampden Park, 16th April 1904

Celtic 3   (Quinn 3)
Rangers 2   (Speedie 2)

Attendance 65,000

SCOTTISH DIVISION 1 1904-05

CELTIC	**26**	**18**	**5**	**3**	**68**	**31**	**41**
Rangers	26	19	3	4	83	28	41
Third Lanark	26	14	7	5	60	28	35
Airdrieonians	26	11	5	10	38	45	27
Hibernian	26	9	8	9	39	39	26
Partick Thistle	26	12	2	12	36	56	26
Dundee	26	10	5	11	38	32	25
Heart of Midlothian	26	11	3	12	46	44	25
Kilmarnock	26	9	5	12	29	45	23
St. Mirren	26	9	4	13	33	36	22
Port Glasgow Athletic	26	8	5	13	30	51	21
Queen's Park	26	6	8	12	28	45	20
Greenock Morton	26	7	4	15	27	50	18
Motherwell	26	6	2	18	28	53	14

SCOTTISH DIVISION 2 1904-05

Clyde	22	13	6	3	38	22	32
Falkirk	**22**	**12**	**4**	**6**	**31**	**25**	**28**
Hamilton Academical	22	12	3	7	40	22	27
Leith Athletic	22	10	4	8	36	26	24
Ayr	22	11	1	10	46	37	23
Arthurlie	22	9	5	8	37	42	23
Aberdeen	**22**	**7**	**7**	**8**	**36**	**26**	**21**
Albion Rovers	22	8	4	10	38	53	20
East Stirlingshire	22	7	5	10	38	38	19
Raith Rovers	22	9	1	12	30	34	19
Abercorn	22	8	1	13	31	45	17
St. Bernard's	22	3	5	14	23	54	11

1905 Scottish F.A. Cup

Semi-finals

| Airdrieonians vs Third Lanark | 1-2 |
| Celtic vs Rangers | 0-2 |

Final

Hampden Park, 8th April 1905

Third Lanark 0
Rangers 0

Attendance 55,000

Replay

Hampden Park, 15th April 1905

Third Lanark 3   (Wilson 2, Johnstone)
Rangers 1   (Smith)

Attendance 40,000

SCOTTISH DIVISION 1 1905-06

CELTIC	**30**	**24**	**1**	**5**	**76**	**19**	**49**
Heart of Midlothian	30	18	7	5	64	27	43
Airdrieonians	30	15	8	7	53	31	38
Rangers	30	15	7	8	58	48	37
Partick Thistle	30	15	6	9	44	40	36
Third Lanark	30	16	2	12	62	38	34
Dundee	30	11	12	7	40	34	34
St. Mirren	30	13	5	12	41	37	31
Motherwell	30	9	8	13	50	64	26
Greenock Morton	30	10	6	14	35	54	26
Hibernian	30	10	5	15	35	40	25
Aberdeen	30	8	8	14	37	49	24
Falkirk	30	9	5	16	54	69	23
Kilmarnock	30	8	4	18	46	68	20
Port Glasgow Athletic	30	6	8	16	38	68	20
Queen's Park	30	5	4	21	41	88	14

SCOTTISH DIVISION 2 1905-06

Leith Athletic	22	15	4	3	46	22	34
Clyde	**22**	**11**	**9**	**2**	**38**	**21**	**31**
Albion Rovers	22	12	3	7	48	33	27
Hamilton Academical	**22**	**12**	**2**	**8**	**45**	**33**	**26**
St. Bernard's	22	9	4	9	42	34	22
Arthurlie	22	10	2	10	46	45	22
Ayr	22	9	3	10	44	51	21
Raith Rovers	22	6	7	9	38	42	19
Cowdenbeath	22	7	3	12	27	40	17
Abercorn	22	6	5	11	31	46	17
Vale of Leven	22	6	4	12	33	50	16
East Stirlingshire	22	1	10	11	26	47	12

1906 Scottish F.A. Cup

Semi-finals

Port Glasgow Athletic vs Heart of Midlothian	0-2
St. Mirren vs Third Lanark	1-1, 0-0, 0-1

Final

Ibrox Park, 28th April 1906

Heart of Midlothian 1   (G. Wilson)

Third Lanark 0

Attendance 25,000

SCOTTISH DIVISION 1 1906-07

CELTIC	**34**	**23**	**9**	**2**	**80**	**30**	**55**
Dundee	34	18	12	4	53	26	48
Rangers	34	19	7	8	69	33	45
Airdrieonians	34	18	6	10	59	44	42
Falkirk	34	17	7	10	73	58	41
Third Lanark	34	15	9	10	57	48	39
St. Mirren	34	12	13	9	50	44	37
Clyde	34	15	6	13	47	52	36
Heart of Midlothian	34	11	13	10	46	43	35
Motherwell	34	12	9	13	45	48	33
Aberdeen	34	10	10	14	48	55	30
Hibernian	34	10	10	14	40	49	30
Greenock Morton	34	11	6	17	41	50	28
Partick Thistle	34	9	8	17	40	60	26
Queen's Park	34	9	6	19	51	66	24
Hamilton Academical	34	8	5	21	40	64	21
Kilmarnock	34	8	5	21	40	72	21
Port Glasgow Athletic	34	7	7	20	30	67	21

SCOTTISH DIVISION 2 1906-07

St. Bernard's	22	14	4	4	41	24	32
Vale of Leven	22	13	1	8	54	35	27
Arthurlie	22	12	3	7	51	39	27
Dumbarton	22	11	3	8	52	35	25
Leith Athletic	22	10	4	8	40	35	24
Albion Rovers	22	10	3	9	43	36	23
Cowdenbeath	22	10	5	7	36	39	23
Ayr	22	7	6	9	34	38	20
Abercorn	22	5	7	10	29	47	17
Raith Rovers	22	6	4	12	39	48	16
East Stirlingshire	22	6	4	12	36	48	16
Ayr Parkhouse	22	5	2	15	32	63	12

Cowdenbeath had 2 points deducted

1907 Scottish F.A. Cup

Semi-finals

Celtic vs Hibernian	0-0, 0-0, 3-0
Heart of Midlothian vs Queen's Park	1-0

Final

Hampden Park, 20th April 1907

Celtic 3   (Orr (pen), Somers 2)

Heart of Midlothian 0

Attendance 50,000

SCOTTISH DIVISION 1 1907-08

CELTIC	**34**	**24**	**7**	**3**	**86**	**27**	**55**
Falkirk	34	22	7	5	103	41	51
Rangers	34	21	8	5	74	40	50
Dundee	34	20	8	6	71	28	48
Hibernian	34	17	8	9	55	42	42
Airdrieonians	34	18	5	11	58	41	41
St. Mirren	34	13	10	11	50	59	36
Aberdeen	34	13	9	12	45	44	35
Third Lanark	34	13	7	14	45	50	33
Motherwell	34	12	7	15	61	53	31
Hamilton Academical	34	10	8	16	54	65	28
Heart of Midlothian	34	11	6	17	50	62	28
Greenock Morton	34	9	9	16	43	66	27
Partick Thistle	34	8	9	17	43	69	25
Kilmarnock	34	6	13	15	38	61	25
Queen's Park	34	7	8	19	54	84	22
Clyde	34	5	8	21	36	75	18
Port Glasgow Athletic	34	5	7	22	39	98	17

SCOTTISH DIVISION 2 1907-08

Raith Rovers	22	14	2	6	37	23	30
Dumbarton	22	12	5	5	49	32	27
Ayr	22	11	5	6	39	33	27
Abercorn	22	9	5	8	33	30	23
East Stirlingshire	22	9	5	8	30	32	23
Ayr Parkhouse	22	11	0	11	38	37	22
Leith Athletic	22	8	5	9	41	40	21
St. Bernard's	22	8	5	9	31	32	21
Albion Rovers	22	7	5	10	36	48	19
Vale of Leven	22	5	8	9	25	31	18
Arthurlie	22	6	5	11	33	45	17
Cowdenbeath	22	5	4	13	26	35	14

Dumbarton had 2 points deducted

1908 Scottish F.A. Cup

Semi-finals

Aberdeen vs Celtic	0-1
Kilmarnock vs St. Mirren	0-0, 0-2

Final

Hampden Park, 18th April 1908

Celtic 5   (Bennett 2, Hamilton, Somers, Quinn)

St. Mirren 1   (Cunningham)

Attendance 55,000

SCOTTISH DIVISION 1 1908-09

CELTIC	34	23	5	6	71	24	51
Dundee	34	22	6	6	70	32	50
Clyde	34	21	6	7	61	37	48
Rangers	34	19	7	8	91	38	45
Airdrieonians	34	16	9	9	67	46	41
Hibernian	34	16	7	11	40	32	39
St. Mirren	34	15	6	13	53	45	36
Aberdeen	34	15	6	13	61	53	36
Falkirk	34	13	7	14	58	56	33
Kilmarnock	34	13	7	14	47	61	33
Third Lanark	34	11	10	13	56	49	32
Heart of Midlothian	34	12	8	14	54	49	32
Port Glasgow Athletic	34	10	8	16	39	52	28
Motherwell	34	11	6	17	47	73	28
Queen's Park	34	6	13	15	42	65	25
Hamilton Academical	34	6	12	16	42	72	24
Greenock Morton	34	8	7	19	39	90	23
Partick Thistle	34	2	4	28	38	102	8

SCOTTISH DIVISION 1 1909-10

CELTIC	34	24	6	4	63	22	54
Falkirk	34	22	8	4	71	28	52
Rangers	34	20	6	8	70	35	46
Aberdeen	34	16	8	10	44	29	40
Clyde	34	14	9	11	47	40	37
Dundee	34	14	8	12	52	44	36
Third Lanark	34	13	8	13	62	44	34
Hibernian	34	14	6	14	33	40	34
Airdrieonians	34	12	9	13	46	57	33
Motherwell	34	12	8	14	59	60	32
Kilmarnock	34	12	8	14	53	59	32
Heart of Midlothian	34	12	7	15	59	50	31
St. Mirren	34	13	5	16	48	58	31
Queen's Park	34	12	6	16	54	74	30
Hamilton Academical	34	11	6	17	50	67	28
Partick Thistle	34	8	10	16	45	59	26
Greenock Morton	34	11	3	20	38	60	25
Port Glasgow Athletic	*34*	*3*	*5*	*26*	*25*	*93*	*11*

SCOTTISH DIVISION 2 1908-09

Abercorn	22	13	5	4	39	16	31
Raith Rovers	22	11	6	5	46	22	28
Vale of Leven	22	12	4	6	38	25	28
Dumbarton	22	10	5	7	34	34	25
Ayr	22	10	3	9	43	36	23
Leith Athletic	22	10	3	9	37	33	23
Ayr Parkhouse	22	8	5	9	29	31	21
St. Bernard's	22	9	3	10	34	37	21
East Stirlingshire	22	9	3	10	27	33	21
Albion Rovers	22	9	2	11	36	47	20
Cowdenbeath	22	4	4	14	19	42	12
Arthurlie	22	5	1	16	29	55	11

SCOTTISH DIVISION 2 1909-10

Leith Athletic	22	13	7	2	43	18	33
Raith Rovers	**22**	**14**	**5**	**3**	**35**	**20**	**33**
St. Bernard's	22	12	3	7	43	31	27
Dumbarton	22	9	5	8	44	38	23
Abercorn	22	7	8	7	38	39	22
Vale of Leven	22	8	5	9	36	38	21
Ayr	22	9	3	10	37	40	21
East Stirlingshire	22	9	2	11	37	43	20
Albion Rovers	22	7	5	10	34	39	19
Arthurlie	22	6	5	11	34	47	17
Cowdenbeath	22	7	3	12	22	34	17
Ayr Parkhouse	22	4	3	15	27	43	11

Ayr merged with Ayr Parkhouse to become Ayr United for the next season

1909 Scottish F.A. Cup

Semi-final

Celtic vs Clyde	0-0, 2-0
Falkirk vs Rangers	0-1

Final

Hampden Park, 10th April 1909

Celtic 2   *(Quinn, Munro)*

Rangers 2   *(Gilchrist, Bennett)*

Attendance 70,000

Replay

Hampden Park, 17th April 1909

Celtic 1   *(Quinn)*

Rangers 1   *(Gordon)*

Attendance 60,000

When, as stated in the rules, extra time was not played at the end of the game, the crowd rioted and over a hundred people were injured. As a result, both clubs refused to play a third match and the Scottish F.A. agreed that the trophy would not be awarded for this season.

1910 Scottish F.A. Cup

Semi-finals

Hibernian vs Dundee	0-0, 0-0, 0-1
Clyde vs Celtic	3-1

Final

Ibrox Park, 9th April 1910

Dundee 2   *(Hunter, Langlands)*

Clyde 2   *(Chalmers, Booth)*

Attendance 60,000

Replay

Ibrox Park, 16th April 1910

Dundee 0

Clyde 0   *(aet.)*

Attendance 22,000

2nd Replay

Ibrox Park, 20th April 1910

Dundee 2   *(Bellamy, Hunter)*

Clyde 1   *(Chalmers)*

Attendance 25,000

SCOTTISH DIVISION 1 1910-11

RANGERS	34	23	6	5	90	34	52
Aberdeen	34	19	10	5	53	28	48
Falkirk	34	17	10	7	65	42	44
Partick Thistle	34	17	8	9	50	41	42
Celtic	34	15	11	8	48	18	41
Dundee	34	18	5	11	54	42	41
Clyde	34	14	11	9	45	36	39
Third Lanark	34	16	7	11	59	53	39
Hibernian	34	15	6	13	44	48	36
Kilmarnock	34	12	10	12	42	45	34
Airdrieonians	34	12	9	13	49	53	33
St. Mirren	34	12	7	15	46	57	31
Greenock Morton	34	9	11	14	49	51	29
Heart of Midlothian	34	8	8	18	42	59	24
Raith Rovers	34	7	10	17	36	55	24
Hamilton Academical	34	8	5	21	31	60	21
Motherwell	34	8	4	22	37	66	20
Queen's Park	34	5	4	25	28	80	14

SCOTTISH DIVISION 2 1910-11

Dumbarton	22	15	1	6	52	30	31
Ayr United	22	12	3	7	54	36	27
Albion Rovers	22	10	5	7	26	21	25
Leith Athletic	22	10	5	7	44	43	25
Cowdenbeath	22	9	5	8	31	27	23
St. Bernard's	22	10	2	10	36	41	22
East Stirlingshire	22	7	6	9	28	34	20
Dundee Hibernians	22	7	5	10	29	36	19
Arthurlie	22	7	5	10	26	33	19
Abercorn	22	9	1	12	39	50	19
Port Glasgow Athletic	*22*	*8*	*2*	*12*	*27*	*33*	*18*
Vale of Leven	22	4	8	10	21	29	16

1911 Scottish F.A. Cup

Semi-finals

Celtic vs Aberdeen	1-0
Hamilton Academical vs Dundee	3-2

Final

Ibrox Park, 8th April 1911

Celtic 0
Hamilton Academical 0

Attendance 45,000

Replay

Ibrox Park, 15th April 1911

Celtic 2 (Quinn, McAteer)
Hamilton Academical 0

Attendance 25,000

SCOTTISH DIVISION 1 1911-12

RANGERS	34	24	3	7	86	34	51
Celtic	34	17	11	6	58	33	45
Clyde	34	19	4	11	56	32	42
Heart of Midlothian	34	16	8	10	54	40	40
Partick Thistle	34	16	8	10	47	40	40
Greenock Morton	34	14	9	11	44	44	37
Falkirk	34	15	6	13	46	43	36
Dundee	34	13	9	12	52	41	35
Aberdeen	34	14	7	13	44	44	35
Airdrieonians	34	12	8	14	40	41	32
Third Lanark	34	12	7	15	40	57	31
Hamilton Academical	34	11	8	15	32	44	30
Hibernian	34	12	5	17	44	47	29
Motherwell	34	11	5	18	34	44	27
Raith Rovers	34	9	9	16	39	59	27
Kilmarnock	34	11	4	19	38	60	26
Queen's Park	34	8	9	17	29	53	25
St. Mirren	34	7	10	17	32	59	24

SCOTTISH DIVISION 2 1911-12

Ayr United	22	16	3	3	54	24	35
Abercorn	22	13	4	5	43	22	30
Dumbarton	22	13	1	8	47	31	27
Cowdenbeath	22	12	2	8	39	31	26
St. Johnstone	22	10	4	8	29	27	24
St. Bernard's	22	9	5	8	38	36	23
Leith Athletic	22	9	4	9	31	34	22
Arthurlie	22	7	5	10	30	30	19
East Stirlingshire	22	7	3	12	21	31	17
Dundee Hibernians	22	5	5	12	21	41	15
Vale of Leven	22	6	1	15	26	50	13
Albion Rovers	22	6	1	15	19	41	13

1912 Scottish F.A. Cup

Semi-finals

Celtic vs Heart of Midlothian	3-0
Clyde vs Third Lanark	3-1

Final

Ibrox Park, 6th April 1912

Celtic 2 (McMenemy, Gallacher)
Clyde 0

Attendance 50,000

SCOTTISH DIVISION 1 1912-13

RANGERS	34	24	5	5	76	41	53
Celtic	34	22	5	7	53	28	49
Heart of Midlothian	34	17	7	10	71	43	41
Airdrieonians	34	15	11	8	64	46	41
Falkirk	34	14	12	8	56	38	40
Motherwell	34	12	13	9	47	39	37
Aberdeen	34	14	9	11	47	40	37
Hibernian	34	16	5	13	63	54	37
Clyde	34	13	9	12	41	44	35
Hamilton Academical	34	12	8	14	44	47	32
Kilmarnock	34	10	11	13	37	54	31
St. Mirren	34	10	10	14	50	60	30
Greenock Morton	34	11	7	16	50	59	29
Dundee	34	8	13	13	33	46	29
Third Lanark	34	8	12	14	31	41	28
Raith Rovers	34	8	10	16	46	60	26
Partick Thistle	34	10	4	20	40	55	24
Queen's Park	34	5	3	26	34	88	13

SCOTTISH DIVISION 2 1912-13

Ayr United	26	13	8	5	45	19	34
Dunfermline Athletic	26	13	7	6	45	27	33
East Stirlingshire	26	12	8	6	43	27	32
Abercorn	26	12	7	7	33	31	31
Cowdenbeath	26	12	6	8	36	27	30
Dumbarton	26	12	5	9	38	30	29
St. Bernard's	26	12	3	11	36	34	27
Johnstone	26	9	6	11	31	43	24
Albion Rovers	26	10	3	13	38	40	23
Dundee Hibernians	26	6	10	10	34	43	22
St. Johnstone	26	7	7	12	29	38	21
Vale of Leven	26	8	5	13	28	44	21
Arthurlie	26	7	5	14	37	49	19
Leith Athletic	26	5	8	13	26	47	18

1913 Scottish F.A. Cup

Semi-finals

Falkirk vs Heart of Midlothian	1-0
Raith Rovers vs Clyde	1-1, 1-0

Final

Celtic Park, 12th April 1913

Falkirk 2   (Robertson, Logan)
Raith Rovers 0

Attendance 45,000

SCOTTISH DIVISION 1 1913-14

CELTIC	38	30	5	3	81	14	65
Rangers	38	27	5	6	79	31	59
Heart of Midlothian	38	23	8	7	70	29	54
Greenock Morton	38	26	2	10	76	51	54
Falkirk	38	20	9	9	69	51	49
Airdrieonians	38	18	12	8	72	43	48
Dundee	38	19	5	14	64	53	43
Third Lanark	38	13	10	15	42	51	36
Clyde	38	11	11	16	44	44	33
Ayr United	38	13	7	18	56	72	33
Raith Rovers	38	13	6	19	56	57	32
Kilmarnock	38	11	9	18	48	68	31
Hibernian	38	12	6	20	58	75	30
Aberdeen	38	10	10	18	38	55	30
Partick Thistle	38	10	9	19	37	51	29
Queen's Park	38	10	9	19	52	84	29
Hamilton Academical	38	11	6	21	46	66	28
Motherwell	38	11	6	21	49	65	28
Dumbarton	38	10	7	21	45	87	27
St. Mirren	38	8	6	24	38	73	22

SCOTTISH DIVISION 2 1913-14

Cowdenbeath	22	13	5	4	34	17	31
Albion Rovers	22	10	7	5	38	33	27
Dunfermline Athletic	22	11	4	7	46	28	26
Dundee Hibernians	22	11	4	7	36	31	26
St. Johnstone	22	9	5	8	48	38	23
Abercorn	22	10	3	9	32	32	23
St. Bernard's	22	8	6	8	39	31	22
East Stirlingshire	22	7	8	7	40	36	22
Arthurlie	22	8	4	10	35	37	20
Leith Athletic	22	5	9	8	31	37	19
Vale of Leven	22	5	3	14	23	47	13
Johnstone	22	4	4	14	20	55	12

1914 Scottish F.A. Cup

Semi-finals

Celtic vs Third Lanark	2-0
Hibernian vs St. Mirren	3-1

Final

Ibrox Park, 11th April 1914

Celtic 0
Hibernian 0

Attendance 56,000

Replay

Ibrox Park, 16th April 1914

Celtic 4   (McColl 2, Browning 2)
Hibernian 1   (Smith)

Attendance 40,000

SCOTTISH DIVISION 'A' 1914-15

CELTIC	38	30	5	3	91	25	65
Heart of Midlothian	38	27	7	4	83	32	61
Rangers	38	23	4	11	74	47	50
Greenock Morton	38	18	12	8	74	48	48
Ayr United	38	20	8	10	55	40	48
Falkirk	38	16	7	15	48	48	39
Hamilton Academical	38	16	6	16	60	55	38
Partick Thistle	38	15	8	15	56	58	38
St. Mirren	38	14	8	16	56	65	36
Airdrieonians	38	14	7	17	54	60	35
Hibernian	38	12	11	15	59	66	35
Kilmarnock	38	15	4	19	55	59	34
Dumbarton	38	13	8	17	51	66	34
Aberdeen	38	11	11	16	39	52	33
Dundee	38	12	9	17	43	61	33
Third Lanark	38	10	12	16	51	57	32
Clyde	38	12	6	20	44	59	30
Motherwell	38	10	10	18	49	66	30
Raith Rovers	38	9	10	19	53	68	28
Queen's Park	38	4	5	29	27	90	13

SCOTTISH DIVISION 'B' 1914-15

Cowdenbeath	26	16	5	5	49	17	37
St. Bernards	26	18	1	7	66	34	37
Leith Athletic	26	15	7	4	54	31	37
East Stirlingshire	26	13	5	8	52	44	31
Clydebank	26	13	4	9	67	37	30
Dunfermline Athletic	26	13	2	11	49	39	28
Johnstone	26	11	5	10	41	51	27
St. Johnstone	26	10	6	10	56	53	26
Albion Rovers	26	9	7	10	37	42	25
Lochgelly United	26	9	3	14	43	60	21
Dundee Hibernians	26	8	3	15	48	61	19
Abercorn	26	5	7	14	35	65	17
Arthurlie	26	6	4	16	36	66	16
Vale of Leven	26	4	5	17	33	66	13

SCOTTISH LEAGUE 1915-16

CELTIC	38	32	3	3	116	23	67
Rangers	38	25	6	7	87	39	56
*Greenock Morton	37	22	7	8	86	35	51
Ayr United	38	20	8	10	72	45	48
Partick Thistle	38	19	8	11	65	41	46
*Heart of Midlothian	37	20	6	11	66	45	46
Hamilton Academical	38	19	3	16	68	76	41
Dundee	38	18	4	16	56	49	40
Dumbarton	38	13	11	14	53	64	37
Kilmarnock	38	12	11	15	46	49	35
Aberdeen	38	11	12	15	51	64	34
Falkirk	38	12	9	17	45	61	33
St. Mirren	38	13	4	21	50	67	30
Motherwell	38	11	8	19	55	81	30
Airdrieonians	38	11	8	19	44	74	30
Third Lanark	38	9	11	18	40	56	29
Clyde	38	11	7	20	49	71	29
Queen's Park	38	11	6	21	53	100	28
Hibernian	38	9	7	22	44	71	25
Raith Rovers	38	9	5	24	30	65	23

Greenock Morton and Heart of Midlothian played only once

SCOTTISH LEAGUE 1916-17

CELTIC	38	27	10	1	79	17	64
Greenock Morton	38	24	6	8	72	39	54
Rangers	38	24	5	9	68	32	53
Airdrieonians	38	21	8	9	71	38	50
Third Lanark	38	19	11	8	53	37	49
Kilmarnock	38	18	7	13	69	45	43
St. Mirren	38	15	10	13	49	43	40
Motherwell	38	16	6	16	57	59	38
Partick Thistle	38	14	7	17	44	43	35
Dumbarton	38	12	11	15	56	73	35
Hamilton Academical	38	13	9	16	54	73	35
Falkirk	38	12	10	16	57	57	34
Clyde	38	10	14	14	41	53	34
Heart of Midlothian	38	14	4	20	44	59	32
Ayr United	38	12	7	19	47	59	31
Dundee	38	13	4	21	58	71	30
Hibernian	38	10	10	18	57	72	30
Queen's Park	38	11	7	20	56	81	29
Raith Rovers	38	8	7	23	42	91	23
Aberdeen	38	7	7	24	36	68	21

Aberdeen, Dundee and Raith Rovers all withdrew from the League for the next season due to travelling difficulties caused by war-time restrictions and conditions

SCOTTISH LEAGUE 1917-18

RANGERS	34	25	6	3	66	24	56
Celtic	34	24	7	3	66	26	55
Kilmarnock	34	19	5	10	69	41	43
Greenock Morton	34	17	9	8	53	42	43
Motherwell	34	16	9	9	70	51	41
Partick Thistle	34	14	12	8	51	37	40
Queen's Park	34	14	6	14	64	63	34
Dumbarton	34	13	8	13	48	49	34
Clydebank	34	14	5	15	55	56	33
Heart of Midlothian	34	14	4	16	41	58	32
St. Mirren	34	11	7	16	42	50	29
Hamilton Academical	34	11	6	17	52	63	28
Third Lanark	34	10	7	17	56	62	27
Falkirk	34	9	9	16	38	58	27
Airdrieonians	34	10	6	18	46	58	26
Hibernian	34	8	9	17	42	57	25
Clyde	34	9	2	23	37	72	20
Ayr United	34	5	9	20	32	61	19

SCOTTISH LEAGUE 1918-19

CELTIC	34	26	6	2	71	22	58
Rangers	34	26	5	3	86	16	57
Greenock Morton	34	18	11	5	76	38	47
Partick Thistle	34	17	7	10	62	43	41
Motherwell	34	14	10	10	51	40	38
Ayr United	34	15	8	11	62	53	38
Heart of Midlothian	34	14	9	11	59	52	37
Queen's Park	34	15	5	14	59	57	35
Kilmarnock	34	14	7	13	61	59	35
Clydebank	34	12	8	14	52	65	32
St. Mirren	34	10	12	12	43	55	32
Third Lanark	34	11	9	14	60	62	31
Airdrieonians	34	9	11	14	45	54	29
Hamilton Academical	34	11	5	18	49	75	27
Dumbarton	34	7	8	19	31	58	22
Falkirk	34	6	8	20	46	73	20
Clyde	34	7	6	21	45	75	20
Hibernian	34	5	3	26	30	91	13

SCOTTISH LEAGUE 1919-20

RANGERS	42	31	9	2	106	25	71
Celtic	42	29	10	3	89	31	68
Motherwell	42	23	11	8	73	53	57
Dundee	42	22	6	14	79	65	50
Clydebank	42	20	8	14	78	54	48
Greenock Morton	42	16	13	13	71	48	45
Airdrieonians	42	17	10	15	57	43	44
Third Lanark	42	16	11	15	56	62	43
Kilmarnock	42	20	3	19	59	74	43
Ayr United	42	15	10	17	72	69	40
Dumbarton	42	13	13	16	57	65	39
Queen's Park	42	14	10	18	67	73	38
Partick Thistle	42	13	12	17	51	62	38
St. Mirren	42	15	8	19	63	81	38
Clyde	42	14	9	19	64	71	37
Heart of Midlothian	42	14	9	19	57	72	37
Aberdeen	42	11	13	18	46	64	35
Hibernian	42	13	7	22	60	79	33
Raith Rovers	42	11	10	21	61	83	32
Falkirk	42	10	11	21	45	74	31
Hamilton Academical	42	11	7	24	56	86	29
Albion Rovers	42	10	8	24	43	77	28

1920 Scottish F.A. Cup

Semi-finals

Kilmarnock vs Greenock Morton	3-2
Albion Rovers vs Rangers	0-0, 1-1, 2-0

Final

Hampden Park, 17th April 1920

Kilmarnock 3 (Culley, Shortt, J.R. Smith)

Albion Rovers 2 (Watson, Hillhouse)

Attendance 97,000

SCOTTISH LEAGUE 1920-21

RANGERS	42	35	6	1	91	24	76
Celtic	42	30	6	6	86	35	66
Heart of Midlothian	42	20	10	12	74	49	50
Dundee	42	19	11	12	54	48	49
Motherwell	42	19	10	13	75	51	48
Partick Thistle	42	17	12	13	53	39	46
Clyde	42	21	3	18	63	62	45
Third Lanark	42	19	6	17	74	61	44
Greenock Morton	42	15	14	13	66	58	44
Airdrieonians	42	17	9	16	71	64	43
Aberdeen	42	14	14	14	53	54	42
Kilmarnock	42	17	8	17	62	68	42
Hibernian	42	16	9	17	58	57	41
Ayr United	42	14	12	16	62	69	40
Hamilton Academical	42	14	12	16	44	57	40
Raith Rovers	42	16	5	21	54	58	37
Albion Rovers	42	11	12	19	57	68	34
Falkirk	42	11	12	19	54	72	34
Queen's Park	42	11	11	20	45	80	33
Clydebank	42	7	14	21	47	72	28
Dumbarton	42	10	4	28	41	89	24
St. Mirren	42	7	4	31	43	92	18

1921 Scottish F.A. Cup

Semi-finals

Partick Thistle vs Heart of Midlothian	0-0, 0-0, 2-0
Rangers vs Albion Rovers	4-1

Final

Celtic Park, 16th April 1921

Partick Thistle 1   (Blair)

Rangers 0

Attendance 28,000

SCOTTISH DIVISION 1 1921-22

CELTIC	42	27	13	2	83	20	67
Rangers	42	28	10	4	83	26	66
Raith Rovers	42	19	13	10	66	43	51
Dundee	42	19	11	12	57	40	49
Falkirk	42	16	17	9	48	38	49
Partick Thistle	42	20	8	14	57	53	48
Hibernian	42	16	14	12	55	44	46
St. Mirren	42	17	12	13	71	61	46
Third Lanark	42	17	12	13	58	52	46
Clyde	42	16	12	14	60	51	44
Albion Rovers	42	17	10	15	55	51	44
Greenock Morton	42	16	10	16	58	57	42
Motherwell	42	16	7	19	63	58	39
Ayr United	42	13	12	17	55	63	38
Aberdeen	42	13	9	20	48	54	35
Airdrieonians	42	12	11	19	46	56	35
Kilmarnock	42	13	9	20	56	83	35
Hamilton Academical	42	9	16	17	51	62	34
Heart of Midlothian	42	11	10	21	50	60	32
Dumbarton	*42*	*10*	*10*	*22*	*46*	*81*	*30*
Queen's Park	*42*	*9*	*10*	*23*	*38*	*82*	*28*
Clydebank	*42*	*6*	*8*	*28*	*34*	*103*	*20*

SCOTTISH DIVISION 2 1921-22

Alloa Athletic	38	26	8	4	81	32	60
Cowdenbeath	38	19	9	10	56	30	47
Armadale	38	20	5	13	64	49	45
Vale of Leven	38	17	10	11	56	43	44
Bathgate	38	16	11	11	56	41	43
Bo'ness	38	16	7	15	57	49	39
Broxburn United	38	14	11	13	43	43	39
Dunfermline Athletic	38	14	10	14	56	42	38
St. Bernard's	38	15	8	15	50	49	38
Stenhousemuir	38	14	10	14	50	51	38
Johnstone	38	14	10	14	46	59	38
East Fife	38	15	7	16	55	54	37
St. Johnstone	38	12	11	15	41	52	35
Forfar Athletic	38	11	12	15	44	53	34
East Stirlingshire	38	12	10	16	43	60	34
Arbroath	38	11	11	16	45	56	33
King's Park	38	10	12	16	47	65	32
Lochgelly United	38	11	9	18	46	56	31
Dundee Hibernians	*38*	*10*	*8*	*20*	*47*	*65*	*28*
Clackmannan	*38*	*10*	*7*	*21*	*41*	*75*	*27*

1922 Scottish F.A. Cup

Semi-finals

Greenock Morton vs Aberdeen	3-1
Rangers vs Partick Thistle	2-0

Final

Hampden Park, 15th April 1922

Greenock Morton 1   (Gourlay)

Rangers 0

Attendance 75,000

SCOTTISH DIVISION 1 1922-23

RANGERS	38	23	9	6	67	29	55
Airdrieonians	38	20	10	8	58	38	50
Celtic	38	19	8	11	52	39	46
Falkirk	38	14	17	7	44	32	45
Aberdeen	38	15	12	11	46	34	42
St. Mirren	38	15	12	11	54	44	42
Dundee	38	17	7	14	51	45	41
Hibernian	38	17	7	14	45	40	41
Raith Rovers	38	13	13	12	31	43	39
Ayr United	38	13	12	13	43	44	38
Partick Thistle	38	14	9	15	51	48	37
Heart of Midlothian	38	11	15	12	51	50	37
Motherwell	38	13	10	15	59	60	36
Greenock Morton	38	12	11	15	44	47	35
Kilmarnock	38	14	7	17	57	66	35
Clyde	38	12	9	17	36	44	33
Third Lanark	38	11	8	19	40	59	30
Hamilton Academical	38	11	7	20	43	59	29
Albion Rovers	*38*	*8*	*10*	*20*	*38*	*64*	*26*
Alloa Athletic	*38*	*6*	*11*	*21*	*27*	*52*	*23*

SCOTTISH DIVISION 2 1922-23

Queen's Park	38	24	9	5	73	31	57
Clydebank	38	21	10	7	69	29	52
St. Johnstone	38	19	12	7	60	39	48
Dumbarton	38	17	8	13	61	40	42
Bathgate	38	16	9	13	67	55	41
Armadale	38	15	11	12	63	52	41
Bo'ness	38	12	17	9	48	46	41
Broxburn United	38	14	12	12	40	43	40
East Fife	38	16	7	15	48	42	39
Lochgelly United	38	16	5	17	41	64	37
Cowdenbeath	38	16	6	16	56	52	36
King's Park	38	14	6	18	46	60	34
Dunfermline Athletic	38	11	11	16	47	44	33
Stenhousemuir	38	13	7	18	53	67	33
Forfar Athletic	38	13	7	18	51	73	33
Johnstone	38	13	6	19	41	62	32
Vale of Leven	38	11	8	19	50	59	30
St. Bernard's	38	8	15	15	39	50	29
East Stirlingshire	*38*	*10*	*8*	*20*	*48*	*69*	*28*
Arbroath	38	8	12	18	45	69	28

St. Johnstone, Cowdenbeath and St. Bernard's all had 2 points deducted for fielding ineligible players

1923 Scottish F.A. Cup

Semi-finals

Celtic vs Motherwell	2-0
Hibernian vs Third Lanark	1-0

Final

Hampden Park, 31st March 1923

Celtic 1 (Cassidy)

Hibernian 0

Attendance 80,000

SCOTTISH DIVISION 1 1923-24

RANGERS	38	25	9	4	72	22	59
Airdrieonians	38	20	10	8	72	46	50
Celtic	38	17	12	9	56	33	46
Raith Rovers	38	18	7	13	56	38	43
Dundee	38	15	13	10	70	57	43
St. Mirren	38	15	12	11	53	45	42
Hibernian	38	15	11	12	66	52	41
Partick Thistle	38	15	9	14	58	55	39
Heart of Midlothian	38	14	10	14	61	50	38
Motherwell	38	15	7	16	58	63	37
Greenock Morton	38	16	5	17	48	54	37
Hamilton Academical	38	15	6	17	52	57	36
Aberdeen	38	13	10	15	37	41	36
Ayr United	38	12	10	16	38	60	34
Falkirk	38	13	6	19	46	53	32
Kilmarnock	38	12	8	18	48	65	32
Queen's Park	38	11	9	18	43	60	31
Third Lanark	38	11	8	19	54	78	30
Clyde	*38*	*10*	*9*	*19*	*40*	*70*	*29*
Clydebank	*38*	*10*	*5*	*23*	*42*	*71*	*25*

SCOTTISH DIVISION 2 1923-24

St. Johnstone	38	22	12	4	79	33	56
Cowdenbeath	38	23	9	6	78	33	55
Bathgate	38	16	12	10	58	49	44
Stenhousemuir	38	16	11	11	58	45	43
Albion Rovers	38	15	12	11	67	53	42
King's Park	38	16	10	12	67	56	42
Dunfermline Athletic	38	14	11	13	52	45	39
Johnstone	38	16	7	15	60	56	39
Dundee United	38	12	15	11	41	41	39
Dumbarton	38	17	5	16	55	58	39
Armadale	38	16	6	16	56	63	38
East Fife	38	14	9	15	54	47	37
Bo'ness	38	13	11	14	45	52	37
Forfar Athletic	38	14	7	17	43	68	35
Broxburn United	38	13	8	17	50	56	34
Alloa Athletic	38	14	6	18	44	53	34
Arbroath	38	12	8	18	49	51	32
St. Bernard's	38	11	10	17	49	54	32
Vale of Leven	*38*	*11*	*9*	*18*	*41*	*67*	*31*
Lochgelly United	*38*	*4*	*4*	*30*	*20*	*86*	*12*

SCOTTISH DIVISION 3 1923-24

Arthurlie	30	21	5	4	59	24	47
East Stirlingshire	30	17	8	5	63	36	42
Queen of the South	30	14	10	6	64	31	38
Montrose	30	15	6	9	60	48	36
Dykehead	30	16	1	13	55	41	33
Nithsdale Wanderers	30	13	7	10	42	35	33
Beith	30	14	4	12	49	41	32
Mid-Annandale	30	13	5	12	59	48	31
Royal Albert	30	12	4	14	44	53	28
Dumbarton Harp	30	10	8	12	40	51	28
Solway Star	30	9	9	12	42	48	27
Clackmannan	30	10	7	13	37	54	27
Galston	30	11	3	16	53	70	25
Peebles Rovers	30	7	8	15	43	56	22
Helensburgh	30	5	7	18	46	72	17
Brechin City	30	4	6	20	28	76	14

1924 Scottish F.A. Cup

Semi-finals

Airdrieonians vs Falkirk	2-1
Aberdeen vs Hibernian	0-0, 0-0, 0-1

Final

Ibrox Park, 19th April 1924

Airdrieonians 2 (Russell 2)

Hibernian 0

Attendance 59,218

SCOTTISH DIVISION 1 1924-25

RANGERS	38	25	10	3	76	26	60
Airdrieonians	38	25	7	6	85	31	57
Hibernian	38	22	8	8	78	43	52
Celtic	38	18	8	12	77	44	44
Cowdenbeath	38	16	10	12	76	65	42
St. Mirren	38	18	4	16	65	63	40
Partick Thistle	38	14	10	14	60	61	38
Dundee	38	14	8	16	48	55	36
Raith Rovers	38	14	8	16	52	60	36
Heart of Midlothian	38	12	11	15	65	69	35
St. Johnstone	38	12	11	15	56	71	35
Kilmarnock	38	12	9	17	53	64	33
Hamilton Academical	38	15	3	20	50	63	33
Greenock Morton	38	12	9	17	46	69	33
Aberdeen	38	11	10	17	46	56	32
Falkirk	38	12	8	18	44	54	32
Queen's Park	38	12	8	18	50	71	32
Motherwell	38	10	10	18	55	64	30
Ayr United	*38*	*11*	*8*	*19*	*43*	*65*	*30*
Third Lanark	*38*	*11*	*8*	*19*	*53*	*84*	*30*

SCOTTISH DIVISION 2 1924-25

Dundee United	38	20	10	8	58	44	50
Clydebank	38	20	8	10	65	42	48
Clyde	38	20	7	11	72	39	47
Alloa Athletic	38	17	11	10	57	33	45
Arbroath	38	16	10	12	47	46	42
Bo'ness	38	16	9	13	71	48	41
Broxburn United	38	16	9	13	48	54	41
Dumbarton	38	15	10	13	45	44	40
East Fife	38	17	5	16	66	58	39
King's Park	38	15	8	15	54	46	38
Stenhousemuir	38	15	7	16	51	58	37
Arthurlie	38	14	8	16	56	60	36
Dunfermline Athletic	38	14	7	17	62	57	35
Armadale	38	15	5	18	55	62	35
Albion Rovers	38	15	5	18	46	61	35
Bathgate	38	12	10	16	58	74	34
St. Bernard's	38	14	4	20	52	70	32
East Stirlingshire	38	11	8	19	58	72	30
Johnstone	*38*	*12*	*4*	*22*	*53*	*85*	*28*
Forfar Athletic	*38*	*10*	*7*	*21*	*46*	*67*	*27*

SCOTTISH DIVISION 3 1924-25

Nithsdale Wanderers	30	18	7	5	81	40	43
Queen of the South	30	17	6	7	67	32	40
Solway Star	30	15	10	5	41	28	40
Vale of Leven	30	17	4	9	61	43	38
Lochgelly United	30	15	4	11	59	41	34
Leith Athletic	30	13	5	12	48	42	31
Helensburgh	30	12	7	11	68	60	31
Peebles Rovers	30	12	7	11	64	57	31
Royal Albert	30	9	8	13	48	61	26
Clackmannan	30	10	6	14	35	48	26
Galston	30	10	6	14	39	70	26
Dykehead	29	7	11	12	30	47	25
Beith	30	9	6	15	62	74	24
Brechin City	29	9	4	16	51	61	24
Mid-Annandale	30	7	7	16	47	70	21
Montrose	30	8	4	18	39	66	20
* Dumbarton Harp	*17*	*5*	*3*	*9*	*25*	*47*	*13*

Dykehead vs Brechin City was not played but Brechin City were
awarded the points
Dumbarton Harp's results were expunged from the records

1925 Scottish F.A. Cup

Semi-finals

Celtic vs Rangers	5-0
Dundee vs Hamilton Academical	1-1, 2-0

Final

Hampden Park, 11th April 1925

Celtic 2   (Gallacher, McGrory)

Dundee 1   (McLean)

Attendance 75,137

SCOTTISH DIVISION 1 1925-26

CELTIC	38	25	8	5	97	40	58
Airdrieonians	38	23	4	11	95	54	50
Heart of Midlothian	38	21	8	9	87	56	50
St. Mirren	38	20	7	11	62	52	47
Motherwell	38	19	8	11	67	46	46
Rangers	38	19	6	13	79	55	44
Cowdenbeath	38	18	6	14	87	68	42
Falkirk	38	14	14	10	61	57	42
Kilmarnock	38	17	7	14	79	77	41
Dundee	38	14	9	15	47	59	37
Aberdeen	38	13	10	15	49	54	36
Hamilton Academical	38	13	9	16	68	79	35
Queen's Park	38	15	4	19	70	81	34
Partick Thistle	38	10	13	15	64	73	33
Greenock Morton	38	12	7	19	57	84	31
Hibernian	38	12	6	20	72	77	30
Dundee United	38	11	6	21	52	74	28
St. Johnstone	38	9	10	19	43	78	28
Raith Rovers	*38*	*11*	*4*	*23*	*46*	*81*	*26*
Clydebank	*38*	*7*	*8*	*23*	*55*	*92*	*22*

SCOTTISH DIVISION 2 1925-26

Dunfermline Athletic	38	26	7	5	109	43	59
Clyde	38	24	5	9	87	51	53
Ayr United	38	20	12	6	77	39	52
East Fife	38	20	9	9	98	73	49
Stenhousemuir	38	19	10	9	74	52	48
Third Lanark	38	19	8	11	72	47	46
Arthurlie	38	17	5	16	81	75	39
Bo'ness	38	17	5	16	65	70	39
Albion Rovers	38	16	6	16	78	71	38
Arbroath	38	17	4	17	80	73	38
Dumbarton	38	14	10	14	54	78	38
Nithsdale Wanderers	38	15	7	16	79	82	37
King's Park	38	14	9	15	67	73	37
St. Bernard's	38	15	5	18	86	82	35
Armadale	38	14	5	19	82	101	33
Alloa Athletic	38	11	8	19	54	63	30
Queen of the South	38	10	8	20	64	88	28
East Stirlingshire	38	10	7	21	59	89	27
Bathgate	38	7	6	25	60	105	20
Broxburn United	*38*	*4*	*6*	*28*	*55*	*126*	*14*

SCOTTISH DIVISION 3 1925-26

Helensburgh	30	16	6	8	66	47	38
Leith Athletic	29	16	5	8	73	41	37
Forfar Athletic	28	16	3	9	61	42	35
Dykehead	28	14	5	9	62	47	33
Royal Albert	28	16	1	11	75	61	33
Mid-Annandale	29	14	3	12	50	54	31
Vale of Leven	26	14	2	10	78	55	30
Montrose	26	12	3	11	56	58	28
Brechin City	28	12	3	13	67	73	27
Lochgelly United	29	9	9	11	58	63	27
Solway Star	29	9	6	14	50	62	24
Beith	27	9	4	14	58	68	22
Johnstone	29	7	6	16	55	74	20
Clackmannan	25	5	8	12	42	74	18
Peebles Rovers	26	9	0	17	52	76	18
Galston	15	4	4	7	38	46	12

Galston resigned from the League after 15 games. Other games were not played for various reasons and it was decided to dissolve Division 3 at the end of the season

1926 Scottish F.A. Cup

Semi-finals

St. Mirren vs Rangers	1-0
Celtic vs Aberdeen	2-1

Final

Hampden Park, 10th April 1926

St. Mirren 2 (McCrae, Howieson)

Celtic 0

Attendance 98,620

SCOTTISH DIVISION 1 1926-27

RANGERS	**38**	**23**	**10**	**5**	**85**	**41**	**56**
Motherwell	38	23	5	10	81	52	51
Celtic	38	21	7	10	101	55	49
Airdrieonians	38	18	9	11	97	64	45
Dundee	38	17	9	12	77	51	43
Falkirk	38	16	10	12	77	60	42
Cowdenbeath	38	18	6	14	74	60	42
Aberdeen	38	13	14	11	73	72	40
Hibernian	38	16	7	15	62	71	39
St. Mirren	38	16	5	17	78	76	37
Partick Thistle	38	15	6	17	89	74	36
Queen's Park	38	15	6	17	74	84	36
Heart of Midlothian	38	12	11	15	65	64	35
St. Johnstone	38	13	9	16	55	69	35
Hamilton Academical	38	13	9	16	60	85	35
Kilmarnock	38	12	8	18	54	71	32
Clyde	38	10	9	19	54	85	29
Dunfermline Athletic	38	10	8	20	53	85	28
Greenock Morton	*38*	*12*	*4*	*22*	*56*	*101*	*28*
Dundee United	*38*	*7*	*8*	*23*	*56*	*101*	*22*

SCOTTISH DIVISION 2 1926-27

Bo'ness	**38**	**23**	**10**	**5**	**86**	**41**	**56**
Raith Rovers	**38**	**21**	**7**	**10**	**92**	**52**	**49**
Clydebank	38	18	9	11	94	75	45
Third Lanark	38	17	10	11	67	48	44
East Stirlingshire	38	18	8	12	93	75	44
Fast Fife	38	19	4	15	103	91	42
Arthurlie	38	18	5	15	90	83	41
Ayr United	38	13	15	10	67	68	41
Forfar Athletic	38	15	7	16	66	79	37
Stenhousemuir	38	12	12	14	69	75	36
Queen of the South	38	16	4	18	72	80	36
King's Park	38	13	9	16	76	75	35
St. Bernard's	38	14	6	18	70	77	34
Armadale	38	12	10	16	69	78	34
Alloa Athletic	38	11	11	16	70	78	33
Albion Rovers	38	11	11	16	74	87	33
Bathgate	38	13	7	18	76	98	33
Dumbarton	38	13	6	19	69	84	32
Arbroath	38	13	6	19	64	82	32
Nithsdale Wanderers	*38*	*7*	*9*	*22*	*59*	*100*	*23*

1927 Scottish F.A. Cup

Semi-finals

Celtic vs Falkirk	1-0
East Fife vs Partick Thistle	2-1

Final

Hampden Park, 16th April 1927

Celtic 3 (Robertson (og), McLean, Connolly)

St. Mirren 1 (Wood)

Attendance 80,070

SCOTTISH DIVISION 1 1927-28

RANGERS	38	26	8	4	109	36	60
Celtic	38	23	9	6	93	39	55
Motherwell	38	23	9	6	92	46	55
Heart of Midlothian	38	20	7	11	89	50	47
St. Mirren	38	18	8	12	77	76	44
Partick Thistle	38	18	7	13	65	67	43
Aberdeen	38	19	5	14	71	61	43
Kilmarnock	38	15	10	13	68	78	40
Cowdenbeath	38	16	7	15	66	68	39
Falkirk	38	16	5	17	76	69	37
St. Johnstone	38	14	8	16	66	67	36
Hibernian	38	13	9	16	73	75	35
Airdrieonians	38	12	11	15	59	69	35
Dundee	38	14	7	17	65	80	35
Clyde	38	10	11	17	46	72	31
Queen's Park	38	12	6	20	69	80	30
Raith Rovers	38	11	7	20	60	89	29
Hamilton Academical	38	11	6	21	67	86	28
Bo'ness	*38*	*9*	*8*	*21*	*48*	*86*	*26*
Dunfermline Athletic	*38*	*4*	*4*	*30*	*41*	*126*	*12*

SCOTTISH DIVISION 1 1928-29

RANGERS	38	30	7	1	107	32	67
Celtic	38	22	7	9	67	44	51
Motherwell	38	20	10	8	85	66	50
Heart of Midlothian	38	19	9	10	91	57	47
Queen's Park	38	18	7	13	100	69	43
Partick Thistle	38	17	7	14	9	70	41
Aberdeen	38	16	8	14	81	69	40
St. Mirren	38	16	8	14	78	74	40
St. Johnstone	38	14	10	14	57	70	38
Kilmarnock	38	14	8	16	79	74	36
Falkirk	38	14	8	16	68	86	36
Hamilton Academical	38	13	9	16	58	83	35
Cowdenbeath	38	14	5	19	55	69	33
Hibernian	38	13	6	19	54	62	32
Airdrieonians	38	12	7	19	56	65	31
Ayr United	38	12	7	19	65	84	31
Clyde	38	12	6	20	47	71	30
Dundee	38	9	11	18	58	68	29
Third Lanark	*38*	*10*	*6*	*22*	*71*	*102*	*26*
Raith Rovers	*38*	*9*	*6*	*23*	*52*	*105*	*24*

SCOTTISH DIVISION 2 1927-28

Ayr United	38	24	6	8	117	60	54
Third Lanark	38	18	9	11	99	66	45
King's Park	38	16	12	10	84	68	44
East Fife	38	18	7	13	87	73	43
Forfar Athletic	38	18	7	13	83	73	43
Dundee United	38	17	9	12	81	73	43
Arthurlie	38	18	4	16	84	90	40
Albion Rovers	38	17	4	17	79	69	38
East Stirlingshire	38	14	10	14	84	76	38
Arbroath	38	16	4	18	84	86	36
Dumbarton	38	16	4	18	66	72	36
Queen of the South	38	15	6	17	92	106	36
Leith Athletic	38	13	9	16	76	71	35
Clydebank	38	16	3	19	78	80	35
Alloa Athletic	38	12	11	15	72	76	35
Stenhousemuir	38	15	5	18	75	81	35
St. Bernard's	38	15	5	18	75	101	35
Greenock Morton	38	13	8	17	65	82	34
Bathgate	38	10	11	17	62	81	31
Armadale	38	8	8	22	53	112	24

SCOTTISH DIVISION 2 1928-29

Dundee United	36	24	3	9	99	55	51
Greenock Morton	36	21	8	7	85	49	50
Arbroath	36	19	9	8	90	60	47
Albion Rovers	36	18	8	10	95	67	44
Leith Athletic	36	18	7	11	78	56	43
St. Bernard's	36	19	9	11	77	55	41
Forfar Athletic	35	14	10	11	69	75	38
East Fife	35	15	6	14	88	77	36
Queen of the South	36	16	4	16	86	79	36
Bo'ness	35	15	5	15	62	62	35
Dunfermline Athletic	36	13	7	16	66	72	33
East Stirlingshire	36	14	4	18	71	75	32
Alloa Athletic	36	12	7	17	64	77	31
Dumbarton	36	11	9	16	59	78	31
King's Park	36	8	13	15	60	84	29
Clydebank	36	11	5	20	70	86	27
Arthurlie	*32*	*9*	*7*	*16*	*51*	*73*	*25*
Stenhousemuir	35	9	6	20	52	90	24
Armadale	36	8	7	21	47	99	23
Bathgate	*28*	*5*	*2*	*21*	*37*	*92*	*12*

Bathgate resigned during the season. Arthurlie also resigned with four games to play, leaving matches against Forfar Athletic, East Fife, Bo'ness and Stenhousemuir unplayed

1928 Scottish F.A. Cup

Semi-finals

Rangers vs Hibernian	3-0
Celtic vs Queen's Park	2-1

Final

Hampden Park, 14th April 1928

Rangers 4 (Meiklejohn (pen), McPhail, Archibald 2)
Celtic 0

Attendance 118,115

1929 Scottish F.A. Cup

Semi-finals

Celtic vs Kilmarnock	0-1
Rangers vs St. Mirren	3-2

Final

Hampden Park, 6th April 1929

Kilmarnock 2 (Aitken, Williamson)
Rangers 0

Attendance 114,708

SCOTTISH DIVISION 1 1929-30

RANGERS	38	28	4	6	94	32	60
Motherwell	38	25	5	8	104	48	55
Aberdeen	38	23	7	8	85	61	53
Celtic	38	22	5	11	88	46	49
St. Mirren	38	18	5	15	73	56	41
Partick Thistle	38	16	9	13	72	61	41
Falkirk	38	16	9	13	62	64	41
Kilmarnock	38	15	9	14	77	73	39
Ayr United	38	16	6	16	70	92	38
Heart of Midlothian	38	14	9	15	69	69	37
Clyde	38	13	11	14	64	69	37
Airdrieonians	38	16	4	18	60	66	36
Hamilton Academical	38	14	7	17	76	81	35
Dundee	38	14	6	18	51	58	34
Queen's Park	38	15	4	19	67	80	34
Cowdenbeath	38	13	7	18	64	74	33
Hibernian	38	9	11	18	45	62	29
Greenock Morton	38	10	7	21	67	95	27
Dundee United	*38*	*7*	*8*	*23*	*56*	*109*	*22*
St. Johnstone	*38*	*6*	*7*	*25*	*48*	*96*	*19*

SCOTTISH DIVISION 1 1930-31

RANGERS	38	27	6	5	96	29	60
Celtic	38	24	10	4	101	34	58
Motherwell	38	24	8	6	102	42	56
Partick Thistle	38	24	5	9	76	44	53
Heart of Midlothian	38	19	6	13	90	63	44
Aberdeen	38	17	7	14	79	63	41
Cowdenbeath	38	17	7	14	58	65	41
Dundee	38	17	5	16	65	63	39
Airdrieonians	38	17	5	16	59	66	39
Hamilton Academical	38	16	5	17	59	57	37
Kilmarnock	38	15	5	18	59	60	35
Clyde	38	15	4	19	60	87	34
Queen's Park	38	13	7	18	71	72	33
Falkirk	38	14	4	20	77	87	32
St. Mirren	38	11	8	19	49	72	30
Greenock Morton	38	11	7	20	58	83	29
Leith Athletic	38	8	11	19	52	85	27
Ayr United	38	8	11	19	53	92	27
Hibernian	*38*	*9*	*7*	*22*	*49*	*81*	*25*
East Fife	*38*	*8*	*4*	*26*	*45*	*113*	*20*

SCOTTISH DIVISION 2 1929-30

Leith Athletic	38	23	11	4	92	42	57
East Fife	38	26	5	7	114	58	57
Albion Rovers	38	24	6	8	101	60	54
Third Lanark	38	23	6	9	92	53	52
Raith Rovers	38	18	8	12	94	67	44
King's Park	38	17	8	13	109	80	42
Queen of the South	38	18	6	14	65	63	42
Forfar Athletic	38	18	5	15	98	95	41
Arbroath	38	16	7	15	83	87	39
Dunfermline Athletic	38	16	6	16	99	85	38
Montrose	38	14	10	14	79	87	38
East Stirlingshire	38	16	4	18	83	75	36
Bo'ness	38	15	4	19	67	95	34
St. Bernard's	38	13	6	19	65	65	32
Armadale	38	13	5	20	56	91	31
Dumbarton	38	14	2	22	77	95	30
Stenhousemuir	38	11	5	22	75	108	27
Clydebank	38	7	10	21	66	92	24
Alloa Athletic	38	9	6	23	55	104	24
Brechin City	38	7	4	27	57	125	18

SCOTTISH DIVISION 2 1930-31

Third Lanark	38	27	7	4	107	42	61
Dundee United	38	21	8	9	93	54	50
Dunfermline Athletic	38	20	7	11	83	50	47
Raith Rovers	38	20	6	12	93	72	46
Queen of the South	38	18	6	14	83	66	42
St. Johnstone	38	18	6	14	76	64	42
East Stirlingshire	38	17	7	14	85	74	41
Montrose	38	19	3	16	75	90	41
Albion Rovers	38	14	11	13	80	83	39
Dumbarton	38	15	8	15	73	72	38
St. Bernard's	38	14	9	15	85	66	37
Forfar Athletic	38	15	6	17	78	83	36
Alloa Athletic	38	15	5	18	65	87	35
King's Park	38	14	6	18	78	70	34
Arbroath	38	15	4	19	83	94	34
Brechin City	38	13	7	18	52	84	33
Stenhousemuir	38	13	6	19	78	98	32
Armadale	38	13	2	23	74	99	28
Clydebank	*38*	*10*	*2*	*26*	*61*	*108*	*22*
Bo'ness	38	9	4	25	54	100	22

1930 Scottish F.A. Cup

Semi-finals

Rangers vs Heart of Midlothian	4-1
Partick Thistle vs Hamilton Academical	3-1

Final

Hampden Park, 12th April 1930

Rangers 0
Partick Thistle 0

Attendance 107,475

Replay

Hampden Park, 16th April 1930

Rangers 2　(Marshall, Craig)
Partick Thistle 1　(Torbet)

Attendance 102,479

1931 Scottish F.A. Cup

Semi-finals

Celtic vs Kilmarnock	3-0
Motherwell vs St. Mirren	1-0

Final

Hampden Park, 11th April 1931

Celtic 2　(McGrory, Craig (og))
Motherwell 2　(Stevenson, McMenemy)

Attendance 105,000

Replay

Hampden Park, 15th April 1931

Celtic 4　(R. Thomson 2, McGrory 2)
Motherwell 2　(Murdoch, Stevenson)

Attendance 98,579

SCOTTISH DIVISION 1 1931-32

MOTHERWELL	38	30	6	2	119	31	66
Rangers	38	28	5	5	118	42	61
Celtic	38	20	8	10	94	50	48
Third Lanark	38	21	4	13	92	81	46
St. Mirren	38	20	4	14	77	56	44
Partick Thistle	38	19	4	15	58	59	42
Aberdeen	38	16	9	13	57	49	41
Heart of Midlothian	38	17	5	16	63	61	39
Kilmarnock	38	16	7	15	68	70	39
Hamilton Academical	38	16	6	16	84	65	38
Dundee	38	14	10	14	61	72	38
Cowdenbeath	38	15	8	15	66	78	38
Clyde	38	13	9	16	58	70	35
Airdrieonians	38	13	6	19	74	81	32
Greenock Morton	38	12	7	19	78	87	31
Queen's Park	38	13	5	20	59	79	31
Ayr United	38	11	7	20	70	90	29
Falkirk	38	11	5	22	70	76	27
Dundee United	*38*	*6*	*7*	*25*	*40*	*118*	*19*
Leith Athletic	*38*	*6*	*4*	*28*	*46*	*137*	*16*

SCOTTISH DIVISION 1 1932-33

RANGERS	38	26	10	2	113	43	62
Motherwell	38	27	5	6	114	53	59
Heart of Midlothian	38	21	8	9	84	51	50
Celtic	38	20	8	10	75	44	48
St. Johnstone	38	17	10	11	70	57	44
Aberdeen	38	18	6	14	85	58	42
St. Mirren	38	18	6	14	73	60	42
Hamilton Academical	38	18	6	14	92	78	42
Queen's Park	38	17	7	14	78	79	41
Partick Thistle	38	17	6	15	75	55	40
Falkirk	38	15	6	17	70	70	36
Clyde	38	15	5	18	69	75	35
Third Lanark	38	14	7	17	70	80	35
Kilmarnock	38	13	9	16	72	86	35
Dundee	38	12	9	17	58	74	33
Ayr United	38	13	4	21	62	96	30
Cowdenbeath	38	10	5	23	65	111	25
Airdrieonians	38	10	3	25	55	102	23
Greenock Morton	*38*	*6*	*9*	*23*	*49*	*97*	*21*
East Stirlingshire	*38*	*7*	*3*	*28*	*55*	*115*	*17*

SCOTTISH DIVISION 2 1931-32

East Stirlingshire	38	26	3	9	111	55	55
St. Johnstone	38	24	7	7	102	52	55
Raith Rovers	38	20	6	12	83	65	46
Stenhousemuir	38	19	8	11	88	76	46
St. Bernard's	38	19	7	12	81	62	45
Forfar Athletic	38	19	7	12	90	79	45
Hibernian	38	18	8	12	73	52	44
East Fife	38	18	5	15	107	77	41
Queen of the South	38	18	5	15	99	91	41
Dunfermline Athletic	38	17	6	15	78	73	40
Arbroath	38	17	5	16	82	78	39
Dumbarton	38	14	10	14	70	68	38
Alloa Athletic	38	14	7	17	73	74	35
Bo'ness	38	15	4	19	70	103	34
King's Park	38	14	5	19	97	93	33
Albion Rovers	38	13	2	23	81	104	28
Montrose	38	11	6	21	60	96	28
Armadale	38	10	5	23	68	102	25
Brechin City	38	9	7	22	52	97	25
Edinburgh City	38	5	7	26	78	146	17

SCOTTISH DIVISION 2 1932-33

Hibernian	34	25	4	5	80	29	54
Queen of the South	34	20	9	5	93	59	49
Dunfermline Athletic	34	20	7	7	89	44	47
Stenhousemuir	34	18	6	10	67	58	42
Albion Rovers	34	19	2	13	82	57	40
Raith Rovers	34	16	4	14	83	67	36
East Fife	34	15	4	15	85	71	34
King's Park	34	13	8	13	85	80	34
Dumbarton	34	14	6	14	69	67	34
Arbroath	34	14	5	15	65	62	33
Alloa Athletic	34	14	5	15	60	58	33
St. Bernard's	34	13	6	15	67	64	32
Dundee United	34	14	4	16	65	67	32
Forfar Athletic	34	12	4	18	68	87	28
Brechin City	34	11	4	19	65	95	26
Leith Athletic	34	10	5	19	43	81	25
Montrose	34	8	5	21	63	89	21
Edinburgh City	34	4	4	26	39	133	12

Bo'ness and Armadale were expelled in November 1932, being unable to meet match guarantee fees for visiting opponents. Their records at the time stood as:

Bo'ness	14	4	2	8	26	50	10
Armadale	17	1	2	4	27	72	4

1932 Scottish F.A. Cup

Semi-finals
Rangers vs Hamilton Academical	5-2
Kilmarnock vs Airdrieonians	3-2

Final
Hampden Park, 16th April 1932

Rangers 1   (McPhail)
Kilmarnock 1   (Maxwell)

Attendance 111,982

Replay
Hampden Park, 20th April 1932

Rangers 3   (Fleming, McPhail, English)
Kilmarnock 0

Attendance 104,600

1933 Scottish F.A. Cup

Semi-finals
Celtic vs Heart of Midlothian	0-0, 2-1
Motherwell vs Clyde	2-0

Final
Hampden Park, 15th April 1933

Celtic 1   (McGrory)
Motherwell 0

Attendance 102,339

SCOTTISH DIVISION 1 1933-34

RANGERS	38	30	6	2	118	41	66
Motherwell	38	29	4	5	97	45	62
Celtic	38	18	11	9	78	53	47
Queen of the South	38	21	3	14	75	78	45
Aberdeen	38	18	8	12	90	57	44
Heart of Midlothian	38	17	10	11	86	59	44
Kilmarnock	38	17	9	12	73	64	43
Ayr United	38	16	10	12	87	92	42
St. Johnstone	38	17	6	15	74	53	40
Falkirk	38	16	6	16	73	68	38
Hamilton Academical	38	15	8	15	65	79	38
Dundee	38	15	6	17	68	64	36
Partick Thistle	38	14	5	19	73	78	33
Clyde	38	10	11	17	56	70	31
Queen's Park	38	13	5	20	65	85	31
Hibernian	38	12	3	23	51	69	27
St. Mirren	38	9	9	20	46	75	27
Airdrieonians	38	10	6	22	59	103	26
Third Lanark	*38*	*8*	*9*	*21*	*62*	*103*	*25*
Cowdenbeath	*38*	*5*	*5*	*28*	*58*	*118*	*15*

SCOTTISH DIVISION 1 1934-35

RANGERS	38	25	5	8	96	46	55
Celtic	38	24	4	10	92	45	52
Heart of Midlothian	38	20	10	8	87	51	50
Hamilton Academical	38	19	10	9	87	67	48
St. Johnstone	38	18	10	10	66	46	46
Aberdeen	38	17	10	11	68	54	44
Motherwell	38	15	10	13	83	64	40
Dundee	38	16	8	14	63	63	40
Kilmarnock	38	16	6	16	76	68	38
Clyde	38	14	10	14	71	69	38
Hibernian	38	14	8	16	59	70	36
Queen's Park	38	13	10	15	61	80	36
Partick Thistle	38	15	5	18	61	68	35
Airdrieonians	38	13	7	18	64	72	33
Dunfermline Athletic	38	13	5	20	56	96	31
Albion Rovers	38	10	9	19	62	77	29
Queen of the South	38	11	7	20	52	72	29
Ayr United	38	12	5	21	61	112	29
St. Mirren	*38*	*11*	*5*	*22*	*49*	*70*	*27*
Falkirk	*38*	*9*	*6*	*23*	*58*	*82*	*24*

SCOTTISH DIVISION 2 1933-34

Albion Rovers	34	20	5	9	74	47	45
Dunfermline Athletic	34	20	4	10	90	52	44
Arbroath	34	20	4	10	83	53	44
Stenhousemuir	34	18	4	12	70	73	40
Greenock Morton	34	17	5	12	67	64	39
Dumbarton	34	17	3	14	67	68	37
King's Park	34	14	8	12	78	70	36
Raith Rovers	34	15	5	14	71	55	35
East Stirlingshire	34	14	7	13	65	74	35
St. Bernard's	34	15	4	15	75	56	34
Forfar Athletic	34	13	7	14	77	71	33
Leith Athletic	34	12	8	14	63	60	32
East Fife	34	12	8	14	71	76	32
Brechin City	34	13	5	16	60	70	31
Alloa Athletic	34	11	9	14	55	68	31
Montrose	34	11	4	19	53	81	26
Dundee United	34	10	4	20	81	88	24
Edinburgh City	34	4	6	24	37	111	14

SCOTTISH DIVISION 2 1934-35

Third Lanark	34	23	6	5	94	43	52
Arbroath	34	23	4	7	78	42	50
St. Bernard's	34	20	7	7	103	47	47
Dundee United	34	18	6	10	105	65	42
Stenhousemuir	34	17	5	12	86	80	39
Greenock Morton	34	17	4	13	88	64	38
King's Park	34	18	2	14	86	71	38
Leith Athletic	34	16	5	13	69	71	37
East Fife	34	16	3	15	79	73	35
Alloa Athletic	34	12	10	12	68	61	34
Forfar Athletic	34	13	8	13	77	73	34
Cowdenbeath	34	13	6	15	84	75	32
Raith Rovers	34	13	3	18	68	73	29
East Stirlingshire	34	11	7	16	57	76	29
Brechin City	34	10	6	18	51	98	26
Dumbarton	34	9	4	21	60	105	22
Montrose	34	7	6	21	58	105	20
Edinburgh City	34	3	2	29	45	134	8

1934 Scottish F.A. Cup

Semi-finals

Rangers vs St. Johnstone	1-0
St. Mirren vs Motherwell	3-1

Final

Hampden Park, 21st April 1934

Rangers 5   (Nicholson 2, McPhail, Main, Smith)
St. Mirren 0

Attendance 113,403

1935 Scottish F.A. Cup

Semi-finals

Rangers vs Heart of Midlothian	1-1, 2-1
Aberdeen vs Hamilton Academical	1-2

Final

Hampden Park, 20th April 1935

Rangers 2   (Smith 2)
Hamilton Academical 1   (Harrison)

Attendance 87,740

SCOTTISH DIVISION 1 1935-36

CELTIC	38	32	2	4	115	33	66
Rangers	38	27	7	4	110	43	61
Aberdeen	38	26	9	3	96	50	61
Motherwell	38	18	12	8	77	58	48
Heart of Midlothian	38	20	7	11	88	55	47
Hamilton Academical	38	15	7	16	77	74	37
St. Johnstone	38	15	7	16	70	81	37
Kilmarnock	38	14	7	17	69	64	35
Partick Thistle	38	12	10	16	64	72	34
Dunfermline Athletic	38	13	8	17	73	92	34
Third Lanark	38	14	5	19	63	71	33
Arbroath	38	11	11	16	46	69	33
Dundee	38	11	10	17	67	80	32
Queen's Park	38	11	10	17	58	75	32
Queen of the South	38	11	9	18	54	72	31
Albion Rovers	38	13	4	21	69	92	30
Hibernian	38	11	7	20	56	82	29
Clyde	38	10	8	20	63	84	28
Airdrieonians	*38*	*9*	*9*	*20*	*68*	*91*	*27*
Ayr United	*38*	*11*	*3*	*24*	*53*	*98*	*25*

SCOTTISH DIVISION 1 1936-37

RANGERS	38	26	9	3	88	32	61
Aberdeen	38	23	8	7	89	44	54
Celtic	38	22	8	8	89	58	52
Motherwell	38	22	7	9	96	54	51
Heart of Midlothian	38	24	3	11	99	60	51
Third Lanark	38	20	6	12	79	61	46
Falkirk	38	19	6	13	98	66	44
Hamilton Academical	38	18	5	15	91	96	41
Dundee	38	12	15	11	58	69	39
Clyde	38	16	6	16	59	70	38
Kilmarnock	38	14	9	15	60	70	37
St. Johnstone	38	14	8	16	74	68	36
Partick Thistle	38	11	12	15	73	68	34
Arbroath	38	13	5	20	57	84	31
Queen's Park	38	9	12	17	51	77	30
St. Mirren	38	11	7	20	68	81	29
Hibernian	38	6	13	19	54	83	25
Queen of the South	38	8	8	22	49	95	24
Dunfermline Athletic	*38*	*5*	*11*	*22*	*65*	*98*	*21*
Albion Rovers	*38*	*5*	*6*	*27*	*53*	*116*	*16*

SCOTTISH DIVISION 2 1935-36

Falkirk	34	28	3	3	132	34	59
St. Mirren	34	25	2	7	114	41	52
Greenock Morton	34	21	6	7	117	60	48
Alloa Athletic	34	19	6	9	65	51	44
St. Bernard's	34	18	4	12	106	78	40
East Fife	34	16	6	12	86	79	38
Dundee United	34	16	5	13	108	81	37
East Stirlingshire	34	13	8	13	70	75	34
Leith Athletic	34	15	3	16	67	77	33
Cowdenbeath	34	13	5	16	79	77	31
Stenhousemuir	34	13	3	18	59	78	29
Montrose	34	13	3	18	58	82	29
Forfar Athletic	34	10	7	17	60	81	27
King's Park	34	11	5	18	55	109	27
Edinburgh City	34	8	9	17	57	83	25
Brechin City	34	8	6	20	57	96	22
Raith Rovers	34	9	3	22	60	96	21
Dumbarton	34	5	6	23	52	121	16

SCOTTISH DIVISION 2 1936-37

Ayr United	34	25	4	5	122	49	54
Greenock Morton	34	23	5	6	110	42	51
St. Bernard's	34	22	4	8	102	51	48
Airdrieonians	34	18	8	8	85	60	44
East Fife	34	15	8	11	76	51	38
Cowdenbeath	34	14	10	10	75	59	38
East Stirlingshire	34	18	2	14	81	78	38
Raith Rovers	34	16	4	14	72	66	36
Alloa Athletic	34	13	7	14	64	65	33
Stenhousemuir	34	14	4	16	82	86	32
Leith Athletic	34	13	5	16	62	65	31
Forfar Athletic	34	11	8	15	73	89	30
Montrose	34	11	6	17	65	100	28
Dundee United	34	9	9	16	72	97	27
Dumbarton	34	11	5	18	57	83	27
Brechin City	34	8	9	17	64	98	25
King's Park	34	11	3	20	61	106	25
Edinburgh City	34	2	3	29	42	120	7

1936 Scottish F.A. Cup

Semi-finals

Rangers vs Clyde	3-0
Falkirk vs Third Lanark	1-3

Final

Hampden Park, 18th April 1936

Rangers 1   (McPhail)

Third Lanark 0

Attendance 88,859

1937 Scottish F.A. Cup

Semi-finals

Celtic vs Clyde	2-0
Aberdeen vs Greenock Morton	2-0

Final

Hampden Park, 24th April 1937

Celtic 2   (Crum, Buchan)

Aberdeen 1   (Armstrong)

Attendance 146,433

SCOTTISH DIVISION 1 1937-38

CELTIC	38	27	7	4	114	42	61
Heart of Midlothian	38	26	6	6	90	50	58
Rangers	38	18	13	7	75	49	49
Falkirk	38	19	9	10	82	52	47
Motherwell	38	17	10	11	78	69	44
Aberdeen	38	15	9	14	74	59	39
Partick Thistle	38	15	9	14	68	70	39
St. Johnstone	38	16	7	15	78	81	39
Third Lanark	38	11	13	14	68	73	35
Hibernian	38	11	13	14	57	65	35
Arbroath	38	11	13	14	58	79	35
Queen's Park	38	11	12	15	59	74	34
Hamilton Academical	38	13	7	18	81	76	33
St. Mirren	38	14	5	19	58	66	33
Clyde	38	10	13	15	68	78	33
Queen of the South	38	11	11	16	58	71	33
Ayr United	38	9	15	14	66	85	33
Kilmarnock	38	12	9	17	65	91	33
Dundee	*38*	*13*	*6*	*19*	*70*	*74*	*32*
Greenock Morton	*38*	*6*	*3*	*29*	*64*	*127*	*15*

SCOTTISH DIVISION 2 1937-38

Raith Rovers	34	27	5	2	142	54	59
Albion Rovers	34	20	8	6	97	50	48
Airdrieonians	34	21	5	8	100	53	47
St. Bernard's	34	20	5	9	75	49	45
East Fife	34	19	5	10	104	61	43
Cowdenbeath	34	17	9	8	115	71	43
Dumbarton	34	17	5	12	85	66	39
Stenhousemuir	34	17	5	12	87	78	39
Dunfermline Athletic	34	17	5	12	82	76	39
Leith Athletic	34	16	5	13	71	56	37
Alloa Athletic	34	11	4	19	78	106	26
King's Park	34	11	4	19	64	96	26
East Stirlingshire	34	9	7	18	55	95	25
Dundee United	34	9	5	20	69	104	23
Forfar Athletic	34	8	6	20	67	100	22
Montrose	34	7	8	19	56	88	22
Edinburgh City	34	7	3	24	77	135	17
Brechin City	34	5	2	27	53	139	12

1938 Scottish F.A. Cup

Semi-finals

Kilmarnock vs Rangers	4-3
St. Bernard's vs East Fife	1-1, 1-1, 1-2

Final

Hampden Park, 23rd April 1938

East Fife 1 (McLeod)
Kilmarnock 1 (McAvoy)

Attendance 80,091

Replay

Hampden Park, 27th April 1938

East Fife 4 (McKerrell 2, McLeod, Miller)
Kilmarnock 2 (aet.) (Thomson (pen), McGrogan)

Attendance 92,716

SCOTTISH DIVISION 1 1938-39

RANGERS	38	25	9	4	112	55	59
Celtic	38	20	8	10	99	53	48
Aberdeen	38	20	6	12	91	61	46
Heart of Midlothian	38	20	5	13	98	70	45
Falkirk	38	19	7	12	73	63	45
Queen of the South	38	17	9	12	69	64	43
Hamilton Academical	38	18	5	15	67	71	41
St. Johnstone	38	17	6	15	85	82	40
Clyde	38	17	5	16	78	70	39
Kilmarnock	38	15	9	14	73	86	39
Partick Thistle	38	17	4	17	74	87	38
Motherwell	38	16	5	17	82	86	37
Hibernian	38	14	7	17	68	69	35
Ayr United	38	13	9	16	76	83	35
Third Lanark	38	12	8	18	80	96	32
Albion Rovers	38	12	6	20	65	90	30
Arbroath	38	11	8	19	54	75	30
St. Mirren	38	11	7	20	57	80	29
Queen's Park	*38*	*11*	*5*	*22*	*57*	*83*	*27*
Raith Rovers	*38*	*10*	*2*	*26*	*65*	*99*	*22*

SCOTTISH DIVISION 2 1938-39

Cowdenbeath	34	28	4	2	120	45	60
Alloa Athletic	34	22	4	8	91	46	48
East Fife	34	21	6	7	99	61	48
Airdrieonians	34	21	5	8	85	57	47
Dunfermline Athletic	34	18	5	11	99	78	41
Dundee	34	15	7	12	99	63	37
St. Bernard's	34	15	6	13	79	79	36
Stenhousemuir	34	15	5	14	74	69	35
Dundee United	34	15	3	16	78	69	33
Brechin City	34	11	9	14	82	106	31
Dumbarton	34	9	12	13	68	76	30
Greenock Morton	34	11	6	17	74	88	28
King's Park	34	12	2	20	87	92	26
Montrose	34	10	5	19	82	96	25
Forfar Athletic	34	11	3	20	74	138	25
Leith Athletic	34	10	4	20	57	83	24
East Stirlingshire	34	9	4	21	89	130	22
Edinburgh City	34	6	4	24	58	119	16

1939 Scottish F.A. Cup

Semi-finals

Clyde vs Hibernian	1-0
Aberdeen vs Motherwell	1-1, 1-3

Final

Hampden Park, 22nd April 1939

Clyde 4 (Wallace, Martin 2, Noble)
Motherwell 0

Attendance 94,799

1945/46 Scottish League Cup

Semi-finals

Aberdeen vs Airdrieonians	2-2, 5-3
Rangers vs Heart of Midlothian	2-1

Final

Hampden Park, 11th May 1946

Aberdeen 3 (Baird, Williamson, Taylor)
Rangers 2 (Duncanson, Thornton)

Attendance 121,000

SCOTTISH DIVISION 'A' 1946-47

RANGERS	30	21	4	5	76	26	46
Hibernian	30	19	6	5	69	33	44
Aberdeen	30	16	7	7	58	41	39
Heart of Midlothian	30	16	6	8	52	43	38
Partick Thistle	30	16	3	11	74	59	35
Greenock Morton	30	12	10	8	58	45	34
Celtic	30	13	6	11	53	55	32
Motherwell	30	12	5	13	58	54	29
Third Lanark	30	11	6	13	56	64	28
Clyde	30	9	9	12	55	65	27
Falkirk	30	8	10	12	62	61	26
Queen of the South	30	9	8	13	44	69	26
Queen's Park	30	8	6	16	47	60	22
St. Mirren	30	9	4	17	47	65	22
Kilmarnock	*30*	*6*	*9*	*15*	*44*	*66*	*21*
Hamilton Academical	*30*	*2*	*7*	*21*	*38*	*85*	*11*

SCOTTISH DIVISION 'B' 1946-47

Dundee	26	21	3	2	113	30	45
Airdrieonians	26	19	4	3	78	38	42
East Fife	26	12	7	7	58	39	31
Albion Rovers	26	10	7	9	50	54	27
Alloa Athletic	26	11	5	10	51	57	27
Raith Rovers	26	10	6	10	45	52	26
Stenhousemuir	26	8	7	11	43	53	23
Dunfermline Athletic	26	10	3	13	50	72	23
St. Johnstone	26	9	4	13	45	47	22
Dundee United	26	9	4	13	53	60	22
Ayr United	26	9	2	15	56	73	20
Arbroath	26	7	6	13	42	63	20
Dumbarton	26	7	4	15	41	54	18
Cowdenbeath	26	6	6	14	44	77	18

SCOTTISH DIVISION 'C' 1946-47

Stirling Albion	18	13	4	1	66	22	30
Dundee Reserves	18	12	2	4	60	37	26
Leith Athletic	18	11	3	4	57	33	25
East Stirlingshire	18	10	2	6	54	40	22
St. Johnstone Reserves	18	8	5	5	52	37	21
Forfar Athletic	18	6	2	10	32	46	14
Montrose	18	5	2	11	39	53	12
Brechin City	18	4	4	10	42	60	12
Dundee United Reserves	18	3	3	12	42	77	9
Edinburgh City	18	3	3	12	36	75	9

1947 Scottish F.A. Cup

Semi-finals

Aberdeen vs Arbroath	2-0
Hibernian vs Motherwell	2-1

Final

Hampden Park, 19th April 1947

Aberdeen 2 (Hamilton, Williams)
Hibernian 1 (Cuthbertson)

Attendance 82,140

1946/47 Scottish League Cup

Semi-finals

Rangers vs Hibernian	3-1
Aberdeen vs Heart of Midlothian	6-2

Final

Hampden Park, 5th April 1947

Rangers 4 (Duncanson 2, Williamson, Gillick)
Aberdeen 0

Attendance 82,700

SCOTTISH DIVISION 'A' 1947-48

HIBERNIAN	30	22	4	4	86	27	48
Rangers	30	21	4	5	64	28	46
Partick Thistle	30	16	4	10	61	42	36
Dundee	30	15	3	12	67	51	33
St. Mirren	30	13	5	12	54	58	31
Clyde	30	12	7	11	52	57	31
Falkirk	30	10	10	10	55	48	30
Motherwell	30	13	3	14	45	47	29
Heart of Midlothian	30	10	8	12	37	42	28
Aberdeen	30	10	7	13	45	45	27
Third Lanark	30	10	6	14	56	73	26
Celtic	30	10	5	15	41	56	25
Queen of the South	30	10	5	15	49	74	25
Greenock Morton	30	9	6	15	47	43	24
Airdrieonians	*30*	*7*	*7*	*16*	*39*	*78*	*21*
Queen's Park	*30*	*9*	*2*	*19*	*45*	*75*	*20*

SCOTTISH DIVISION 'B' 1947-48

East Fife	30	25	3	2	103	36	53
Albion Rovers	30	19	4	7	58	49	42
Hamilton Academical	30	17	6	7	75	45	40
Raith Rovers	30	14	6	10	83	66	34
Cowdenbeath	30	12	8	10	56	53	32
Kilmarnock	30	13	4	13	72	62	30
Dunfermline Athletic	30	13	3	14	72	71	29
Stirling Albion	30	11	6	13	85	66	28
St. Johnstone	30	11	5	14	69	63	27
Ayr United	30	9	9	12	59	61	27
Dumbarton	30	9	7	14	66	79	25
Alloa Athletic	30	10	6	14	53	77	24
Arbroath	30	10	3	17	55	62	23
Stenhousemuir	30	6	11	13	53	83	23
Dundee United	30	10	2	18	58	88	22
Leith Athletic	*30*	*6*	*7*	*17*	*45*	*84*	*19*

Alloa Athletic had 2 points deducted

SCOTTISH DIVISION 'C' 1947-48

East Stirlingshire	22	18	3	1	72	26	39
East Fife Reserves	22	16	3	3	63	38	35
Forfar Athletic	22	14	4	4	69	40	32
Kilmarnock Reserves	22	10	3	9	52	41	23
St. Johnstone Reserves	22	9	4	9	44	51	22
Dundee United Reserves	22	9	2	11	56	57	20
Montrose	22	7	5	10	43	70	19
Arbroath Reserves	22	7	4	11	45	57	18
Leith Athletic Reserves	22	7	3	12	44	60	17
Brechin City	22	6	4	12	43	54	16
Edinburgh City	22	6	3	13	54	60	15
Raith Rovers Reserves	22	3	2	17	36	67	8

1948 Scottish F.A. Cup

Semi-finals

Rangers vs Hibernian	1-0
Greenock Morton vs Celtic	1-0

Final

Hampden Park, 17th April 1948

Rangers 1 (Gillick)
Greenock Morton 1 (aet.) (Whyte)

Attendance 131,629

Replay

Hampden Park, 21st April 1948

Rangers 1 (Williamson)
Greenock Morton 0 (aet.)

Attendance 133,570

1947/48 Scottish League Cup

Semi-finals

Aberdeen vs East Fife	0-1
Falkirk vs Rangers	1-0

Final

Hampden Park, 25th October 1947

East Fife 0
Falkirk 0 (aet.)

Attendance 53,785

Replay

Hampden Park, 1st November 1947

East Fife 4 (Duncan 3, Adams)
Falkirk 1 (Aikman)

Attendance 31,000

SCOTTISH DIVISION 'A' 1948-49

RANGERS	30	20	6	4	63	32	46
Dundee	30	20	5	5	71	48	45
Hibernian	30	17	5	8	75	52	39
East Fife	30	16	3	11	64	46	35
Falkirk	30	12	8	10	70	54	32
Celtic	30	12	7	11	48	40	31
Third Lanark	30	13	5	12	56	52	31
Heart of Midlothian	30	12	6	12	64	54	30
St. Mirren	30	13	4	13	51	47	30
Queen of the South	30	11	8	11	47	53	30
Partick Thistle	30	9	9	12	50	63	27
Motherwell	30	10	5	15	44	49	25
Aberdeen	30	7	11	12	39	48	25
Clyde	30	9	6	15	50	67	24
Greenock Morton	*30*	*7*	*8*	*15*	*39*	*51*	*22*
Albion Rovers	*30*	*3*	*2*	*25*	*30*	*105*	*8*

SCOTTISH DIVISION 'B' 1948-49

Raith Rovers	**30**	**20**	**2**	**8**	**80**	**44**	**72**
Stirling Albion	**30**	**20**	**2**	**8**	**71**	**47**	**72**
Airdrieonians	30	16	9	5	76	42	41
Dunfermline Athletic	30	16	9	5	80	58	41
Queen's Park	30	14	7	9	66	49	35
St. Johnstone	30	14	4	12	58	51	32
Arbroath	30	12	8	10	62	56	32
Dundee United	30	10	7	13	60	67	27
Ayr United	30	10	7	13	51	70	27
Hamilton Academical	30	9	8	13	48	57	26
Kilmarnock	30	9	7	14	58	61	25
Stenhousemuir	30	8	8	14	50	54	24
Cowdenbeath	30	9	5	16	53	58	23
Alloa Athletic	30	10	3	17	42	85	23
Dumbarton	30	8	6	16	52	79	22
East Stirlingshire	**30**	**6**	**6**	**18**	**38**	**67**	**18**

SCOTTISH DIVISION 'C' 1948-49

Forfar Athletic	**22**	**17**	**1**	**4**	**80**	**37**	**35**
Leith Athletic	22	15	3	4	76	29	33
Brechin City	22	13	4	5	67	38	30
Montrose	22	10	5	7	59	50	25
Queen's Park Strollers	22	9	6	7	52	52	24
Airdrieonians Reserves	22	9	4	9	66	66	22
St. Johnstone Reserves	22	9	4	9	42	44	22
Dundee United Reserves	22	10	2	10	58	67	22
Raith Rovers Reserves	22	6	7	9	56	60	19
Kilmarnock Reserves	22	5	3	14	41	54	13
Dunfermline Athletic Reserves	22	4	3	15	43	84	11
Edinburgh City	*22*	*2*	*4*	*16*	*26*	*85*	*8*

1949 Scottish F.A. Cup

Semi-final

Rangers vs East Fife	3-0
Clyde vs Dundee	2-2, 2-1

Final

Hampden Park, 23rd April 1949

Rangers 4 (Young 2 (2 pens), Williamson, Duncanson)
Clyde 1 (Galletly)

Attendance 102,162

1948/49 Scottish League Cup

Semi-finals

Rangers vs Dundee	4-1
Raith Rovers vs Hamilton Academical	2-0

Final

Hampden Park, 12th March 1949

Rangers 2 (Gillick, Paton)
Raith Rovers 0

Attendance 57,540

SCOTTISH DIVISION 'A' 1949-50

RANGERS	30	22	6	2	58	26	50
Hibernian	30	22	5	3	86	34	49
Heart of Midlothian	30	20	3	7	86	40	43
East Fife	30	15	7	8	58	43	37
Celtic	30	14	7	9	51	50	35
Dundee	30	12	7	11	49	46	31
Partick Thistle	30	13	3	14	55	45	29
Aberdeen	30	11	4	15	48	56	26
Raith Rovers	30	9	8	13	45	54	26
Motherwell	30	10	5	15	53	58	25
St. Mirren	30	8	9	13	42	49	25
Third Lanark	30	11	3	16	44	62	25
Clyde	30	10	4	16	56	73	24
Falkirk	30	7	10	13	48	72	24
Queen of the South	*30*	*5*	*6*	*19*	*31*	*63*	*16*
Stirling Albion	*30*	*6*	*3*	*21*	*38*	*77*	*15*

SCOTTISH DIVISION 'A' 1950-51

HIBERNIAN	30	22	4	4	78	26	48
Rangers	30	17	4	9	64	37	38
Dundee	30	15	8	7	47	30	38
Heart of Midlothian	30	16	5	9	72	45	37
Aberdeen	30	15	5	10	61	50	35
Partick Thistle	30	13	7	10	57	48	33
Celtic	30	12	5	13	48	46	29
Raith Rovers	30	13	2	15	52	52	28
Motherwell	30	11	6	13	58	65	28
East Fife	30	10	8	12	48	66	28
St. Mirren	30	9	7	14	35	51	25
Greenock Morton	30	10	4	16	47	59	24
Third Lanark	30	11	2	17	40	51	24
Airdrieonians	30	10	4	16	52	67	24
Clyde	*30*	*8*	*7*	*15*	*37*	*57*	*23*
Falkirk	*30*	*7*	*4*	*19*	*35*	*81*	*18*

SCOTTISH DIVISION 'B' 1949-50

Greenock Morton	30	20	7	3	77	33	47
Airdrieonians	30	19	6	5	79	40	44
Dunfermline Athletic	30	16	4	10	71	57	36
St. Johnstone	30	15	6	9	64	56	36
Cowdenbeath	30	16	3	11	63	56	35
Hamilton Academical	30	14	6	10	57	44	34
Dundee United	30	14	5	11	74	56	33
Kilmarnock	30	14	5	11	50	43	33
Queen's Park	30	12	7	11	63	59	31
Forfar Athletic	30	11	8	11	53	56	30
Albion Rovers	30	10	7	13	49	61	27
Stenhousemuir	30	8	8	14	54	72	24
Ayr United	30	8	6	16	53	80	22
Arbroath	30	5	9	16	47	69	19
Dumbarton	30	6	4	20	39	62	16
Alloa Athletic	30	5	3	22	47	96	13

SCOTTISH DIVISION 'B' 1950-51

Queen of the South	30	21	3	6	69	35	45
Stirling Albion	30	21	3	6	78	44	45
Ayr United	30	15	6	9	64	40	36
Dundee United	30	16	4	10	78	58	36
St. Johnstone	30	14	5	11	68	53	33
Queen's Park	30	13	7	10	56	53	33
Hamilton Academical	30	12	8	10	65	49	32
Albion Rovers	30	14	4	12	56	51	32
Dumbarton	30	12	5	13	52	53	29
Dunfermline Athletic	30	12	4	14	58	73	28
Cowdenbeath	30	12	3	15	61	57	27
Kilmarnock	30	8	8	14	44	49	24
Arbroath	30	8	5	17	46	78	21
Forfar Athletic	30	9	3	18	43	76	21
Stenhousemuir	30	9	2	19	51	80	20
Alloa Athletic	30	7	4	19	58	98	18

1950 Scottish F.A. Cup

Semi-final

Rangers vs Queen of the South	1-1, 3-0
East Fife vs Partick Thistle	2-1

Final

Hampden Park, 22nd April 1950

Rangers 3　(Findlay, Thornton 2)

East Fife 0

Attendance 120,015

1951 Scottish F.A. Cup

Semi-final

Celtic vs Raith Rovers	3-2
Hibernian vs Motherwell	1-3

Final

Hampden Park, 21st April 1951

Celtic 1　(McPhail)

Motherwell 0

Attendance 133,343

1949/50 Scottish League Cup

Semi-finals

East Fife vs Rangers	2-1
Dunfermline Athletic vs Hibernian	2-1

Final

Hampden Park, 29th October 1949

East Fife 3　(Fleming, Duncan, Morris)

Dunfermline Athletic 0

Attendance 39,744

1950/51 Scottish League Cup

Semi-finals

Motherwell vs Ayr United	4-3
Hibernian vs Queen of the South	3-1

Final

Hampden Park, 28th October 1950

Motherwell 3　(Kelly, Forrest, Watters)

Hibernian 0

Attendance 64,074

SCOTTISH DIVISION 'A' 1951-52

HIBERNIAN	30	20	5	5	92	36	45
Rangers	30	16	9	5	61	31	41
East Fife	30	17	3	10	71	49	37
Heart of Midlothian	30	14	7	9	69	53	35
Raith Rovers	30	14	5	11	43	42	33
Partick Thistle	30	12	7	11	48	51	31
Motherwell	30	12	7	11	51	57	31
Dundee	30	11	6	13	53	52	28
Celtic	30	10	8	12	52	55	28
Queen of the South	30	10	8	12	50	60	28
Aberdeen	30	10	7	13	65	58	27
Third Lanark	30	9	8	13	51	62	26
Airdrieonians	30	11	4	15	54	69	26
St. Mirren	30	10	5	15	43	58	25
Greenock Morton	*30*	*9*	*6*	*15*	*49*	*56*	*24*
Stirling Albion	*30*	*5*	*5*	*20*	*36*	*99*	*15*

SCOTTISH DIVISION 'B' 1951-52

Clyde	**30**	**19**	**6**	**5**	**100**	**45**	**44**
Falkirk	**30**	**18**	**7**	**5**	**80**	**34**	**43**
Ayr United	30	17	5	8	55	45	39
Dundee United	30	16	5	9	75	60	37
Kilmarnock	30	16	2	12	62	48	34
Dunfermline Athletic	30	15	2	13	74	65	32
Alloa Athletic	30	13	6	11	55	49	32
Cowdenbeath	30	12	8	10	66	67	32
Hamilton Academical	30	12	6	12	47	51	30
Dumbarton	30	10	8	12	51	57	28
St. Johnstone	30	9	7	14	62	68	25
Forfar Athletic	30	10	4	16	59	97	24
Stenhousemuir	30	8	6	16	57	74	22
Albion Rovers	30	6	10	14	39	57	22
Queen's Park	30	8	4	18	40	62	20
Arbroath	30	6	4	20	40	83	16

1952 Scottish F.A. Cup

Semi-finals

Motherwell vs Heart of Midlothian	1-1, 1-1, 3-1
Dundee vs Third Lanark	2-0

Final

Hampden Park, 19th April 1952

Motherwell 4   (Watson, Redpath, Humphries, Kelly)

Dundee 0

Attendance 136,274

1951/52 Scottish League Cup

Semi-finals

Dundee vs Motherwell	5-1
Rangers vs Celtic	3-0

Final

Hampden Park, 27th October 1951

Dundee 3   (Flavell, Pattillo, Boyd)

Rangers 2   (Findlay, Thornton)

Attendance 92,325

SCOTTISH DIVISION 'A' 1952-53

RANGERS	30	18	7	5	80	39	43
Hibernian	30	19	5	6	93	51	43
East Fife	30	16	7	7	72	48	39
Heart of Midlothian	30	12	6	12	59	50	30
Clyde	30	13	4	13	78	78	30
St. Mirren	30	11	8	11	52	58	30
Dundee	30	9	11	8	44	37	29
Celtic	30	11	7	12	51	54	29
Partick Thistle	30	10	9	11	55	63	29
Queen of the South	30	10	8	12	43	61	28
Aberdeen	30	11	5	14	64	68	27
Raith Rovers	30	9	8	13	47	53	26
Falkirk	30	11	4	15	53	63	26
Airdrieonians	30	10	6	14	53	75	26
Motherwell	*30*	*10*	*5*	*15*	*57*	*80*	*25*
Third Lanark	*30*	*8*	*4*	*18*	*52*	*75*	*20*

SCOTTISH DIVISION 'B' 1952-53

Stirling Albion	**30**	**20**	**4**	**6**	**64**	**43**	**44**
Hamilton Academical	**30**	**20**	**3**	**7**	**72**	**40**	**43**
Queen's Park	30	15	7	8	70	46	37
Kilmarnock	30	17	2	11	74	48	36
Ayr United	30	17	2	11	76	56	36
Greenock Morton	30	15	3	12	79	57	33
Arbroath	30	13	7	10	52	57	33
Dundee United	30	12	5	13	52	56	29
Alloa Athletic	30	12	5	13	63	68	29
Dumbarton	30	11	6	13	58	67	28
Dunfermline Athletic	30	9	9	12	51	58	27
Stenhousemuir	30	10	6	14	56	65	26
Cowdenbeath	30	8	7	15	37	54	23
St. Johnstone	30	8	6	16	41	63	22
Forfar Athletic	30	8	4	18	54	88	20
Albion Rovers	30	5	4	21	44	77	14

1953 Scottish F.A. Cup

Semi-finals

Rangers vs Heart of Midlothian	2-1
Third Lanark vs Aberdeen	1-1, 1-2

Final

Hampden Park, 25th April 1953

Rangers 1   (Prentice)

Aberdeen 1   (Yorston)

Attendance 129,761

Replay

Hampden Park, 29th April 1953

Rangers 1   (Simpson)

Aberdeen 0

Attendance 112,619

1952/53 Scottish League Cup

Semi-finals

Dundee vs Hibernian	2-1
Kilmarnock vs Rangers	1-0

Final

Hampden Park, 25th October 1952

Dundee 2   (Flavell 2)

Kilmarnock 0

Attendance 51,830

SCOTTISH DIVISION 'A' 1953-54

CELTIC	**30**	**20**	**3**	**7**	**72**	**29**	**43**
Heart of Midlothian	30	16	6	8	70	45	38
Partick Thistle	30	17	1	12	76	54	35
Rangers	30	13	8	9	56	35	34
Hibernian	30	15	4	11	72	51	34
East Fife	30	13	8	9	55	45	34
Dundee	30	14	6	10	46	47	34
Clyde	30	15	4	11	64	67	34
Aberdeen	30	15	3	12	66	51	33
Queen of the South	30	14	4	12	72	53	32
St. Mirren	30	12	4	14	44	54	28
Raith Rovers	30	10	6	14	56	60	26
Falkirk	30	9	7	14	47	61	25
Stirling Albion	30	10	4	16	39	62	24
Airdrieonians	*30*	*5*	*5*	*20*	*41*	*92*	*15*
Hamilton Academical	*30*	*4*	*3*	*23*	*29*	*94*	*11*

SCOTTISH DIVISION 'A' 1954-55

ABERDEEN	**30**	**24**	**1**	**5**	**73**	**26**	**49**
Celtic	30	19	8	3	76	37	46
Rangers	30	19	3	8	67	33	41
Heart of Midlothian	30	16	7	7	74	45	39
Hibernian	30	15	4	11	64	54	34
St. Mirren	30	12	8	10	55	54	32
Clyde	30	11	9	10	59	50	31
Dundee	30	13	4	13	48	48	30
Partick Thistle	30	11	7	12	49	61	29
Kilmarnock	30	10	6	14	46	58	26
East Fife	30	9	6	15	51	62	24
Falkirk	30	8	8	14	42	54	24
Queen of the South	30	9	6	15	38	56	24
Raith Rovers	30	10	3	17	49	57	23
Motherwell	30	9	4	17	42	62	22
Stirling Albion	30	2	2	26	29	105	6

SCOTTISH DIVISION 'B' 1953-54

Motherwell	**30**	**21**	**3**	**6**	**109**	**43**	**45**
Kilmarnock	**30**	**19**	**4**	**7**	**71**	**39**	**42**
Third Lanark	30	13	10	7	78	48	36
Stenhousemuir	30	14	8	8	66	58	36
Greenock Morton	30	15	3	12	85	65	33
St. Johnstone	30	14	3	13	80	71	31
Albion Rovers	30	12	7	11	55	63	31
Dunfermline Athletic	30	11	9	10	48	57	31
Ayr United	30	11	8	11	50	56	30
Queen's Park	30	9	9	12	56	51	27
Alloa Athletic	30	7	10	13	50	72	24
Forfar Athletic	30	10	4	16	38	69	24
Cowdenbeath	30	9	5	16	67	81	23
Arbroath	30	8	7	15	53	67	23
Dundee United	30	8	6	16	54	79	22
Dumbarton	*30*	*7*	*8*	*15*	*51*	*92*	*22*

SCOTTISH DIVISION 'B' 1954-55

Airdrieonians	**30**	**18**	**10**	**2**	**103**	**61**	**46**
Dunfermline Athletic	**30**	**19**	**4**	**7**	**72**	**40**	**42**
Hamilton Academical	30	17	5	8	74	51	39
Queen's Park	30	15	5	10	65	36	35
Third Lanark	30	13	7	10	63	49	33
Stenhousemuir	30	12	8	10	70	51	32
St. Johnstone	30	15	2	13	60	51	32
Ayr United	30	14	4	12	61	73	32
Greenock Morton	30	12	5	13	58	69	29
Forfar Athletic	30	11	6	13	63	80	28
Albion Rovers	30	8	10	12	50	69	26
Arbroath	30	8	8	14	55	72	24
Dundee United	30	8	6	16	55	70	22
Cowdenbeath	30	8	5	17	55	72	21
Alloa Athletic	30	7	6	17	51	75	20
Brechin City	30	8	3	19	53	89	19

1954 Scottish F.A. Cup

Semi-finals

Celtic vs Motherwell	2-2, 3-1
Rangers vs Aberdeen	0-6

Final

Hampden Park, 24th April 1954

Celtic 2 (Young (og), Fallon)
Aberdeen 1 (Buckley)

Attendance 130,060

1953/54 Scottish League Cup

Semi-finals

East Fife vs Hibernian	3-2
Partick Thistle vs Rangers	2-0

Final

Hampden Park, 24th October 1953

East Fife 3 (Gardiner, Fleming, Christie)
Partick Thistle 2 (Walker, McKenzie)

Attendance 38,529

1955 Scottish F.A. Cup

Semi-finals

Aberdeen vs Clyde	2-2, 0-1
Airdrieonians vs Celtic	2-2, 0-2

Final

Hampden Park, 23rd April 1955

Clyde 1 (Robertson)
Celtic 1 (Walsh)

Attendance 106,234

Replay

Hampden Park, 27th April 1955

Clyde 1 (Ring)
Celtic 0

Attendance 68,831

1954/55 Scottish League Cup

Semi-finals

Airdrieonians vs Heart of Midlothian	1-4
East Fife vs Motherwell	1-2

Final

Hampden Park, 23rd October 1954

Heart of Midlothian 4   (Bauld 3, Wardhaugh)
Motherwell 2   (Redpath (pen), Bain)

Attendance 55,640

1955/56 Scottish League Cup

Semi-finals

Rangers vs Aberdeen	1-2
Motherwell vs St. Mirren	3-3, 0-2

Final

Hampden Park, 22nd October 1955

Aberdeen 2   (Mallan (og), Leggat)
St. Mirren 1   (Holmes)

Attendance 44,106

SCOTTISH DIVISION 'A' 1955-56

RANGERS	34	22	8	4	85	27	52
Aberdeen	34	18	10	6	87	50	46
Heart of Midlothian	34	19	7	8	99	47	45
Hibernian	34	19	7	8	86	50	45
Celtic	34	16	9	9	55	39	41
Queen of the South	34	16	5	13	69	73	37
Airdrieonians	34	14	8	12	85	96	36
Kilmarnock	34	12	10	12	52	45	34
Partick Thistle	34	13	7	14	62	60	33
Motherwell	34	11	11	12	53	59	33
Raith Rovers	34	12	9	13	58	75	33
East Fife	34	13	5	16	61	69	31
Dundee	34	12	6	16	56	65	30
Falkirk	34	11	6	17	58	75	28
St. Mirren	34	10	7	17	57	70	27
Dunfermline Athletic	34	10	6	18	42	82	26
Clyde	*34*	*8*	*6*	*20*	*50*	*74*	*22*
Stirling Albion	*34*	*4*	*5*	*25*	*23*	*82*	*13*

SCOTTISH DIVISION 1 1956-57

RANGERS	34	26	3	5	96	48	55
Heart of Midlothian	34	24	5	5	81	48	53
Kilmarnock	34	16	10	8	57	39	42
Raith Rovers	34	16	7	11	84	58	39
Celtic	34	15	8	11	58	43	38
Aberdeen	34	18	2	14	79	59	38
Motherwell	34	16	5	13	75	66	37
Partick Thistle	34	13	8	13	53	51	34
Hibernian	34	12	9	13	69	56	33
Dundee	34	13	6	15	55	61	32
Airdrieonians	34	13	4	17	77	89	30
St. Mirren	34	12	6	16	58	72	30
Queen's Park	34	11	7	16	55	59	29
Falkirk	34	10	8	16	51	70	28
East Fife	34	10	6	18	59	82	26
Queen of the South	34	10	5	19	54	96	25
Dunfermline Athletic	*34*	*9*	*6*	*19*	*54*	*74*	*24*
Ayr United	*34*	*7*	*5*	*22*	*48*	*89*	*19*

SCOTTISH DIVISION 'B' 1955-56

Queen's Park	36	23	8	5	78	28	54
Ayr United	36	24	3	9	103	55	51
St. Johnstone	36	21	7	8	86	45	49
Dumbarton	36	21	5	10	83	62	47
Stenhousemuir	36	20	4	12	82	54	44
Brechin City	36	18	6	12	60	56	42
Cowdenbeath	36	16	7	13	80	85	39
Dundee United	36	12	14	10	78	65	38
Greenock Morton	36	15	6	15	71	69	36
Third Lanark	36	16	3	17	80	64	35
Hamilton Academical	36	13	7	16	86	84	33
Stranraer	36	14	5	17	77	92	33
Alloa Athletic	36	12	7	17	67	73	31
Berwick Rangers	36	11	9	16	52	77	31
Forfar Athletic	36	10	9	17	62	75	29
East Stirlingshire	36	9	10	17	66	94	28
Albion Rovers	36	8	11	17	58	82	27
Arbroath	36	10	6	20	47	67	26
Montrose	36	4	3	29	44	133	11

SCOTTISH DIVISION 2 1956-57

Clyde	36	29	6	1	112	39	64
Third Lanark	36	24	3	9	105	51	51
Cowdenbeath	36	20	5	11	87	65	45
Greenock Morton	36	18	7	11	81	70	43
Albion Rovers	36	18	6	12	98	80	42
Brechin City	36	15	10	11	72	68	40
Stranraer	36	15	10	11	79	77	40
Stirling Albion	36	17	5	14	81	64	39
Dumbarton	36	17	4	15	101	70	38
Arbroath	36	17	4	15	79	57	38
Hamilton Academical	36	14	8	14	69	68	36
St. Johnstone	36	14	6	16	79	80	34
Dundee United	36	14	6	16	75	80	34
Stenhousemuir	36	13	6	17	71	81	32
Alloa Athletic	36	11	5	20	66	99	27
Forfar Athletic	36	9	5	22	75	100	23
Montrose	36	7	7	22	54	124	21
Berwick Rangers	36	7	6	23	58	114	20
East Stirlingshire	36	5	7	24	56	121	17

1956 Scottish F.A. Cup

Semi-finals

Heart of Midlothian vs Raith Rovers	0-0, 3-0
Celtic vs Clyde	2-1

Final

Hampden Park, 21st April 1956

Heart of Midlothian 3   (Crawford 2, Conn)
Celtic 1   (Haughney)

Attendance 132,840

1957 Scottish F.A. Cup

Semi-finals
Falkirk vs Raith Rovers   2-2, 2-0
Celtic vs Kilmarnock   1-1, 1-3

Final
Hampden Park, 20th April 1957

Falkirk 1   (Prentice (pen))
Kilmarnock 1   (Curlett)

Attendance 81,375

Replay
Hampden Park, 24th April 1957

Falkirk 2   (Merchant, Moran)
Kilmarnock 1   (Curlett)

Attendance 79,960

1956/57 Scottish League Cup

Semi-finals
Celtic vs Clyde   2-0
Partick Thistle vs Dundee   0-0, 3-2

Final
Hampden Park, 27th October 1956

Celtic 0
Partick Thistle 0 (aet.)

Attendance 59,000

Replay
Hampden Park, 31st October 1956

Celtic 3   (McPhail 2, Collins)
Partick Thistle 0

Attendance not known

SCOTTISH DIVISION 1 1957-58

HEART OF MIDLOTHIAN	34	29	4	1	132	29	62
Rangers	34	22	5	7	89	49	49
Celtic	34	19	8	7	84	47	46
Clyde	34	18	6	10	84	61	42
Kilmarnock	34	14	9	11	60	55	37
Partick Thistle	34	17	3	14	69	71	37
Raith Rovers	34	14	7	13	66	56	35
Motherwell	34	12	8	14	68	67	32
Hibernian	34	13	5	16	59	60	31
Falkirk	34	11	9	14	64	82	31
Dundee	34	13	5	16	49	65	31
Aberdeen	34	14	2	18	68	76	30
St. Mirren	34	11	8	15	59	66	30
Third Lanark	34	13	4	17	69	88	30
Queen of the South	34	12	5	17	61	72	29
Airdrieonians	34	13	2	19	71	92	28
East Fife	*34*	*10*	*3*	*21*	*45*	*88*	*23*
Queen's Park	*34*	*4*	*1*	*29*	*41*	*114*	*9*

SCOTTISH DIVISION 2 1957-58

Stirling Albion	36	25	5	6	105	48	55
Dunfermline Athletic	36	24	5	7	120	42	53
Arbroath	36	21	5	10	89	72	47
Dumbarton	36	20	4	12	92	57	44
Ayr United	36	18	6	12	98	81	42
Cowdenbeath	36	17	8	11	100	85	42
Brechin City	36	16	8	12	80	81	40
Alloa Athletic	36	15	9	12	88	78	39
Dundee United	36	12	9	15	81	77	33
Hamilton Academical	36	12	9	15	70	79	33
St. Johnstone	36	12	9	15	67	85	33
Forfar Athletic	36	13	6	17	70	71	32
Greenock Morton	36	12	8	16	77	83	32
Montrose	36	13	6	17	55	72	32
East Stirlingshire	36	12	5	19	55	79	29
Stenhousemuir	36	12	5	19	68	98	29
Albion Rovers	36	12	5	19	53	79	29
Stranraer	36	9	7	20	54	83	25
Berwick Rangers	36	5	5	26	37	109	15

1958 Scottish F.A. Cup

Semi-finals
Clyde vs Motherwell   3-2
Rangers vs Hibernian   2-2, 1-2

Final
Hampden Park, 26th April 1958

Clyde 1   (Coyle)
Hibernian 0

Attendance 95,123

1957/58 Scottish League Cup

Semi-finals
Clyde vs Celtic   2-4
Rangers vs Brechin City   4-0

Final
Hampden Park, 19th October 1957

Celtic 7   (Mochan 2, Wilson, McPhail 3, Fernie (pen))
Rangers 1   (Simpson)

Attendance 82,293

SCOTTISH DIVISION 1 1958-59

RANGERS	34	21	8	5	92	51	50
Heart of Midlothian	34	21	6	7	92	51	48
Motherwell	34	18	8	8	83	50	44
Dundee	34	16	9	9	61	51	41
Airdrieonians	34	15	7	12	64	62	37
Celtic	34	14	8	12	70	53	36
St. Mirren	34	14	7	13	71	74	35
Kilmarnock	34	13	8	13	58	51	34
Partick Thistle	34	14	6	14	59	66	34
Hibernian	34	13	6	15	68	70	32
Third Lanark	34	11	10	13	74	83	32
Stirling Albion	34	11	8	15	54	64	30
Aberdeen	34	12	5	17	63	66	29
Raith Rovers	34	10	9	15	60	70	29
Clyde	34	12	4	18	62	66	28
Dunfermline Athletic	34	10	8	16	68	87	28
Falkirk	*34*	*10*	*7*	*17*	*58*	*79*	*27*
Queen of the South	*34*	*6*	*6*	*22*	*38*	*101*	*18*

SCOTTISH DIVISION 2 1958-59

Ayr United	36	28	4	4	115	48	60
Arbroath	36	23	5	8	86	59	51
Stenhousemuir	36	20	6	10	87	68	46
Dumbarton	36	19	7	10	94	61	45
Brechin City	36	16	10	10	79	65	42
St. Johnstone	36	15	10	11	54	44	40
Hamilton Academical	36	15	8	13	76	62	38
East Fife	36	15	8	13	83	81	38
Berwick Rangers	36	16	6	14	63	66	38
Albion Rovers	36	14	7	15	84	79	35
Greenock Morton	36	13	8	15	68	85	34
Forfar Athletic	36	12	9	15	73	87	33
Alloa Athletic	36	12	7	17	76	81	31
Cowdenbeath	36	13	5	18	67	79	31
East Stirlingshire	36	10	8	18	50	77	28
Stranraer	36	8	11	17	63	76	27
Dundee United	36	9	7	20	62	86	25
Queen's Park	36	9	6	21	53	80	24
Montrose	36	6	6	24	49	96	18

1959 Scottish F.A. Cup

Semi-finals

St. Mirren vs Celtic	4-0
Third Lanark vs Aberdeen	1-1, 0-1

Final

Hampden Park, 25th April 1959

St. Mirren 3 (Bryceland, Miller, Baker)
Aberdeen 1 (Baird)

Attendance 108,591

1958/59 Scottish League Cup

Semi-finals

Heart of Midlothian vs Kilmarnock	3-0
Celtic vs Partick Thistle	1-2

Final

Hampden Park, 25th October 1958

Heart of Midlothian 5 (Bauld 2, Murray 2, Hamilton)
Partick Thistle 1 (Smith)

Attendance 59,960

SCOTTISH DIVISION 1 1959-60

HEART OF MIDLOTHIAN	34	23	8	3	102	51	54
Kilmarnock	34	24	2	8	67	45	50
Rangers	34	17	8	9	72	38	42
Dundee	34	16	10	8	70	49	42
Motherwell	34	16	8	10	71	61	40
Clyde	34	15	9	10	77	69	39
Hibernian	34	14	7	13	106	85	35
Ayr United	34	14	6	14	65	73	34
Celtic	34	12	9	13	73	59	33
Partick Thistle	34	14	4	16	54	78	32
Raith Rovers	34	14	3	17	64	62	31
Third Lanark	34	13	4	17	75	83	30
Dunfermline Athletic	34	10	9	15	72	80	29
St. Mirren	34	11	6	17	78	86	28
Aberdeen	34	11	6	17	54	72	28
Airdrieonians	34	11	6	17	56	80	28
Stirling Albion	*34*	*7*	*8*	*19*	*55*	*72*	*22*
Arbroath	*34*	*6*	*7*	*23*	*38*	*106*	*15*

SCOTTISH DIVISION 2 1959-60

St. Johnstone	36	24	5	7	87	47	53
Dundee United	36	22	6	8	90	45	50
Queen of the South	36	21	7	8	94	52	49
Hamilton Academical	36	21	6	9	91	62	48
Stenhousemuir	36	20	4	12	86	67	44
Dumbarton	36	18	7	11	67	53	43
Montrose	36	19	5	12	60	52	43
Falkirk	36	15	9	12	77	43	39
Berwick Rangers	36	16	5	15	62	55	37
Albion Rovers	36	14	8	14	71	78	36
Queen's Park	36	17	2	17	65	79	36
Brechin City	36	14	6	16	66	66	34
Alloa Athletic	36	13	5	18	70	85	31
Greenock Morton	36	10	8	18	67	79	28
East Stirlingshire	36	10	8	18	68	82	28
Forfar Athletic	36	10	8	18	53	84	28
Stranraer	36	10	3	23	53	77	23
East Fife	36	7	6	23	50	84	20
Cowdenbeath	36	6	2	28	42	124	14

1960 Scottish F.A. Cup

Semi-finals

Rangers vs Celtic	1-1, 4-1
Clyde vs Kilmarnock	0-2

Final

Hampden Park, 23rd April 1960

Rangers 2 (Millar 2)
Kilmarnock 0

Attendance 108,017

1959/60 Scottish League Cup

Semi-finals

Heart of Midlothian vs Cowdenbeath	9-3
Third Lanark vs Arbroath	3-0

Final

Hampden Park, 24th October 1959

Heart of Midlothian 2 (Hamilton, Young)
Third Lanark 1 (Gray)

Attendance 57,994

SCOTTISH DIVISION 1 1960-61

RANGERS	34	23	5	6	88	46	51
Kilmarnock	34	21	8	5	77	45	50
Third Lanark	34	20	2	12	100	80	42
Celtic	34	15	9	10	64	46	39
Motherwell	34	15	8	11	70	57	38
Aberdeen	34	14	8	12	72	72	36
Heart of Midlothian	34	13	8	13	51	53	34
Hibernian	34	15	4	15	66	69	34
Dundee United	34	13	7	14	60	58	33
Dundee	34	13	6	15	61	53	32
Partick Thistle	34	13	6	15	59	69	32
Dunfermline Athletic	34	12	7	15	65	81	31
Airdrieonians	34	10	10	14	61	71	30
St. Mirren	34	11	7	16	53	58	29
St. Johnstone	34	10	9	15	47	63	29
Raith Rovers	34	10	7	17	46	67	27
Clyde	*34*	*6*	*11*	*17*	*55*	*77*	*23*
Ayr United	*34*	*5*	*12*	*17*	*51*	*81*	*22*

SCOTTISH DIVISION 2 1960-61

Stirling Albion	36	24	7	5	89	37	55
Falkirk	36	24	6	6	100	40	54
Stenhousemuir	36	24	2	10	99	69	50
Stranraer	36	19	6	11	83	55	44
Queen of the South	36	20	3	13	77	52	43
Hamilton Academical	36	17	7	12	84	80	41
Montrose	36	19	2	15	75	65	40
Cowdenbeath	36	17	6	13	71	65	40
Berwick Rangers	36	14	9	13	62	69	37
Dumbarton	36	15	5	16	78	82	35
Alloa Athletic	36	13	7	16	78	68	33
Arbroath	36	13	7	16	56	76	33
East Fife	36	14	4	18	70	80	32
Brechin City	36	9	9	18	60	78	27
Queen's Park	36	10	6	20	61	87	26
East Stirlingshire	36	9	7	20	59	100	25
Albion Rovers	36	9	6	21	60	89	24
Forfar Athletic	36	10	4	22	65	98	24
Greenock Morton	36	5	11	20	56	93	21

1961 Scottish F.A. Cup

Semi-finals

Celtic vs Airdrieonians   4-0
Dunfermline Athletic vs St. Mirren   0-0, 1-0

Final

Hampden Park, 22nd April 1961

Dunfermline Athletic 0
Celtic 0

Attendance 113,328

Replay

Hampden Park, 26th April 1961

Dunfermline Athletic 2   (Thomson, Dickson)
Celtic 0

Attendance 87,866

1960/61 Scottish League Cup

Semi-finals

Rangers vs Queen of the South   7-0
Kilmarnock vs Hamilton Academical   5-1

Final

Hampden Park, 29th October 1960

Rangers 2   (Brand, Scott)
Kilmarnock 0

Attendance 82,063

SCOTTISH DIVISION 1 1961-62

DUNDEE	34	25	4	5	80	46	54
Rangers	34	22	7	5	8	31	51
Celtic	34	19	8	7	81	37	46
Dunfermline Athletic	34	19	5	10	77	46	43
Kilmarnock	34	16	10	8	74	58	42
Heart of Midlothian	34	16	6	12	54	49	38
Partick Thistle	34	16	3	15	60	55	35
Hibernian	34	14	5	15	58	72	33
Motherwell	34	13	6	15	65	62	32
Dundee United	34	13	6	15	70	71	32
Third Lanark	34	13	5	16	59	60	31
Aberdeen	34	10	9	15	60	73	29
Raith Rovers	34	10	7	17	51	73	27
Falkirk	34	11	4	19	45	68	26
Airdrieonians	34	9	7	18	57	78	25
St. Mirren	34	10	5	19	52	80	25
St. Johnstone	*34*	*9*	*7*	*18*	*35*	*61*	*25*
Stirling Albion	*34*	*6*	*6*	*22*	*34*	*76*	*18*

SCOTTISH DIVISION 2 1961-62

Clyde	36	15	4	7	108	47	54
Queen of the South	36	24	5	7	78	33	53
Greenock Morton	36	19	6	11	78	64	44
Alloa Athletic	36	17	8	11	92	78	42
Montrose	36	15	11	10	63	50	41
Arbroath	36	17	7	12	66	59	41
Stranraer	36	14	11	11	61	62	39
Berwick Rangers	36	16	6	14	83	70	38
Ayr United	36	15	8	13	71	63	38
East Fife	36	15	7	14	60	59	37
East Stirlingshire	36	15	4	17	70	81	34
Queen's Park	36	12	9	15	64	62	33
Hamilton Academical	36	14	5	17	78	79	33
Cowdenbeath	36	11	9	16	65	77	31
Stenhousemuir	36	13	5	18	69	86	31
Forfar Athletic	36	11	8	17	68	76	30
Dumbarton	36	9	10	17	49	66	28
Albion Rovers	36	10	5	21	42	74	25
Brechin City	36	5	2	29	44	123	12

1962 Scottish F.A. Cup

Semi-finals

Rangers vs Motherwell   3-1
Celtic vs St. Mirren   1-3

Final

Hampden Park, 21st April 1962

Rangers 2   (Brand, Wilson)
St. Mirren 0

Attendance 127,940

1961/62 Scottish League Cup

Semi-finals

Rangers vs St. Johnstone	3-2
Heart of Midlothian vs Stirling Albion	2-1

Final

Hampden Park, 28th October 1961

Rangers 1 (Millar (pen))
Heart of Midlothian 0 (aet.) (Cumming (pen))

Attendance 88,635

Replay

Hampden Park, 18th December 1961

Rangers 3 (Millar, Brand, McMillan)
Heart of Midlothian 1 (Davidson)

Attendance 47,500

1963 Scottish F.A. Cup

Semi-finals

Rangers vs Dundee United	5-2
Raith Rovers vs Celtic	2-5

Final

Hampden Park, 4th May 1963

Rangers 1 (Brand)
Celtic 1 (Murdoch)

Attendance 129,643

Replay

Hampden Park, 15th May 1963

Rangers 3 (Wilson, Brand 2)
Celtic 0

Attendance 120,273

SCOTTISH DIVISION 1 1962-63

RANGERS	34	25	7	2	94	28	57
Kilmarnock	34	20	8	6	92	40	48
Partick Thistle	34	20	6	8	66	44	46
Celtic	34	19	6	9	76	44	44
Heart of Midlothian	34	17	9	8	85	59	43
Aberdeen	34	17	7	10	70	47	41
Dundee United	34	15	11	8	67	52	41
Dunfermline Athletic	34	13	8	13	50	47	34
Dundee	34	12	9	13	60	49	33
Motherwell	34	10	11	13	60	63	31
Airdrieonians	34	14	2	18	52	76	30
St. Mirren	34	10	8	16	52	72	28
Falkirk	34	12	3	19	54	69	27
Third Lanark	34	9	8	17	56	68	26
Queen of the South	34	10	6	18	36	75	26
Hibernian	34	8	9	17	47	67	25
Clyde	*34*	*9*	*5*	*20*	*49*	*83*	*23*
Raith Rovers	*34*	*2*	*5*	*27*	*35*	*118*	*9*

SCOTTISH DIVISION 2 1962-63

St. Johnstone	36	25	5	6	83	37	55
East Stirlingshire	36	20	9	7	80	50	49
Greenock Morton	36	23	2	11	100	49	48
Hamilton Academical	36	18	8	10	69	56	44
Stranraer	36	16	10	10	81	70	42
Arbroath	36	18	4	14	74	51	40
Albion Rovers	36	18	2	16	72	79	38
Cowdenbeath	36	15	7	14	72	61	37
Alloa Athletic	36	15	6	15	57	56	36
Stirling Albion	36	16	4	16	74	75	36
East Fife	36	15	6	15	60	69	36
Dumbarton	36	15	4	17	64	64	34
Ayr United	36	13	8	15	68	77	34
Queen's Park	36	13	6	17	68	72	32
Montrose	36	13	5	18	57	70	31
Stenhousemuir	36	13	5	18	54	75	31
Berwick Rangers	36	11	7	18	57	77	29
Forfar Athletic	36	9	5	22	73	99	23
Brechin City	36	3	3	30	39	113	9

1962/63 Scottish League Cup

Semi-finals

St. Johnstone vs Heart of Midlothian	0-4
Rangers vs Kilmarnock	2-3

Final

Hampden Park, 27th October 1962

Heart of Midlothian 1 (Davidson)
Kilmarnock 0

Attendance 51,280

SCOTTISH DIVISION 1 1963-64

RANGERS	34	25	5	4	85	31	55
Kilmarnock	34	22	5	7	77	40	49
Celtic	34	19	9	6	89	34	47
Heart of Midlothian	34	19	9	6	74	40	47
Dunfermline Athletic	34	18	9	7	64	33	45
Dundee	34	20	5	9	94	50	45
Partick Thistle	34	15	5	14	55	54	35
Dundee United	34	13	8	13	65	49	34
Aberdeen	34	12	8	14	53	53	32
Hibernian	34	12	6	16	59	66	30
Motherwell	34	9	11	14	51	62	29
St. Mirren	34	12	5	17	44	74	29
St. Johnstone	34	11	6	17	54	70	28
Falkirk	34	11	6	17	54	84	28
Airdrieonians	34	11	4	19	52	97	26
Third Lanark	34	9	7	18	47	78	25
Queen of the South	*34*	*5*	*6*	*23*	*40*	*92*	*16*
East Stirlingshire	*34*	*5*	*2*	*27*	*37*	*91*	*12*

At the end of this season East Stirlingshire merged with Clydebank Juniors to form East Stirlingshire Clydebank with home games played alternately at Falkirk and Clydebank

SCOTTISH DIVISION 2 1963-64

Greenock Morton	36	32	3	1	135	37	67
Clyde	36	22	9	5	81	44	53
Arbroath	36	20	6	10	79	46	46
East Fife	36	16	13	7	92	57	45
Montrose	36	19	6	11	79	57	44
Dumbarton	36	16	6	14	67	59	38
Queen's Park	36	17	4	15	57	54	38
Stranraer	36	16	6	14	71	73	38
Albion Rovers	36	12	12	12	67	71	36
Raith Rovers	36	15	5	16	70	61	35
Stenhousemuir	36	15	5	16	83	75	35
Berwick Rangers	36	10	10	16	68	84	30
Hamilton Academical	36	12	6	18	65	81	30
Ayr United	36	12	5	19	58	83	29
Brechin City	36	10	8	18	61	98	28
Alloa Athletic	36	11	5	20	64	92	27
Cowdenbeath	36	7	11	18	46	72	25
Forfar Athletic	36	6	8	22	57	104	20
Stirling Albion	36	6	8	22	47	99	20

SCOTTISH DIVISION 2 1964-65

Stirling Albion	36	26	7	3	84	41	59
Hamilton Academical	36	21	8	7	86	53	50
Queen of the South	36	16	13	7	84	50	45
Queen's Park	36	17	9	10	57	41	43
East Stirlingshire Clydebank	36	15	10	11	64	50	40
Stranraer	36	17	6	13	74	64	40
Arbroath	36	13	13	10	56	51	39
Berwick Rangers	36	15	9	12	73	70	39
East Fife	36	15	7	14	78	77	37
Alloa Athletic	36	14	8	14	71	81	36
Albion Rovers	36	14	5	17	56	60	33
Cowdenbeath	36	11	10	15	55	62	32
Raith Rovers	36	9	14	13	54	61	32
Dumbarton	36	13	6	17	55	67	32
Stenhousemuir	36	11	8	17	49	74	30
Montrose	36	10	9	17	80	91	29
Forfar Athletic	36	9	7	20	63	89	25
Ayr United	36	9	6	21	49	67	24
Brechin City	36	6	7	23	53	102	19

At the end of this season East Stirlingshire Clydebank split to form East Stirlingshire FC and Clydebank FC once again. Clydebank were not initially elected into the League.

1964 Scottish F.A. Cup

Semi-finals

Rangers vs Dunfermline Athletic	1-0
Kilmarnock vs Dundee	0-4

Final

Hampden Park, 25th April 1964

Rangers 3 (Millar 2, Brand)
Dundee 1 (Cameron)

Attendance 120,982

1965 Scottish F.A. Cup

Semi-finals

Celtic vs Motherwell	2-2, 3-0
Hibernian vs Dunfermline Athletic	0-2

Final

Hampden Park, 24th April 1965

Celtic 3 (Auld 2, McNeill)
Dunfermline Athletic 2 (Melrose, McLaughlin)

Attendance 108,800

1963/64 Scottish League Cup

Semi-finals

Rangers vs Berwick Rangers	3-1
Greenock Morton vs Hibernian	1-1, 1-0

Final

Hampden Park, 26th October 1963

Rangers 5 (Forrest 4, Willoughby)
Greenock Morton 0

Attendance 105,907

1964/65 Scottish League Cup

Semi-finals

Dundee United vs Rangers	1-2
Celtic v Greenock Morton	2-0

Final

Hampden Park, 24th October 1964

Rangers 2 (Forrest 2)
Celtic 1 (Johnstone)

Attendance 91,423

SCOTTISH DIVISION 1 1964-65

KILMARNOCK	34	22	6	6	62	33	50
Heart of Midlothian	34	22	6	6	90	49	50
Dunfermline Athletic	34	22	5	7	83	36	49
Hibernian	34	21	4	9	75	47	46
Rangers	34	18	8	8	78	35	44
Dundee	34	15	10	9	86	63	40
Clyde	34	17	6	11	64	58	40
Celtic	34	16	5	13	76	57	37
Dundee United	34	15	6	13	59	51	36
Greenock Morton	34	13	7	14	54	54	33
Partick Thistle	34	11	10	13	57	58	32
Aberdeen	34	12	8	14	59	75	32
St. Johnstone	34	9	11	14	57	62	29
Motherwell	34	10	8	16	45	54	28
St. Mirren	34	9	6	19	38	70	24
Falkirk	34	7	7	20	43	85	21
Airdrieonians	*34*	*5*	*4*	*25*	*48*	*110*	*14*
Third Lanark	*34*	*3*	*1*	*30*	*22*	*99*	*7*

SCOTTISH DIVISION 1 1965-66

CELTIC	34	27	3	4	106	30	57
Rangers	34	25	5	4	91	29	55
Kilmarnock	34	20	5	9	73	46	45
Dunfermline Athletic	34	19	6	9	94	55	44
Dundee United	34	19	5	10	79	51	43
Hibernian	34	16	6	12	81	55	38
Heart of Midlothian	34	13	12	9	56	48	38
Aberdeen	34	15	6	13	61	54	36
Dundee	34	14	6	14	61	61	34
Falkirk	34	15	1	18	48	72	31
Clyde	34	13	4	17	62	64	30
Partick Thistle	34	10	10	14	55	64	30
Motherwell	34	12	4	18	52	69	28
St. Johnstone	34	9	8	17	58	81	26
Stirling Albion	34	9	8	17	40	68	26
St. Mirren	34	9	4	21	44	82	22
Greenock Morton	*34*	*8*	*5*	*21*	*42*	*84*	*21*
Hamilton Academical	*34*	*3*	*2*	*29*	*27*	*117*	*8*

SCOTTISH DIVISION 2 1965-66

Ayr United	36	22	9	5	78	37	53
Airdrieonians	36	22	6	8	107	56	50
Queen of the South	36	18	11	7	83	53	47
East Fife	36	20	4	12	72	55	44
Raith Rovers	36	16	11	9	71	43	43
Arbroath	36	15	13	8	72	52	43
Albion Rovers	36	18	7	11	58	54	43
Alloa Athletic	36	14	10	12	65	65	38
Montrose	36	15	7	14	67	63	37
Cowdenbeath	36	15	7	14	69	68	37
Berwick Rangers	36	12	11	13	69	58	35
Dumbarton	36	14	7	15	63	61	35
Queen's Park	36	13	7	16	62	65	33
Third Lanark	36	12	8	16	55	65	32
Stranraer	36	9	10	17	64	83	28
Brechin City	36	10	7	19	52	92	27
East Stirlingshire	36	9	5	22	59	91	23
Stenhousemuir	36	6	7	23	47	93	19
Forfar Athletic	36	7	3	26	61	120	17

1966 Scottish F.A. Cup

Semi-finals

Aberdeen vs Rangers	0-0, 1-2
Celtic vs Dunfermline Athletic	2-0

Final

Hampden Park, 23rd April 1966

Rangers 0
Celtic 0

Attendance 126,559

Replay

Hampden Park, 27th April 1966

Rangers 1   (Johansen)
Celtic 0

Attendance 96,862

1965/66 Scottish League Cup

Semi-finals

Celtic vs Hibernian	2-2, 4-0
Rangers vs Kilmarnock	6-4

Final

Hampden Park, 23rd October 1965

Celtic 2   (Hughes 2 (2 pens))
Rangers 1   (Young (og))

Attendance 107,609

SCOTTISH DIVISION 1 1966-67

CELTIC	34	26	6	2	111	33	58
Rangers	34	24	7	3	92	31	55
Clyde	34	20	6	8	64	48	46
Aberdeen	34	17	8	9	72	38	42
Hibernian	34	19	4	11	72	49	42
Dundee	34	16	9	9	74	51	41
Kilmarnock	34	16	8	10	59	46	40
Dunfermline Athletic	34	14	10	10	72	52	38
Dundee United	34	14	9	11	68	62	37
Motherwell	34	10	11	13	59	60	31
Heart of Midlothian	34	11	8	15	38	48	30
Partick Thistle	34	9	12	13	49	68	30
Airdrieonians	34	11	6	17	41	53	28
Falkirk	34	11	4	19	33	70	26
St. Johnstone	34	10	5	19	53	73	25
Stirling Albion	34	5	9	20	31	85	19
St. Mirren	*34*	*4*	*7*	*23*	*25*	*81*	*15*
Ayr United	*34*	*1*	*7*	*26*	*20*	*86*	*9*

SCOTTISH DIVISION 2 1966-67

Greenock Morton	38	33	3	2	113	20	69
Raith Rovers	38	27	4	7	95	44	58
Arbroath	38	25	7	6	75	32	57
Hamilton Academical	38	18	8	12	74	60	44
East Fife	38	19	4	15	70	63	42
Cowdenbeath	38	16	8	14	70	55	40
Queen's Park	38	15	10	13	78	68	40
Albion Rovers	38	17	6	15	66	62	40
Queen of the South	38	15	9	14	84	76	39
Berwick Rangers	38	16	6	16	63	55	38
Third Lanark	*38*	*13*	*8*	*17*	*67*	*78*	*34*
Montrose	38	13	8	17	63	77	34
Alloa Athletic	38	15	4	19	55	74	34
Dumbarton	38	12	9	17	55	64	33
Stranraer	38	13	7	18	57	73	33
Forfar Athletic	38	12	3	23	74	106	27
Stenhousemuir	38	9	9	20	62	104	27
Clydebank	38	8	8	22	59	92	24
East Stirlingshire	38	7	10	21	44	87	24
Brechin City	38	8	7	23	58	93	23

At the end of the season Third Lanark resigned from the League due to financial problems

1967 Scottish F.A. Cup

Semi-finals

Celtic vs Clyde	0-0, 2-0
Dundee United vs Aberdeen	0-1

Final

Hampden Park, 29th April 1967

Celtic 2   (Wallace 2)
Aberdeen 0

Attendance 126,102

1966/67 Scottish League Cup

Semi-finals

Celtic vs Airdrieonians	2-0
Rangers vs Aberdeen	2-2, 2-0

Final

Hampden Park, 29th October 1966

Celtic 1   (Lennox)
Rangers 0

Attendance 94,532

SCOTTISH DIVISION 1 1967-68

CELTIC	34	30	3	1	106	24	63
Rangers	34	28	5	1	93	34	61
Hibernian	34	20	5	9	67	49	45
Dunfermline Athletic	34	17	5	12	64	41	39
Aberdeen	34	16	5	13	63	48	37
Greenock Morton	34	15	6	13	57	53	36
Kilmarnock	34	13	8	13	59	57	34
Clyde	34	15	4	15	55	55	34
Dundee	34	13	7	14	62	59	33
Partick Thistle	34	12	7	15	51	67	31
Dundee United	34	10	11	13	53	72	31
Heart of Midlothian	34	13	4	17	56	61	30
Airdrieonians	34	10	9	15	45	58	29
St. Johnstone	34	10	7	17	43	52	27
Falkirk	34	7	12	15	36	50	26
Raith Rovers	34	9	7	18	58	86	25
Motherwell	*34*	*6*	*7*	*21*	*40*	*66*	*19*
Stirling Albion	*34*	*4*	*4*	*26*	*29*	*105*	*12*

SCOTTISH DIVISION 1 1968-69

CELTIC	34	23	8	3	89	32	54
Rangers	34	21	7	6	81	32	49
Dunfermline Athletic	34	19	7	8	63	45	45
Kilmarnock	34	15	14	5	50	32	44
Dundee United	34	17	9	8	61	49	43
St. Johnstone	34	16	5	13	66	59	37
Airdrieonians	34	13	11	10	46	44	37
Heart of Midlothian	34	14	8	12	52	54	36
Dundee	34	10	12	12	47	48	32
Greenock Morton	34	12	8	14	58	68	32
St. Mirren	34	11	10	13	40	54	32
Hibernian	34	12	7	15	60	59	31
Clyde	34	9	13	12	35	50	31
Partick Thistle	34	9	10	15	39	53	28
Aberdeen	34	9	8	17	50	59	26
Raith Rovers	34	8	5	21	45	67	21
Falkirk	*34*	*5*	*8*	*21*	*33*	*69*	*18*
Arbroath	*34*	*5*	*6*	*23*	*41*	*82*	*16*

SCOTTISH DIVISION 2 1967-68

St. Mirren	**36**	**27**	**8**	**1**	**100**	**23**	**62**
Arbroath	**36**	**24**	**5**	**7**	**87**	**34**	**53**
East Fife	36	21	7	8	71	47	49
Queen's Park	36	20	8	8	76	47	48
Ayr United	36	18	6	12	69	48	42
Queen of the South	36	16	6	14	73	57	38
Forfar Athletic	36	14	10	12	57	63	38
Albion Rovers	36	14	9	13	62	55	37
Clydebank	36	13	8	15	62	73	34
Dumbarton	36	11	11	14	63	74	33
Hamilton Academical	36	13	7	16	49	58	33
Cowdenbeath	36	12	8	16	57	62	32
Montrose	36	10	11	15	54	64	31
Berwick Rangers	36	13	4	19	34	54	30
East Stirlingshire	36	9	10	17	61	74	28
Brechin City	36	8	12	16	45	62	28
Alloa Athletic	36	11	6	19	42	69	28
Stranraer	36	8	4	24	41	80	20
Stenhousemuir	36	7	6	23	34	93	20

SCOTTISH DIVISION 2 1968-69

Motherwell	**36**	**30**	**4**	**2**	**112**	**23**	**64**
Ayr United	**36**	**23**	**7**	**6**	**82**	**31**	**53**
East Fife	36	21	6	9	82	45	48
Stirling Albion	36	21	6	9	67	40	48
Queen of the South	36	20	7	9	75	41	47
Forfar Athletic	36	18	7	11	71	56	47
Albion Rovers	36	19	5	12	60	56	43
Stranraer	36	17	7	12	57	45	41
East Stirlingshire	36	17	5	14	70	62	39
Montrose	36	15	4	17	59	71	34
Queen's Park	36	13	7	16	50	59	33
Cowdenbeath	36	12	5	19	54	67	29
Clydebank	36	6	15	15	52	67	27
Dumbarton	36	11	5	20	46	69	27
Hamilton Academical	36	8	8	20	37	72	24
Berwick Rangers	36	7	9	20	42	70	23
Brechin City	36	8	6	22	40	78	22
Alloa Athletic	36	7	7	22	45	79	21
Stenhousemuir	36	6	6	24	55	125	18

1968 Scottish F.A. Cup

Semi-finals

Dunfermline Athletic vs St. Johnstone	1-1, 2-1
Heart of Midlothian vs Greenock Morton	1-1, 2-1

Final

Hampden Park, 27th April 1968

Dunfermline Athletic 3   (Gardner 2, Lister (pen))
Heart of Midlothian 1   (Lunn (og))

Attendance 56,365

1969 Scottish F.A. Cup

Semi-finals

Celtic vs Greenock Morton	4-1
Rangers vs Aberdeen	6-1

Final

Hampden Park, 26th April 1969

Celtic 4   (McNeill, Lennox, Connelly, Chalmers)
Rangers 0

Attendance 132,874

1967/68 Scottish League Cup

Semi-finals

Ayr United vs Celtic	3-3, 1-2
Motherwell vs St. Johnstone	0-2

Final

Hampden Park, 28th October 1967

Celtic 5   (Chalmers 2, Wallace, Lennox, Hughes)
Dundee 3   (G. McLean 2, J. McLean)

Attendance 66,660

1968/69 Scottish League Cup

Semi-finals

Celtic vs Clyde	1-0
Dundee vs Hibernian	1-2

Final

Hampden Park, 5th April 1969

Celtic 6   (Lennox 3, Wallace, Auld, Craig)
Hibernian 2   (O'Rourke, Stevenson)

Attendance 74,240

SCOTTISH DIVISION 1 1969-70

CELTIC	34	27	3	4	96	33	57
Rangers	34	19	7	8	67	40	45
Hibernian	34	19	6	9	65	40	44
Heart of Midlothian	34	13	12	9	50	36	38
Dundee United	34	16	6	12	62	64	38
Dundee	34	15	6	13	49	44	36
Kilmarnock	34	13	10	11	62	57	36
Aberdeen	34	14	7	13	55	45	35
Dunfermline Athletic	34	15	5	14	45	45	35
Greenock Morton	34	13	9	12	52	52	35
Motherwell	34	11	10	13	49	51	32
Airdrieonians	34	12	8	14	59	64	32
St. Johnstone	34	11	9	14	50	62	31
Ayr United	34	12	6	16	37	52	30
St. Mirren	34	8	9	17	39	54	25
Clyde	34	9	7	18	34	56	25
Raith Rovers	*34*	*5*	*11*	*18*	*32*	*67*	*21*
Partick Thistle	*34*	*5*	*7*	*22*	*41*	*82*	*17*

SCOTTISH DIVISION 1 1970-71

CELTIC	34	25	6	3	89	23	56
Aberdeen	34	24	6	4	68	18	54
St. Johnstone	34	19	6	9	59	44	44
Rangers	34	16	9	9	58	34	41
Dundee	34	14	10	10	53	45	38
Dundee United	34	14	8	12	53	54	36
Falkirk	34	13	9	12	46	53	35
Greenock Morton	34	13	8	13	44	44	34
Airdrieonians	34	13	8	13	60	65	34
Motherwell	34	13	8	13	43	47	34
Heart of Midlothian	34	13	7	14	41	40	33
Hibernian	34	10	10	14	47	53	30
Kilmarnock	34	10	8	16	43	67	28
Ayr United	34	9	8	17	37	54	26
Clyde	34	8	10	16	33	59	26
Dunfermline Athletic	34	6	11	17	44	56	23
St. Mirren	*34*	*7*	*9*	*18*	*38*	*56*	*23*
Cowdenbeath	*34*	*7*	*3*	*24*	*33*	*77*	*17*

SCOTTISH DIVISION 2 1969-70

Falkirk	36	25	6	5	94	34	56
Cowdenbeath	36	24	7	5	81	35	55
Queen of the South	36	22	6	8	72	49	50
Stirlingshire	36	18	10	8	70	40	46
Arbroath	36	20	4	12	76	39	44
Alloa Athletic	36	19	5	12	62	41	43
Dumbarton	36	17	6	13	55	46	40
Montrose	36	15	7	14	57	55	37
Berwick Rangers	36	15	5	16	67	55	35
East Fife	36	15	4	17	59	63	34
Albion Rovers	36	14	5	17	53	64	33
East Stirlingshire	36	14	5	17	58	75	33
Clydebank	36	10	10	16	47	65	30
Brechin City	36	11	6	19	47	74	28
Queen's Park	36	10	6	20	38	62	26
Stenhousemuir	36	10	6	20	47	89	26
Stranraer	36	9	7	20	56	75	25
Forfar Athletic	36	11	1	24	55	83	23
Hamilton Academical	36	8	4	24	42	92	20

SCOTTISH DIVISION 2 1970-71

Partick Thistle	36	23	10	3	78	26	56
East Fife	36	22	7	7	86	44	51
Arbroath	36	19	8	9	80	52	46
Dumbarton	36	19	6	11	87	46	44
Clydebank	36	17	8	11	57	43	42
Montrose	36	17	7	12	78	64	41
Albion Rovers	36	15	9	12	53	52	39
Raith Rovers	36	15	9	12	62	62	39
Stranraer	36	14	8	14	54	52	36
Stenhousemuir	36	14	8	14	64	70	36
Queen of the South	36	13	9	14	50	56	35
Stirling Albion	36	12	8	16	61	61	32
Queen's Park	36	13	4	19	51	72	30
Berwick Rangers	36	10	10	16	42	60	30
Forfar Athletic	36	9	11	16	63	75	29
Alloa Athletic	36	9	11	16	56	86	29
East Stirlingshire	36	9	9	18	57	86	27
Hamilton Academical	36	8	7	21	50	79	25
Brechin City	36	6	7	23	30	73	19

1970 Scottish F.A. Cup

Semi-finals

Aberdeen vs Kilmarnock	1-0
Celtic vs Dundee	2-1

Final

Hampden Park, 11th April 1970

Aberdeen 3   (Harper (pen), McKay 2)

Celtic 1   (Lennox)

Attendance 108,434

1969/70 Scottish League Cup

Semi-finals

Ayr United vs Celtic	3-3, 1-2
Motherwell vs St. Johnstone	0-2

Final

Hampden Park, 25th October 1969

Celtic 1   (Auld)

St. Johnstone 0

Attendance 73,067

1971 Scottish F.A. Cup

Semi-finals

Celtic vs Airdrieonians	3-3, 2-0
Hibernian vs Rangers	0-0, 1-2

Final

Hampden Park, 8th May 1971

Celtic 1   (Lennox)

Rangers 1   (D. Johnstone)

Attendance 120,092

Replay

Hampden Park, 12th May 1971

Celtic 2   (Macari, Hood (pen))

Rangers 1   (Craig (og))

Attendance 103,332

1970/71 Scottish League Cup

Semi-finals

Cowdenbeath vs Rangers	0-2
Celtic vs Dumbarton	0-0, 4-3

Final

Hampden Park, 24th October 1970

Rangers 1 (D. Johnstone)

Celtic 0

Attendance 106,263

1971/72 Scottish League Cup

Semi-finals

Falkirk vs Partick Thistle	0-2
Celtic vs St. Mirren	3-0

Final

Hampden Park, 23rd October 1971

Partick Thistle 4 (Rae, Lawrie, McQuade, Bone)

Celtic 1 (Dalglish)

Attendance 62,740

SCOTTISH DIVISION 1 1971-72

CELTIC	34	28	4	2	96	28	60
Aberdeen	34	21	8	5	80	26	50
Rangers	34	21	2	11	71	38	44
Hibernian	34	19	6	9	62	34	44
Dundee	34	14	13	7	59	38	41
Heart of Midlothian	34	13	13	8	53	49	39
Partick Thistle	34	12	10	12	53	54	34
St. Johnstone	34	12	8	14	52	58	32
Dundee United	34	12	7	15	55	70	31
Motherwell	34	11	7	16	49	69	29
Kilmarnock	34	11	6	17	49	64	28
Ayr United	34	9	10	15	40	58	28
Greenock Morton	34	10	7	17	46	52	27
Falkirk	34	10	7	17	44	60	27
Airdrieonians	34	7	12	15	44	76	26
East Fife	34	5	15	14	34	61	25
Clyde	*34*	*7*	*10*	*17*	*36*	*66*	*24*
Dunfermline Athletic	*34*	*7*	*9*	*18*	*31*	*50*	*23*

SCOTTISH DIVISION 1 1972-73

CELTIC	34	26	5	3	93	28	57
Rangers	34	26	4	4	74	30	56
Hibernian	34	19	7	8	74	33	45
Aberdeen	34	16	11	7	61	34	43
Dundee	34	17	9	8	68	43	43
Ayr United	34	16	8	10	50	51	40
Dundee United	34	17	5	12	56	51	39
Motherwell	34	11	9	14	38	48	31
East Fife	34	11	8	15	46	54	30
Heart of Midlothian	34	12	6	16	39	50	30
St. Johnstone	34	10	9	15	52	67	29
Greenock Morton	34	10	8	16	47	53	28
Partick Thistle	34	10	8	16	40	53	28
Falkirk	34	7	12	15	38	56	26
Arbroath	34	9	8	17	39	63	26
Dumbarton	34	6	11	17	43	72	23
Kilmarnock	*34*	*7*	*8*	*19*	*40*	*71*	*22*
Airdrieonians	*34*	*4*	*8*	*22*	*34*	*75*	*16*

SCOTTISH DIVISION 2 1971-72

Dumbarton	36	24	4	8	89	51	52
Arbroath	36	22	8	6	71	41	52
Stirling Albion	36	21	8	7	75	37	50
St. Mirren	36	24	2	10	84	47	50
Cowdenbeath	36	19	10	7	69	28	48
Stranraer	36	18	8	10	70	62	44
Queen of the South	36	17	9	10	56	38	43
East Stirlingshire	36	17	7	12	60	58	41
Clydebank	36	14	11	11	60	52	39
Montrose	36	15	6	15	73	54	36
Raith Rovers	36	13	8	15	56	65	34
Queen's Park	36	12	9	15	47	61	33
Berwick Rangers	36	14	4	18	53	50	32
Stenhousemuir	36	10	8	18	41	58	28
Brechin City	36	8	7	21	41	79	23
Alloa Athletic	36	9	4	23	41	75	22
Forfar Athletic	36	6	9	21	32	84	21
Albion Rovers	36	7	6	23	36	61	20
Hamilton Academical	36	4	8	24	31	93	16

SCOTTISH DIVISION 2 1972-73

Clyde	36	23	10	3	68	28	56
Dunfermline Athletic	36	23	6	7	95	32	52
Raith Rovers	36	19	9	8	73	42	47
Stirling Albion	36	19	9	8	70	39	47
St. Mirren	36	19	7	10	79	50	45
Montrose	36	18	8	10	82	58	44
Cowdenbeath	36	14	10	12	57	53	38
Hamilton Academical	36	16	6	14	67	63	38
Berwick Rangers	36	16	5	15	45	54	37
Stenhousemuir	36	14	8	14	44	41	36
Queen of the South	36	13	8	15	45	52	34
Alloa Athletic	36	11	11	14	45	49	33
East Stirlingshire	36	12	8	16	52	69	32
Queen's Park	36	9	12	15	44	61	30
Stranraer	36	13	4	19	56	78	30
Forfar Athletic	36	10	9	17	38	66	29
Clydebank	36	9	6	21	48	72	21
Albion Rovers	36	5	8	23	35	83	18
Brechin City	36	5	4	27	46	99	14

1972 Scottish F.A. Cup

Semi-finals

Celtic vs Kilmarnock	3-1
Rangers vs Hibernian	1-1, 0-2

Final

Hampden Park, 6th May 1972

Celtic 6 (Dean 3, Macari 2, McNeill)

Hibernian 1 (Gordon)

Attendance 106,102

1973 Scottish F.A. Cup

Semi-finals

Ayr United vs Rangers	0-2
Celtic vs Dundee	0-0, 3-0

Final

Hampden Park, 5th May 1973

Rangers 3 (Parlane, Conn, Forsyth)

Celtic 2 (Dalglish, Connelly (pen))

Attendance 122,714

1972/73 Scottish League Cup

Semi-finals
Hibernian vs Rangers	1-0
Aberdeen vs Celtic	2-3

Final
Hampden Park, 9th December 1972

Hibernian 2 (Stanton, O'Rourke)

Celtic 1 (Dalglish)

Attendance 71,696

1973/74 Scottish League Cup

Semi-finals
Dundee vs Kilmarnock	1-0
Celtic vs Rangers	3-1

Final
Hampden Park, 15th December 1973

Dundee 1 (Wallace)

Celtic 0

Attendance 27,974

SCOTTISH DIVISION 1 1973-74

CELTIC	34	23	7	4	82	27	53
Hibernian	34	20	9	5	75	42	49
Rangers	34	21	6	7	67	34	48
Aberdeen	34	13	16	5	46	26	42
Dundee	34	16	7	11	67	48	39
Heart of Midlothian	34	14	10	10	54	43	38
Ayr United	34	15	8	11	44	40	38
Dundee United	34	15	7	12	55	51	37
Motherwell	34	14	7	13	45	40	35
Dumbarton	34	11	7	16	43	58	29
Partick Thistle	34	9	10	15	33	46	28
St. Johnstone	34	9	10	15	41	60	28
Arbroath	34	10	7	17	52	69	27
Greenock Morton	34	8	10	16	37	49	26
Clyde	34	8	9	17	29	65	25
Dunfermline Athletic	34	8	8	18	43	65	24
East Fife	*34*	*9*	*6*	*19*	*26*	*51*	*24*
Falkirk	*34*	*4*	*14*	*16*	*33*	*58*	*22*

SCOTTISH DIVISION 1 1974-75

RANGERS	34	25	6	3	86	33	56
Hibernian	34	20	9	5	69	37	49
Celtic	34	20	5	9	81	41	45
Dundee United	34	19	7	8	72	43	45
Aberdeen	34	16	9	9	66	43	41
Dundee	34	16	6	12	48	42	38
Ayr United	34	14	8	12	50	61	36
Heart of Midlothian	34	11	13	10	47	52	35
St. Johnstone	34	11	12	11	41	44	34
Motherwell	34	14	5	15	52	57	33
Airdrieonians	34	11	9	14	43	55	31
Kilmarnock	34	8	15	11	52	68	31
Partick Thistle	34	10	10	14	48	62	30
Dumbarton	34	7	10	17	44	55	24
Dunfermline Athletic	34	7	9	18	46	66	23
Clyde	34	6	10	18	40	63	22
Greenock Morton	34	6	10	18	31	62	22
Arbroath	34	5	7	22	34	66	17

SCOTTISH DIVISION 2 1973-74

Airdrieonians	36	28	4	4	102	25	60
Kilmarnock	36	26	6	4	96	44	58
Hamilton Academical	36	24	7	5	68	38	55
Queen of the South	36	20	7	9	73	41	47
Raith Rovers	36	18	9	9	69	48	45
Berwick Rangers	36	16	13	7	53	35	45
Stirling Albion	36	17	6	13	76	50	40
Montrose	36	15	7	14	71	64	37
Stranraer	36	14	8	14	64	70	36
Clydebank	36	13	8	15	47	48	34
St. Mirren	36	12	10	14	62	66	34
Alloa Athletic	36	15	4	17	47	58	34
Cowdenbeath	36	11	9	16	59	85	31
Queen's Park	36	12	4	20	42	64	28
Stenhousemuir	36	11	5	20	44	59	27
East Stirlingshire	36	9	5	22	47	73	23
Albion Rovers	36	7	6	23	38	72	20
Forfar Athletic	36	5	6	25	42	94	16
Brechin City	36	5	4	27	33	99	14

SCOTTISH DIVISION 2 1974-75

Falkirk	38	26	2	10	76	29	54
Queen of the South	38	23	7	8	77	33	53
Montrose	38	23	7	8	70	37	53
Hamilton Academical	38	21	7	10	69	30	49
East Fife	38	20	7	11	57	42	47
St. Mirren	38	19	8	11	74	52	46
Clydebank	38	18	8	12	50	40	44
Stirling Albion	38	17	9	12	67	55	43
East Stirlingshire	38	16	8	14	56	52	40
Berwick Rangers	38	17	6	15	53	49	40
Stenhousemuir	38	14	11	13	52	42	39
Albion Rovers	38	16	7	15	72	64	39
Raith Rovers	38	14	9	15	48	44	37
Stranraer	38	12	11	15	47	65	35
Alloa Athletic	38	11	11	16	49	56	33
Queen's Park	38	10	10	18	41	54	30
Brechin City	38	9	7	22	44	85	25
Meadowbank Thistle	38	9	5	24	26	87	23
Cowdenbeath	38	5	12	22	39	73	21
Forfar Athletic	38	1	7	30	27	102	9

1974 Scottish F.A. Cup

Semi-finals
Celtic vs Dundee	1-0
Heart of Midlothian vs Dundee United	1-1, 2-4

Final
Hampden Park, 4th May 1974

Celtic 3 (Hood, Murray, Deans)

Dundee United 0

Attendance 75,959

1975 Scottish F.A. Cup

Semi-finals
Celtic vs Dundee	1-0
Airdrieonians vs Motherwell	1-1, 1-0

Final
Hampden Park, 3rd May 1975

Celtic 3 (Wilson 2, McCluskey (pen))

Airdrieonians 1 (McCann)

Attendance 75,457

1974/75 Scottish League Cup

Semi-finals

Celtic vs Airdrieonians	1-0
Falkirk vs Hibernian	0-1

Final

Hampden Park, 26th October 1974

Celtic 6   (Johnstone, Deans 3, Wilson, Murray)
Hibernian 3   (Harper 3)

Attendance 53,848

1976 Scottish F.A. Cup

Semi-finals

Motherwell vs Rangers	2-3
Dumbarton vs Heart of Midlothian	0-0, 0-3

Final

Hampden Park, 1st May 1976

Rangers 3   (Johnstone 2, McDonald)
Heart of Midlothian 1   (Shaw)

Attendance 85,250

1975/76 Scottish League Cup

Semi-finals

Montrose vs Rangers	1-5
Celtic vs Partick Thistle	1-0

Final

Hampden Park, 25th October 1975

Rangers 1   (MacDonald)
Celtic 0

Attendance 58,806

SCOTTISH PREMIER 1975-76

RANGERS	36	23	8	5	60	24	54
Celtic	36	21	6	9	71	42	48
Hibernian	36	18	7	11	55	43	43
Motherwell	36	16	8	12	56	48	40
Heart of Midlothian	36	13	9	14	39	45	35
Ayr United	36	14	5	17	46	59	33
Aberdeen	36	11	10	15	49	50	32
Dundee United	36	12	8	16	46	48	32
Dundee	*36*	*11*	*10*	*15*	*49*	*62*	*32*
St. Johnstone	*36*	*3*	*5*	*28*	*29*	*79*	*11*

SCOTTISH DIVISION 1 1975-76

Partick Thistle	26	17	7	2	47	19	41
Kilmarnock	26	16	3	7	44	29	35
Montrose	26	12	6	8	53	43	30
Dumbarton	26	12	4	10	35	46	28
Arbroath	26	11	4	11	41	39	26
St. Mirren	26	9	8	9	37	37	26
Airdrieonians	26	7	11	8	44	41	25
Falkirk	26	10	5	11	38	35	25
Hamilton Academical	26	7	10	9	37	37	24
Queen of the South	26	9	6	11	41	47	24
Greenock Morton	26	7	9	10	31	40	23
East Fife	26	8	7	11	39	53	23
Dunfermline Athletic	*26*	*5*	*10*	*11*	*30*	*51*	*20*
Clyde	*26*	*5*	*4*	*17*	*34*	*52*	*14*

SCOTTISH PREMIER 1976-77

CELTIC	36	23	9	4	79	39	55
Rangers	36	18	10	8	62	37	46
Aberdeen	36	16	11	9	56	42	43
Dundee United	36	16	9	11	54	45	41
Partick Thistle	36	11	13	12	40	44	35
Hibernian	36	8	18	10	34	35	34
Motherwell	36	10	12	14	57	60	32
Ayr United	36	11	8	17	44	68	30
Heart of Midlothian	*36*	*7*	*13*	*16*	*49*	*66*	*27*
Kilmarnock	*36*	*4*	*9*	*23*	*32*	*71*	*17*

SCOTTISH DIVISION 2 1975-76

Clydebank	26	17	6	3	44	13	40
Raith Rovers	26	15	10	1	45	22	40
Alloa Athletic	26	14	7	5	44	28	35
Queen's Park	26	10	9	7	41	33	29
Cowdenbeath	26	11	7	8	44	43	29
Stirling Albion	26	9	7	10	41	33	25
Stranraer	26	11	3	12	49	43	25
East Stirlingshire	26	8	8	10	33	33	24
Albion Rovers	26	7	10	9	35	38	24
Stenhousemuir	26	9	5	12	39	44	23
Berwick Rangers	26	7	5	14	32	44	19
Forfar Athletic	26	4	10	12	28	48	18
Brechin City	26	6	5	15	28	52	17
Meadowbank Thistle	26	5	6	15	24	53	16

SCOTTISH DIVISION 1 1976-77

St. Mirren	39	25	12	2	91	38	62
Clydebank	39	24	10	5	89	38	58
Dundee	39	21	9	9	90	55	51
Greenock Morton	39	20	10	9	77	52	50
Montrose	39	16	9	14	61	62	41
Airdrieonians	39	13	12	14	63	58	38
Dumbarton	39	14	9	16	63	68	37
Arbroath	39	17	3	19	46	62	37
Queen of the South	39	11	13	15	58	65	35
Hamilton Academical	39	11	10	18	44	59	32
St. Johnstone	39	8	13	18	42	64	29
East Fife	39	8	13	18	40	71	29
Raith Rovers	*39*	*8*	*11*	*20*	*45*	*68*	*27*
Falkirk	*39*	*6*	*8*	*25*	*36*	*85*	*20*

SCOTTISH DIVISION 2 1976-77

Stirling Albion	39	22	11	6	59	29	55
Alloa Athletic	39	19	13	7	73	45	51
Dunfermline Athletic	39	20	10	9	52	36	50
Stranraer	39	20	6	13	74	53	46
Queen's Park	39	17	11	11	65	51	45
Albion Rovers	39	15	12	12	74	61	42
Clyde	39	15	11	13	68	64	41
Berwick Rangers	39	13	10	16	37	51	36
Stenhousemuir	39	15	5	19	38	49	35
East Stirlingshire	39	12	8	19	47	63	32
Meadowbank Thistle	39	8	16	15	41	57	32
Cowdenbeath	39	13	5	21	46	64	31
Brechin City	39	7	12	20	51	77	26
Forfar Athletic	39	7	10	22	43	68	24

1977 Scottish F.A. Cup

Semi-finals

Celtic vs Dundee	2-0
Rangers vs Heart of Midlothian	2-0

Final

Hampden Park, 7th May 1977

Celtic 1   (Lynch (pen))
Rangers 0

Attendance 54,252

1976/77 Scottish League Cup

Semi-finals

Aberdeen vs Rangers	5-1
Celtic vs Heart of Midlothian	2-1

Final

Hampden Park, 6th November 1976

Aberdeen 2   (Jarvie, Robb)
Celtic 1   (Dalglish (pen))

Attendance 69,707

SCOTTISH PREMIER 1977-78

RANGERS	36	24	7	5	76	39	55
Aberdeen	36	22	9	5	68	29	53
Dundee United	36	16	8	12	42	32	40
Hibernian	36	15	7	14	51	43	37
Celtic	36	15	6	15	63	54	36
Motherwell	36	13	7	16	45	52	33
Partick Thistle	36	14	5	17	52	64	33
St. Mirren	36	11	8	17	52	63	30
Ayr United	36	9	6	21	36	68	24
Clydebank	36	6	7	23	23	64	19

SCOTTISH DIVISION 1 1977-78

Greenock Morton	39	25	8	6	85	42	58
Heart of Midlothian	39	24	10	5	77	42	58
Dundee	39	25	7	7	91	44	57
Dumbarton	39	16	17	6	65	48	49
Stirling Albion	39	15	12	12	60	52	42
Kilmarnock	39	14	12	13	52	46	40
Hamilton Academical	39	12	12	15	54	56	36
St. Johnstone	39	15	6	18	52	64	36
Arbroath	39	11	13	15	42	55	35
Airdrieonians	39	12	10	17	50	64	34
Montrose	39	10	9	20	55	71	29
Queen of the South	39	8	13	18	44	68	29
Alloa Athletic	39	8	8	23	44	84	24
East Fife	39	4	11	24	39	74	19

SCOTTISH DIVISION 2 1977-78

Clyde	39	21	11	7	71	32	53
Raith Rovers	39	19	15	5	63	34	53
Dunfermline Athletic	39	18	12	9	64	41	48
Berwick Rangers	39	16	16	7	68	51	48
Falkirk	39	15	14	10	51	46	44
Forfar Athletic	39	17	8	14	61	55	42
Queen's Park	39	13	15	11	52	51	41
Albion Rovers	39	16	8	15	68	68	40
East Stirlingshire	39	15	8	16	55	65	38
Cowdenbeath	39	13	8	18	75	78	34
Stranraer	39	13	7	19	54	63	33
Stenhousemuir	39	10	10	19	43	67	30
Meadowbank Thistle	39	6	10	23	43	89	22
Brechin City	39	7	6	26	45	73	20

1978 Scottish F.A. Cup

Semi-finals

Rangers vs Dundee United	2-0
Aberdeen vs Partick Thistle	4-2

Final

Hampden Park, 6th May 1978

Rangers 2   (McDonald, Johnstone)
Aberdeen 1   (Ritchie)

Attendance 61,563

1977/78 Scottish League Cup

Semi-finals

Forfar Athletic vs Rangers	2-5
Celtic vs Heart of Midlothian	2-0

Final

Hampden Park, 18th March 1978

Rangers 2   (Cooper, Smith)
Celtic 1 (aet.)   (Edvaldsson)

Attendance 60,168

SCOTTISH PREMIER 1978-79

CELTIC	36	21	6	9	61	37	48
Rangers	36	18	9	9	52	35	45
Dundee United	36	18	8	10	56	37	44
Aberdeen	36	13	14	9	59	36	40
Hibernian	36	12	13	11	44	48	37
St. Mirren	36	15	6	15	45	41	36
Greenock Morton	36	12	12	12	52	53	36
Partick Thistle	36	13	8	15	42	39	34
Heart of Midlothian	*36*	*8*	*7*	*21*	*49*	*71*	*23*
Motherwell	*36*	*5*	*7*	*24*	*33*	*86*	*17*

SCOTTISH DIVISION 1 1978-79

Dundee	**39**	**24**	**7**	**8**	**68**	**36**	**55**
Kilmarnock	**39**	**22**	**10**	**7**	**72**	**35**	**54**
Clydebank	39	24	6	9	78	50	54
Ayr United	39	21	5	13	71	52	47
Hamilton Academical	39	17	9	13	62	60	43
Airdrieonians	39	16	8	15	72	61	40
Dumbarton	39	14	11	14	58	49	39
Stirling Albion	39	13	9	17	43	55	35
Clyde	39	13	8	18	54	65	34
Arbroath	39	11	11	17	50	61	33
Raith Rovers	39	12	8	19	47	55	32
St. Johnstone	39	10	11	18	57	66	31
Montrose	*39*	*8*	*9*	*22*	*55*	*92*	*25*
Queen of the South	*39*	*8*	*8*	*23*	*43*	*93*	*24*

SCOTTISH DIVISION 2 1978-79

Berwick Rangers	**39**	**22**	**10**	**7**	**82**	**44**	**54**
Dunfermline Athletic	**39**	**19**	**14**	**6**	**66**	**40**	**52**
Falkirk	39	19	12	8	66	37	50
East Fife	39	17	9	13	64	53	43
Cowdenbeath	39	16	10	13	63	58	42
Alloa Athletic	39	16	9	14	57	62	41
Albion Rovers	39	15	10	14	57	56	40
Forfar Athletic	39	13	12	14	55	52	38
Stranraer	39	18	2	19	52	66	38
Stenhousemuir	39	12	8	19	54	58	32
Brechin City	39	9	14	16	49	65	32
East Stirlingshire	39	12	8	19	61	87	32
Queen's Park	39	8	12	19	46	57	28
Meadowbank Thistle	39	8	8	23	37	74	24

1979 Scottish F.A. Cup

Semi-finals
Partick Thistle vs Rangers	0-0, 0-1
Aberdeen vs Hibernian	1-2

Final
Hampden Park, 12th May 1979

Rangers 0　　　**Hibernian 0**

Attendance 50,610

Replay
Hampden Park, 16th May 1979

Rangers 0　　　**Hibernian 0 (aet.)**

Attendance 33,504

2nd Replay
Hampden Park, 28th May 1979

Rangers 3　(Johnstone 2, Duncan (og))
Hibernian 2 (aet.)　(Higgins, McLeod (pen))

Attendance 30,602

1978/79 Scottish League Cup

Semi-finals
Celtic vs Rangers	2-3
Aberdeen vs Hibernian	1-0

Final
Hampden Park, 31st March 1979

Rangers 2　(MacDonald, Jackson)
Aberdeen 1　(Davidson)

Attendance 54,000

SCOTTISH PREMIER 1979-80

ABERDEEN	**36**	**19**	**10**	**7**	**68**	**36**	**48**
Celtic	36	18	11	7	61	38	47
St. Mirren	36	15	12	9	56	49	42
Dundee United	36	12	13	11	43	30	37
Rangers	36	15	7	14	50	46	37
Greenock Morton	36	14	8	14	51	46	36
Partick Thistle	36	11	14	11	43	47	36
Kilmarnock	36	11	11	14	36	52	33
Dundee	*36*	*10*	*6*	*20*	*47*	*73*	*26*
Hibernian	*36*	*6*	*6*	*24*	*29*	*67*	*18*

SCOTTISH DIVISION 1 1979-80

Heart of Midlothian	**39**	**20**	**13**	**6**	**58**	**39**	**53**
Airdrieonians	**39**	**21**	**9**	**9**	**78**	**47**	**51**
Ayr United	39	16	12	11	64	51	44
Dumbarton	39	19	6	14	59	51	44
Raith Rovers	39	14	15	10	59	46	43
Motherwell	39	16	11	12	59	48	43
Hamilton Academical	39	15	10	14	60	59	40
Stirling Albion	39	13	13	13	40	40	39
Clydebank	39	14	8	17	58	57	36
Dunfermline Athletic	39	11	13	15	39	57	35
St. Johnstone	39	12	10	17	57	74	34
Berwick Rangers	39	8	15	16	57	64	31
Arbroath	*39*	*9*	*10*	*20*	*50*	*79*	*28*
Clyde	*39*	*6*	*13*	*20*	*43*	*69*	*25*

SCOTTISH DIVISION 2 1979-80

Falkirk	**39**	**19**	**12**	**8**	**65**	**35**	**50**
East Stirlingshire	**39**	**21**	**7**	**11**	**55**	**40**	**49**
Forfar Athletic	39	19	8	12	63	51	46
Albion Rovers	39	16	12	11	73	56	44
Queen's Park	39	16	9	14	59	47	41
Stenhousemuir	39	16	9	14	56	51	41
Brechin City	39	15	10	14	61	59	40
Cowdenbeath	39	14	12	13	54	52	40
Montrose	39	14	10	15	60	63	38
East Fife	39	12	9	18	45	57	33
Stranraer	39	12	8	19	51	65	32
Meadowbank Thistle	39	12	8	19	42	70	32
Queen of the South	39	11	9	19	51	69	31
Alloa Athletic	39	11	7	21	44	64	29

1980 Scottish F.A. Cup

Semi-finals

Celtic vs Hibernian	5-0
Aberdeen vs Rangers	0-1

Final

Hampden Park, 10th May 1980

Celtic 1 (McCluskey)
Rangers 0 (aet.)

Attendance 70,303

1979/80 Scottish League Cup

Semi-finals

Dundee United vs Hamilton Academical	6-2
Aberdeen vs Greenock Morton	2-1

Final

Hampden Park, 8th December 1979

Dundee United 0
Aberdeen 0 (aet.)

Attendance 27,173

Replay

Dens Park, Dundee, 12th December 1979

Dundee United 3 (Pettigrew 2, Sturrock)
Aberdeen 0

Attendance 28,933

SCOTTISH PREMIER 1980-81

CELTIC	36	26	4	6	84	37	56
Aberdeen	36	19	11	6	61	26	49
Rangers	36	16	12	8	60	32	44
St. Mirren	36	18	8	10	56	47	44
Dundee United	36	17	9	10	66	42	43
Partick Thistle	36	10	10	16	32	48	30
Airdrieonians	36	10	9	17	36	55	29
Greenock Morton	36	10	8	18	36	58	28
Kilmarnock	*36*	*5*	*9*	*22*	*23*	*65*	*19*
Heart of Midlothian	*36*	*6*	*6*	*24*	*27*	*71*	*18*

SCOTTISH DIVISION 1 1980-81

Hibernian	39	24	9	6	67	24	57
Dundee	39	22	8	9	64	40	52
St. Johnstone	39	20	11	8	64	45	51
Raith Rovers	39	20	10	9	49	32	50
Motherwell	39	19	11	9	65	51	49
Ayr United	39	17	11	11	59	42	45
Hamilton Academical	39	15	7	17	61	57	37
Dumbarton	39	13	11	15	49	50	37
Falkirk	39	13	8	18	39	52	34
Clydebank	39	10	13	16	48	59	33
East Stirlingshire	39	6	17	16	41	56	29
Dunfermline Athletic	39	10	7	22	41	58	27
Stirling Albion	*39*	*6*	*11*	*22*	*18*	*48*	*23*
Berwick Rangers	*39*	*5*	*12*	*22*	*31*	*82*	*22*

SCOTTISH DIVISION 2 1980-81

Queen's Park	39	16	18	5	62	43	50
Queen of the South	39	16	14	9	66	53	46
Cowdenbeath	39	18	9	12	63	48	45
Brechin City	39	15	14	10	52	46	44
Forfar Athletic	39	17	9	13	63	57	43
Alloa Athletic	39	15	12	12	61	54	42
Montrose	39	16	8	15	66	55	40
Clyde	39	14	12	13	68	63	40
Arbroath	39	13	12	14	58	54	38
Stenhousemuir	39	13	11	15	63	58	37
East Fife	39	10	15	14	44	53	35
Albion Rovers	39	13	9	17	59	72	34
Meadowbank Thistle	39	11	7	21	42	64	29
Stranraer	39	7	8	24	36	83	22

1981 Scottish F.A. Cup

Semi-finals

Greenock Morton vs Rangers	1-2
Celtic vs Dundee United	0-0, 2-3

Final

Hampden Park, 9th May 1981

Rangers 0
Dundee United 0 (aet.)

Attendance 53,000

Replay

Hampden Park, 12th May 1981

Rangers 4 (Cooper, Russell, MacDonald 2)
Dundee United 1 (Dodds)

Attendance 43,099

1980/81 Scottish League Cup

Semi-finals

Dundee United vs Celtic (1-1, 3-0)	4-1
Ayr United vs Dundee (1-1, 2-3)	3-4

Final

Dens Park, Dundee, 6th December 1980

Dundee United 3 (Dodds, Sturrock 2)
Dundee 0

Attendance 24,456

SCOTTISH PREMIER 1981-82

CELTIC	36	24	7	5	79	33	55
Aberdeen	36	23	7	6	71	29	53
Rangers	36	16	11	9	57	45	43
Dundee United	36	15	10	11	61	38	40
St. Mirren	36	14	9	13	49	52	37
Hibernian	36	11	14	11	48	40	36
Greenock Morton	36	9	12	15	31	54	30
Dundee	36	11	4	21	46	72	26
Partick Thistle	*36*	*6*	*10*	*20*	*35*	*59*	*22*
Airdrieonians	*36*	*5*	*8*	*23*	*31*	*76*	*18*

SCOTTISH DIVISION 1 1981-82

Motherwell	39	26	9	4	92	36	61
Kilmarnock	39	17	17	5	60	29	51
Heart of Midlothian	39	21	8	10	65	37	50
Clydebank	39	19	8	12	61	53	46
St. Johnstone	39	17	8	14	69	60	42
Ayr United	39	15	12	12	56	50	42
Hamilton Academical	39	16	8	15	52	49	40
Queen's Park	39	13	10	16	41	41	36
Falkirk	39	11	14	14	49	52	36
Dunfermline Athletic	39	11	14	14	46	56	36
Dumbarton	39	13	9	17	49	61	35
Raith Rovers	39	11	7	21	31	59	29
East Stirlingshire	*39*	*7*	*10*	*22*	*38*	*77*	*24*
Queen of the South	*39*	*4*	*10*	*25*	*44*	*93*	*18*

SCOTTISH DIVISION 2 1981-82

Clyde	39	24	11	4	79	38	59
Alloa Athletic	39	19	12	8	66	42	50
Arbroath	39	20	10	9	62	50	50
Berwick Rangers	39	20	8	11	66	38	48
Brechin City	39	18	10	11	61	43	46
Forfar Athletic	39	15	15	9	59	35	45
East Fife	39	14	9	16	48	51	37
Stirling Albion	39	12	11	16	39	44	35
Cowdenbeath	39	11	13	15	51	57	35
Montrose	39	12	8	19	49	74	32
Albion Rovers	39	13	5	21	52	74	31
Meadowbank Thistle	39	10	10	19	49	62	30
Stenhousemuir	39	11	6	22	41	65	28
Stranraer	39	7	6	26	36	85	20

1982 Scottish F.A. Cup

Semi-finals

Aberdeen vs St. Mirren	1-1, 3-2
Forfar Athletic vs Rangers	0-0, 1-3

Final

Hampden Park, 22nd May 1982

Aberdeen 4   (McLeish, McGhee, Strachan, Cooper)
Rangers 1 (aet.)   (McDonald)

Attendance 53,788

SCOTTISH PREMIER 1982-83

DUNDEE UNITED	36	24	8	4	90	35	56
Celtic	36	25	5	6	90	36	55
Aberdeen	36	25	5	6	76	24	55
Rangers	36	13	12	11	52	41	38
St. Mirren	36	11	12	13	47	51	34
Dundee	36	9	11	16	42	53	29
Hibernian	36	11	7	18	35	51	29
Motherwell	36	11	5	20	39	73	27
Greenock Morton	*36*	*6*	*8*	*22*	*30*	*74*	*20*
Kilmarnock	*36*	*3*	*11*	*22*	*28*	*91*	*17*

SCOTTISH DIVISION 1 1982-83

St. Johnstone	39	25	5	9	59	37	55
Heart of Midlothian	39	22	10	7	79	38	54
Clydebank	39	20	10	9	72	49	50
Partick Thistle	39	20	9	10	66	45	49
Airdrieonians	39	16	7	16	62	46	39
Alloa Athletic	39	14	11	14	52	52	39
Falkirk	39	15	6	18	45	55	36
Dumbarton	39	13	10	16	50	59	36
Hamilton Academical	39	11	12	16	54	66	34
Raith Rovers	39	13	8	18	64	63	34
Clyde	39	14	6	19	55	66	34
Ayr United	39	12	8	19	45	61	32
Dunfermline Athletic	*39*	*7*	*17*	*15*	*39*	*69*	*31*
Queen's Park	*39*	*16*	*11*	*22*	*44*	*80*	*23*

SCOTTISH DIVISION 2 1982-83

Brechin City	39	21	3	5	77	38	55
Meadowbank Thistle	39	23	8	8	64	45	54
Arbroath	39	21	7	11	78	51	49
Forfar Athletic	39	18	12	9	58	37	48
Stirling Albion	39	18	10	11	57	41	46
East Fife	39	16	11	12	68	43	43
Queen of the South	39	17	7	15	75	56	42
Cowdenbeath	39	13	12	14	55	53	38
Berwick Rangers	39	13	10	16	47	60	36
Albion Rovers	39	14	6	19	55	6	34
Stenhousemuir	39	7	14	18	43	66	29
Stranraer	39	10	6	23	46	79	27
East Stirlingshire	39	7	9	23	43	79	23
Montrose	39	8	6	25	37	86	22

1981/82 Scottish League Cup

Semi-finals

Dundee United vs Aberdeen (0-1, 3-0)	3-1
St. Mirren vs Rangers (2-2, 1-2)	3-4

Final

Hampden Park, 28th November 1981

Rangers 2   (Cooper, Redford)
Dundee United 1   (Milne)

Attendance 53,777

1983 Scottish F.A. Cup

Semi-finals

Aberdeen vs Celtic	1-0
Rangers vs St. Mirren	1-1, 1-0

Final

Hampden Park, 21st May 1983

Aberdeen 1   (Black)
Rangers 0 (aet.)

Attendance 62,979

1982/83 Scottish League Cup

Semi-finals

Celtic vs Dundee United (2-0, 1-2)   3-2
Rangers vs Heart of Midlothian (2-0, 2-1)   4-1

Final

Hampden Park, 2nd December 1982

Celtic 2   (Nicholas, MacLeod)
Rangers 1   (Bett)

Attendance 55,372

1984 Scottish F.A. Cup

Semi-finals

Aberdeen vs Dundee   2-0
St. Mirren vs Celtic   1-2

Final

Hampden Park, 19th May 1984

Aberdeen 2   (Black, McGhee)
Celtic 1 (aet.)   (P. McStay)

Attendance 58,900

SCOTTISH PREMIER 1983-84

ABERDEEN	36	25	7	4	78	21	57
Celtic	36	21	8	7	80	41	50
Dundee United	36	18	11	7	67	39	47
Rangers	36	15	12	9	53	41	42
Heart of Midlothian	36	10	16	10	38	47	36
St. Mirren	36	9	14	13	55	59	32
Hibernian	36	12	7	17	45	55	31
Dundee	36	11	5	20	50	74	27
St. Johnstone	*36*	*10*	*3*	*23*	*36*	*81*	*23*
Motherwell	*36*	*4*	*7*	*25*	*31*	*75*	*15*

1983/84 Scottish League Cup

Semi-finals

Dundee United vs Rangers (1-1, 0-2)   1-3
Aberdeen vs Celtic (0-0, 0-1)   0-1

Final

Hampden Park, 25th March 1984

Rangers 3   (McCoist 3 (2 pens))
Celtic 2 (aet.)   (McClair, Reid)

Attendance 66,369

SCOTTISH DIVISION 1 1983-84

Greenock Morton	39	21	12	6	75	46	54
Dumbarton	39	20	11	8	66	44	51
Partick Thistle	39	19	8	12	67	50	46
Clydebank	39	16	13	10	62	50	45
Brechin City	39	14	14	11	56	58	42
Kilmarnock	39	16	6	17	57	53	38
Falkirk	39	16	6	17	46	54	38
Clyde	39	12	13	14	53	50	37
Hamilton Academical	39	11	14	14	43	46	36
Airdrieonians	39	13	10	16	45	53	36
Meadowbank Thistle	39	12	10	17	49	69	34
Ayr United	39	10	12	17	56	70	32
Raith Rovers	*39*	*10*	*11*	*18*	*53*	*62*	*31*
Alloa Athletic	*39*	*8*	*10*	*21*	*41*	*64*	*26*

SCOTTISH PREMIER 1984-85

ABERDEEN	36	27	5	4	89	26	59
Celtic	36	22	8	6	77	30	52
Dundee United	36	20	7	9	67	33	47
Rangers	36	13	12	11	47	38	38
St. Mirren	36	17	4	15	51	56	38
Dundee	36	15	7	14	48	50	37
Heart of Midlothian	36	13	5	18	47	64	31
Hibernian	36	10	7	19	38	61	27
Dumbarton	*36*	*6*	*7*	*23*	*29*	*64*	*19*
Greenock Morton	*36*	*5*	*2*	*29*	*29*	*100*	*12*

SCOTTISH DIVISION 1 1984-85

Motherwell	39	21	8	10	62	36	50
Clydebank	39	17	14	8	57	37	48
Falkirk	39	19	7	13	65	54	45
Hamilton Academical	39	16	11	12	48	49	43
Airdrieonians	39	17	8	14	70	59	42
Forfar Athletic	39	14	13	12	54	49	41
Ayr United	39	15	9	15	57	52	39
Clyde	39	14	11	14	47	48	39
Brechin City	39	14	9	16	49	57	37
East Fife	39	12	12	15	55	56	36
Partick Thistle	39	13	9	17	50	55	35
Kilmarnock	39	12	10	17	42	61	34
Meadowbank Thistle	*39*	*11*	*10*	*18*	*50*	*66*	*32*
St. Johnstone	*39*	*10*	*5*	*24*	*51*	*78*	*25*

SCOTTISH DIVISION 2 1983-84

Forfar Athletic	39	27	9	3	73	31	63
East Fife	39	20	7	12	57	42	47
Berwick Rangers	39	16	11	12	60	38	43
Stirling Albion	39	14	14	11	51	42	42
Arbroath	39	18	6	15	51	46	42
Queen of the South	39	16	10	13	51	46	42
Stenhousemuir	39	14	11	14	47	57	39
Stranraer	39	13	12	14	47	47	38
Dunfermline Athletic	39	13	10	16	44	45	36
Queen's Park	39	14	8	17	58	63	36
East Stirlingshire	39	10	11	18	51	66	31
Montrose	39	12	7	20	36	59	31
Cowdenbeath	39	10	9	20	44	58	29
Albion Rovers	39	8	11	20	46	76	27

SCOTTISH DIVISION 2 1984-85

Montrose	39	22	9	8	57	40	53
Alloa Athletic	39	20	10	9	58	40	50
Dunfermline Athletic	39	17	15	7	61	36	49
Cowdenbeath	39	18	11	10	68	39	47
Stenhousemuir	39	15	15	9	45	43	45
Stirling Albion	39	15	13	11	62	47	43
Raith Rovers	39	18	6	15	69	57	42
Queen of the South	39	10	14	15	42	56	34
Albion Rovers	39	13	8	18	49	72	34
Queen's Park	39	12	9	18	48	55	33
Stranraer	39	13	6	20	52	67	32
East Stirlingshire	39	8	15	16	38	53	31
Berwick Rangers	39	8	12	19	36	49	28
Arbroath	39	9	7	23	35	66	25

1985 Scottish F.A. Cup

Semi-finals

Dundee United vs Aberdeen	0-0, 2-1
Motherwell vs Celtic	1-1, 0-3

Final

Hampden Park, 18th May 1985

Celtic 2   (Provan, McGarvey)

Dundee United 0

Attendance 60,346

1984/85 Scottish League Cup

Semi-finals

Heart of Midlothian vs Dundee United (1-2, 1-3)	2-5
Rangers vs Meadowbank Thistle (4-0, 1-1)	5-1

Final

Hampden Park, 28th October 1984

Rangers 1   (Ferguson)

Dundee United 0

Attendance 44,698

SCOTTISH PREMIER 1985-86

CELTIC	36	20	10	6	67	38	50
Heart of Midlothian	36	20	10	6	59	33	50
Dundee United	36	18	11	7	59	31	47
Aberdeen	36	16	12	8	62	31	44
Rangers	36	13	9	14	53	45	35
Dundee	36	14	7	15	45	51	35
St. Mirren	36	13	5	18	42	63	31
Hibernian	36	11	6	19	49	63	28
Motherwell	36	7	6	23	33	66	20
Clydebank	36	6	8	22	29	77	20

SCOTTISH DIVISION 1 1985-86

Hamilton Academical	39	24	8	7	77	44	56
Falkirk	39	17	11	11	57	39	45
Kilmarnock	39	18	8	13	62	49	44
Forfar Athletic	39	17	10	12	51	43	44
East Fife	39	14	15	10	54	46	43
Dumbarton	39	16	11	12	59	52	43
Greenock Morton	39	14	11	14	57	63	39
Partick Thistle	39	10	16	13	53	64	36
Airdrieonians	39	12	11	16	51	50	35
Brechin City	39	13	9	17	58	64	35
Clyde	39	9	17	13	49	59	35
Montrose	39	10	14	15	43	54	34
Ayr United	*39*	*10*	*11*	*18*	*41*	*60*	*31*
Alloa Athletic	*39*	*6*	*14*	*19*	*49*	*74*	*26*

SCOTTISH DIVISION 2 1985-86

Dunfermline Athletic	39	23	11	5	91	47	57
Queen of the South	39	23	9	7	71	36	55
Meadowbank Thistle	39	19	11	9	68	45	49
Queen's Park	39	19	8	12	61	39	46
Stirling Albion	39	18	8	13	57	53	44
St. Johnstone	39	18	6	15	63	55	42
Stenhousemuir	39	16	8	15	55	63	40
Arbroath	39	15	9	15	56	50	39
Raith Rovers	39	15	7	17	67	65	37
Cowdenbeath	39	14	9	16	52	53	37
East Stirlingshire	39	11	6	22	49	69	28
Berwick Rangers	39	7	11	21	45	80	25
Albion Rovers	39	8	8	23	38	86	24
Stranraer	39	9	5	25	41	83	23

1986 Scottish F.A. Cup

Semi-finals

Hibernian vs Aberdeen	0-3
Dundee United vs Heart of Midlothian	0-1

Final

Hampden Park, 10th May 1986

Aberdeen 3   (Hewitt 2, Stark)

Heart of Midlothian 0

Attendance 62,841

1985/86 Scottish League Cup

Semi-finals

Dundee United vs Aberdeen (0-1, 0-1)	0-2
Hibernian vs Rangers (2-0, 0-1)	2-1

Final

Hampden Park, 27th October 1985

Aberdeen 3   (Black 2, Stark)

Hibernian 0

Attendance 40,061

SCOTTISH PREMIER 1986-87

RANGERS	44	31	7	6	85	23	69
Celtic	44	27	9	8	90	41	63
Dundee United	44	24	12	8	66	36	60
Aberdeen	44	21	16	7	63	29	58
Heart of Midlothian	44	21	14	9	64	43	56
Dundee	44	18	12	14	74	57	48
St. Mirren	44	12	12	20	36	51	36
Motherwell	44	11	12	21	43	64	34
Hibernian	44	10	13	21	44	70	33
Falkirk	44	8	10	26	31	70	26
Clydebank	*44*	*6*	*12*	*26*	*35*	*93*	*24*
Hamilton Academical	*44*	*6*	*9*	*29*	*39*	*93*	*21*

1986/87 Scottish League Cup

Semi-finals

Celtic vs Motherwell	2-2

Celtic won 5-4 on penalties

Dundee United vs Rangers	1-2

Final

Hampden Park, 26th October 1986

Rangers 2 (Durrant, Cooper (pen))
Celtic 1 (McClair)

Attendance 74,219

SCOTTISH DIVISION 1 1986-87

Greenock Morton	44	24	9	11	88	56	57
Dunfermline Athletic	44	23	10	11	61	41	56
Dumbarton	44	23	7	14	67	52	53
East Fife	44	15	21	8	68	55	51
Airdrieonians	44	20	11	13	58	46	51
Kilmarnock	44	17	11	16	62	53	45
Forfar Athletic	44	14	15	15	61	63	43
Partick Thistle	44	12	15	17	49	54	39
Clyde	44	11	16	17	48	56	38
Queen of the South	44	11	12	21	50	71	34
Brechin City	*44*	*11*	*10*	*23*	*44*	*72*	*32*
Montrose	*44*	*9*	*11*	*24*	*37*	*74*	*29*

SCOTTISH PREMIER 1987-88

CELTIC	44	31	10	3	79	23	72
Heart of Midlothian	44	23	16	5	74	32	62
Rangers	44	26	8	10	85	34	60
Aberdeen	44	21	17	6	56	25	59
Dundee United	44	16	15	13	54	47	47
Hibernian	44	12	19	13	41	42	43
Dundee	44	17	7	20	70	64	41
Motherwell	44	13	10	21	37	56	36
St. Mirren	44	10	15	19	41	64	35
Falkirk	*44*	*10*	*11*	*23*	*41*	*75*	*31*
Dunfermline Athletic	*44*	*8*	*10*	*26*	*41*	*84*	*26*
Greenock Morton	*44*	*3*	*10*	*31*	*27*	*100*	*16*

SCOTTISH DIVISION 2 1986-87

Meadowbank Thistle	39	23	9	7	69	38	55
Raith Rovers	39	16	20	3	73	44	52
Stirling Albion	39	20	12	7	55	33	52
Ayr United	39	22	8	9	70	49	52
St. Johnstone	39	16	13	10	59	49	45
Alloa Athletic	39	17	7	15	48	50	41
Cowdenbeath	39	16	8	15	59	55	40
Albion Rovers	39	15	9	15	48	51	39
Queen's Park	39	9	19	11	48	49	37
Stranraer	39	9	11	19	41	59	29
Arbroath	39	11	7	21	46	66	29
Stenhousemuir	39	10	9	20	37	58	29
East Stirlingshire	39	6	11	22	33	56	23
Berwick Rangers	39	8	7	24	40	69	23

SCOTTISH DIVISION 1 1987-88

Hamilton Academical	44	22	12	10	67	39	56
Meadowbank Thistle	44	20	12	12	70	51	52
Clydebank	44	21	7	16	59	61	49
Forfar Athletic	44	16	16	12	67	58	48
Raith Rovers	44	19	7	18	81	76	45
Airdrieonians	44	16	13	15	65	68	45
Queen of the South	44	14	15	15	56	67	43
Partick Thistle	44	16	9	19	60	64	41
Clyde	44	17	6	21	73	75	40
Kilmarnock	44	13	11	20	55	60	37
East Fife	*44*	*13*	*10*	*21*	*61*	*76*	*36*
Dumbarton	*44*	*12*	*12*	*20*	*51*	*70*	*36*

1987 Scottish F.A. Cup

Semi-finals

Dundee vs Dundee United	2-3
Heart of Midlothian vs St. Mirren	1-2

Final

Hampden Park, 16th May 1987

St. Mirren 1 (Ferguson)
Dundee United 0 (aet.)

Attendance 51,782

SCOTTISH DIVISION 2 1987-88

Ayr United	39	27	7	5	95	31	61
St. Johnstone	39	25	9	5	74	24	59
Queen's Park	39	21	9	9	64	44	51
Brechin City	39	20	8	11	56	40	48
Stirling Albion	39	18	10	11	60	51	46
East Stirlingshire	39	15	13	11	51	47	43
Alloa Athletic	39	16	8	15	50	46	40
Montrose	39	12	11	16	45	51	35
Arbroath	39	10	14	15	54	66	34
Stenhousemuir	39	12	9	18	49	58	33
Cowdenbeath	39	10	13	16	51	66	33
Albion Rovers	39	10	11	18	45	75	31
Berwick Rangers	39	6	4	29	32	77	16
Stranraer	39	4	8	27	34	84	16

1988 Scottish F.A. Cup

Semi-finals

Celtic vs Heart of Midlothian	2-1
Aberdeen vs Dundee United	0-0, 1-1, 0-1

Final

Hampden Park, 14th May 1988

Celtic 2   (McAvennie 2)

Dundee United 1   (Gallacher)

Attendance 74,000

1987/88 Scottish League Cup

Semi-finals

Aberdeen vs Dundee	2-0
Motherwell vs Rangers	1-3

Final

Hampden Park, 25th October 1987

Rangers 3   (Cooper, Durrant, Fleck)

Aberdeen 3 (aet.)   (Bett (pen), Hewitt, Falconer)

Rangers won 5-3 on penalties

Attendance 71,961

SCOTTISH PREMIER 1988-89

RANGERS	36	26	4	6	62	26	56
Aberdeen	36	18	14	4	51	25	50
Celtic	36	21	4	11	66	44	46
Dundee United	36	16	12	8	44	26	44
Hibernian	36	13	9	14	37	36	35
Heart of Midlothian	36	9	13	14	35	42	31
St. Mirren	36	11	7	18	39	55	29
Dundee	36	9	10	17	34	48	28
Motherwell	36	7	13	16	35	44	27
Hamilton Academical	*36*	*6*	*2*	*28*	*19*	*76*	*14*

SCOTTISH DIVISION 1 1988-89

Dunfermline Athletic	39	22	10	7	60	36	54
Falkirk	39	22	8	9	71	37	52
Clydebank	39	18	12	9	80	55	48
Airdrieonians	39	17	13	9	66	44	47
Greenock Morton	39	16	9	14	46	46	41
St. Johnstone	39	14	12	13	51	42	40
Raith Rovers	39	15	10	14	50	52	40
Partick Thistle	39	13	11	15	57	58	37
Forfar Athletic	39	10	16	13	52	56	36
Meadowbank Thistle	39	13	10	16	45	50	36
Ayr United	39	13	9	17	56	72	35
Clyde	39	9	16	14	40	52	34
Kilmarnock	*39*	*10*	*14*	*15*	*47*	*60*	*34*
Queen of the South	*39*	*2*	*8*	*29*	*38*	*99*	*10*

Queen of the South 2 had points deducted

SCOTTISH DIVISION 2 1988-89

Albion Rovers	39	21	8	10	65	48	50
Alloa Athletic	39	17	11	11	66	48	45
Brechin City	39	15	13	11	58	49	43
Stirling Albion	39	15	12	12	64	55	42
East Fife	39	14	13	12	55	54	41
Montrose	39	15	11	13	54	55	41
Queen's Park	39	10	18	11	50	49	38
Cowdenbeath	39	13	14	12	48	52	38
East Stirlingshire	39	13	11	15	54	58	37
Arbroath	39	11	15	13	56	63	37
Stranraer	39	12	12	15	58	63	36
Dumbarton	39	12	10	17	45	55	34
Berwick Rangers	39	10	13	16	50	59	33
Stenhousemuir	39	9	11	19	44	59	29

Cowdenbeath had 2 points deducted

1989 Scottish F.A. Cup

Semi-finals

Rangers vs St. Johnstone	0-0, 4-0
Celtic vs Hibernian	3-1

Final

Hampden Park, 20th May 1989

Celtic 1   (Miller)

Rangers 0

Attendance 72,069

1988/89 Scottish League Cup

Semi-finals

Aberdeen vs Dundee United	2-0
Heart of Midlothian vs Rangers	0-3

Final

Hampden Park, 23rd October 1988

Rangers 3   (McCoist 2 (1 pen), I. Ferguson)

Aberdeen 2   (Dodds 2)

Attendance 72,122

SCOTTISH PREMIER 1989-90

RANGERS	36	20	11	5	48	19	51
Aberdeen	36	17	10	9	56	33	44
Heart of Midlothian	36	16	12	8	54	35	44
Dundee United	36	11	13	12	36	39	35
Celtic	36	10	14	12	37	37	34
Motherwell	36	11	12	13	43	47	34
Hibernian	36	12	10	14	32	41	34
Dunfermline Athletic	36	11	8	17	37	50	30
St. Mirren	36	10	10	16	28	48	30
Dundee	*36*	*5*	*14*	*17*	*41*	*65*	*24*

SCOTTISH DIVISION 1 1989-90

St. Johnstone	39	25	8	6	81	39	58
Airdrieonians	39	23	8	8	77	45	54
Clydebank	39	17	10	12	74	64	44
Falkirk	39	14	15	10	59	46	43
Raith Rovers	39	15	12	12	57	50	42
Hamilton Academical	39	14	13	12	52	53	41
Meadowbank Thistle	39	13	13	13	41	46	39
Partick Thistle	39	12	14	13	62	53	38
Clyde	39	10	15	14	39	46	35
Ayr United	39	11	13	15	41	62	35
Greenock Morton	39	9	16	14	38	46	34
Forfar Athletic	39	8	15	16	51	65	29
Albion Rovers	*39*	*8*	*11*	*20*	*50*	*78*	*27*
Alloa Athletic	*39*	*6*	*13*	*20*	*41*	*70*	*25*

Forfar Athletic had 2 points deducted for a breach of the rules

SCOTTISH DIVISION 2 1989-90

Brechin City	39	19	11	9	59	44	49
Kilmarnock	39	22	4	13	67	39	48
Stirling Albion	39	20	7	12	73	50	47
Stenhousemuir	39	18	8	13	60	53	44
Berwick Rangers	39	18	5	16	66	57	41
Dumbarton	39	15	10	14	70	73	40
Cowdenbeath	39	13	13	13	58	54	39
Stranraer	39	15	8	16	57	59	38
East Fife	39	12	12	15	60	63	36
Queen of the South	39	11	14	14	58	69	36
Queen's Park	39	13	10	16	40	51	36
Arbroath	39	12	10	17	47	61	34
Montrose	39	10	12	17	53	63	32
East Stirlingshire	39	8	10	21	34	66	26

1990 Scottish F.A. Cup

Semi-finals

Celtic vs Clydebank	2-0
Aberdeen vs Dundee United	4-0

Final

Hampden Park, 12th May 1990

Aberdeen 0
Celtic 0 (aet.)

Aberdeen won 9-8 on penalties   Attendance 60,493

1989/90 Scottish League Cup

Semi-finals

Aberdeen vs Celtic	1-0
Dunfermline Athletic vs Rangers	0-5

Final

Hampden Park, 22nd October 1989

Aberdeen 2 (Mason 2)
Rangers 1 (aet.) (Walters (pen))

Attendance 61,190

SCOTTISH PREMIER 1990-91

RANGERS	36	24	7	5	62	23	55
Aberdeen	36	22	9	5	62	27	53
Celtic	36	17	7	12	52	38	41
Dundee United	36	17	7	12	41	29	41
Heart of Midlothian	36	14	7	15	48	55	35
Motherwell	36	12	9	15	51	50	33
St. Johnstone	36	11	9	16	41	54	31
Dunfermline Athletic	36	8	11	17	38	61	27
Hibernian	36	6	13	17	24	51	25
St. Mirren	36	5	9	22	28	59	19

SCOTTISH DIVISION 1 1990-91

Falkirk	39	21	12	6	70	35	54
Airdrieonians	39	21	11	7	69	43	53
Dundee	39	22	8	9	59	33	52
Partick Thistle	39	16	13	10	56	53	45
Kilmarnock	39	15	13	11	58	48	43
Hamilton Academical	39	16	10	13	50	41	42
Raith Rovers	39	14	9	16	54	64	37
Clydebank	39	13	10	16	65	70	36
Greenock Morton	39	11	13	15	48	55	35
Forfar Athletic	39	9	15	15	50	57	33
Meadowbank Thistle	39	10	13	16	56	68	33
Ayr United	39	10	12	17	47	59	32
Clyde	*39*	*9*	*9*	*21*	*41*	*61*	*27*
Brechin City	*39*	*7*	*10*	*22*	*44*	*80*	*24*

SCOTTISH DIVISION 2 1990-91

Stirling Albion	39	20	14	5	62	24	54
Montrose	39	20	6	13	54	34	46
Cowdenbeath	39	18	9	12	64	50	45
Stenhousemuir	39	16	12	11	56	42	44
Queen's Park	39	17	8	14	48	42	42
Stranraer	39	18	4	17	61	60	40
Dumbarton	39	15	10	14	49	49	40
Berwick Rangers	39	15	10	14	51	57	40
Alloa Athletic	39	13	11	15	51	46	37
East Fife	39	14	9	16	57	65	37
Albion Rovers	39	11	13	15	48	63	35
Queen of the South	39	9	12	18	46	62	30
East Stirlingshire	39	9	11	19	36	71	29
Arbroath	39	8	11	20	41	59	27

1991 Scottish F.A. Cup

Semi-finals

Celtic vs Motherwell	0-0, 2-4
Dundee United vs St. Johnstone	2-1

Final

Hampden Park, 18th May 1991

Motherwell 4 (Ferguson, O'Donnell, Angus, Kirk)
Dundee United 2 (aet.) (Bowman, O'Neil, Jackson)

Attendance 57,319

1990/91 Scottish League Cup

Semi-finals

Aberdeen vs Rangers   0-1
Celtic vs Dundee United   2-0

Final

Hampden Park, 28th October 1990

Rangers 2   (Walters, Gough)
Celtic 1 (aet.)   (Elliott)

Attendance 62,817

SCOTTISH PREMIER 1991-92

RANGERS	44	33	6	5	101	31	72
Heart of Midlothian	44	27	9	8	60	37	63
Celtic	44	26	10	8	88	42	62
Dundee United	44	19	13	12	66	50	51
Hibernian	44	16	17	11	53	45	49
Aberdeen	44	17	14	13	55	42	48
Airdrieonians	44	13	10	21	50	70	36
St. Johnstone	44	13	10	21	52	73	36
Falkirk	44	12	11	21	54	73	35
Motherwell	44	10	14	20	43	61	34
St. Mirren	*44*	*6*	*12*	*26*	*33*	*73*	*24*
Dunfermline Athletic	*44*	*4*	*10*	*30*	*22*	*80*	*18*

SCOTTISH DIVISION 1 1991-92

Dundee	44	23	12	9	80	48	58
Partick Thistle	44	23	11	10	52	36	57
Hamilton Academical	44	22	13	9	72	48	57
Kilmarnock	44	21	12	11	59	37	54
Raith Rovers	44	21	11	12	59	42	53
Ayr United	44	18	11	15	63	55	47
Greenock Morton	44	17	12	15	66	59	46
Stirling Albion	44	14	13	17	50	57	41
Clydebank	44	12	12	20	59	77	36
Meadowbank Thistle	44	7	16	21	37	59	30
Montrose	*44*	*5*	*17*	*22*	*45*	*85*	*27*
Forfar Athletic	*44*	*5*	*12*	*27*	*36*	*85*	*22*

SCOTTISH DIVISION 2 1991-92

Dumbarton	39	20	12	7	65	37	52
Cowdenbeath	39	22	7	10	74	52	51
Alloa Athletic	39	20	10	9	58	38	50
East Fife	39	19	11	9	72	57	49
Clyde	39	18	7	14	61	43	43
East Stirlingshire	39	15	11	13	61	70	41
Arbroath	39	12	14	13	49	48	38
Brechin City	39	13	12	14	54	55	38
Queen's Park	39	14	7	18	59	63	35
Stranraer	39	13	9	17	46	56	35
Queen of the South	39	14	5	20	71	86	33
Berwick Rangers	39	10	11	18	50	65	31
Stenhousemuir	39	11	8	20	46	57	30
Albion Rovers	39	5	10	24	42	81	20

1992 Scottish F.A. Cup

Semi-finals

Celtic vs Rangers   0-1
Airdrieonians vs Heart of Midlothian   0-0, 1-1
Airdrieonians won 4-2 on penalties

Final

Hampden Park, 9th May 1992

Rangers 2   (Hateley, McCoist)
Airdrieonians 1   (Smith)

Attendance 44,045

1991/92 Scottish League Cup

Semi-finals

Airdrieonians vs Dunfermline Athletic   1-1
Dunfermline Athletic won 3-2 on penalties
Hibernian vs Rangers   1-0

Final

Hampden Park, 27th October 1991

Hibernian 2   (McIntyre (pen), Wright)
Dunfermline Athletic 0

Attendance 40,377

SCOTTISH PREMIER 1992-93

RANGERS	44	33	7	4	97	35	73
Aberdeen	44	27	10	7	87	36	64
Celtic	44	24	12	8	68	41	60
Dundee United	44	19	9	16	56	49	47
Heart of Midlothian	44	15	14	15	37	35	44
St. Johnstone	44	10	20	14	52	66	40
Hibernian	44	12	13	19	54	64	37
Partick Thistle	44	12	12	20	50	71	36
Motherwell	44	11	13	20	46	62	35
Dundee	44	11	12	21	48	68	34
Falkirk	*44*	*11*	*7*	*26*	*60*	*86*	*29*
Airdrieonians	*44*	*6*	*17*	*21*	*35*	*70*	*29*

SCOTTISH DIVISION 1 1992-93

Raith Rovers	44	25	15	4	85	41	65
Kilmarnock	44	21	12	11	67	40	54
Dunfermline Athletic	44	22	8	14	64	47	52
St. Mirren	44	21	9	14	62	52	51
Hamilton Academical	44	19	12	13	65	45	50
Greenock Morton	44	19	10	15	65	56	48
Ayr United	44	14	18	12	49	44	46
Clydebank	44	16	13	15	71	66	45
Dumbarton	44	15	7	22	56	71	37
Stirling Albion	44	11	13	20	44	61	35
Meadowbank Thistle	*44*	*11*	*10*	*23*	*51*	*80*	*32*
Cowdenbeath	*44*	*3*	*7*	*34*	*33*	*109*	*13*

SCOTTISH DIVISION 2 1992-93

Clyde	39	22	10	7	77	42	54
Brechin City	39	23	7	9	62	32	53
Stranraer	39	19	15	5	69	44	53
Forfar Athletic	39	18	10	11	74	54	46
Alloa Athletic	39	16	12	11	63	54	44
Arbroath	39	18	8	13	59	50	44
Stenhousemuir	39	15	10	14	59	48	40
Berwick Rangers	39	16	7	16	56	64	39
East Fife	39	14	10	15	70	64	38
Queen of the South	39	12	9	18	57	72	33
Queen's Park	39	8	12	19	51	73	28
Montrose	39	10	7	22	46	71	27
East Stirlingshire	39	8	9	22	50	85	25
Albion Rovers	39	6	10	23	36	76	22

1993 Scottish F.A. Cup

Semi-finals

Hibernian vs Aberdeen	0-1
Rangers vs Heart of Midlothian	2-1

Final

Celtic Park, 29th May 1993

Rangers 2   (Murray, Hateley)
Aberdeen 1   (Richardson)

Attendance 50,715

1992/93 Scottish League Cup

Semi-finals

Aberdeen vs Celtic	1-0
Rangers vs St. Johnstone	3-1

Final

Hampden Park, 25th October 1992

Rangers 2   (McCall, Smith(og))
Aberdeen 1 (aet.)   (Shearer)

Attendance 45,298

SCOTTISH PREMIER 1993-94

RANGERS	44	22	14	8	74	41	58
Aberdeen	44	17	21	6	58	36	55
Motherwell	44	20	14	10	58	43	54
Celtic	44	15	20	9	51	38	50
Hibernian	44	16	15	13	53	48	47
Dundee United	44	11	20	13	47	48	42
Heart of Midlothian	44	11	20	13	37	43	42
Kilmarnock	44	12	16	16	36	45	40
Partick Thistle	44	12	16	16	46	57	40
St. Johnstone	44	10	20	14	35	47	40
Raith Rovers	44	6	19	19	46	80	31
Dundee	44	8	13	23	42	57	29

SCOTTISH DIVISION 1 1993-94

Falkirk	44	26	14	4	81	32	66
Dunfermline Athletic	44	29	7	8	93	35	65
Airdrieonians	44	20	14	10	48	38	54
Hamilton Academical	44	19	12	13	66	54	50
Clydebank	44	18	14	12	56	48	50
St. Mirren	44	21	8	15	61	55	50
Ayr United	44	14	14	16	42	52	42
Dumbarton	44	11	14	19	48	59	36
Stirling Albion	44	13	9	22	41	68	35
Clyde	44	10	12	22	35	58	32
Greenock Morton	44	6	17	21	44	75	29
Brechin City	44	6	7	31	30	81	19

SCOTTISH DIVISION 2 1993-94

Stranraer	39	23	10	6	63	35	56
Berwick Rangers	39	18	12	9	75	46	48
Stenhousemuir	39	19	9	11	62	44	47
Meadowbank Thistle	39	17	13	9	62	48	47
Queen of the South	39	17	9	13	69	48	43
East Fife	39	15	11	13	58	52	41
Alloa Athletic	39	12	17	10	41	39	41
Forfar Athletic	39	14	11	14	58	58	39
East Stirlingshire	39	13	11	15	54	57	37
Montrose	39	14	8	17	56	61	36
Queen's Park	39	12	10	17	52	76	34
Arbroath	39	12	9	18	42	67	33
Albion Rovers	39	7	10	22	37	66	24
Cowdenbeath	39	6	8	25	40	72	20

1994 Scottish F.A. Cup

Semi-finals

Dundee United vs Aberdeen	1-1, 1-0
Kilmarnock vs Rangers	0-0, 1-2

Final

Hampden Park, 21st May 1994

Dundee United 1   (Brewster)
Rangers 0

Attendance 37,450

1993/94 Scottish League Cup

Semi-finals

Dundee United vs Hibernian	0-1
Rangers vs Celtic	1-0

Final

Hampden Park, 24th October 1993

Rangers 2   (Durrant, McCoist)
Hibernian 1   (McPherson (og))

Attendance 47,632

SCOTTISH PREMIER 1994-95

RANGERS	36	20	9	7	60	35	69
Motherwell	36	14	12	10	50	50	54
Hibernian	36	12	17	7	49	37	53
Celtic	36	11	18	7	39	33	51
Falkirk	36	12	12	12	48	47	48
Heart of Midlothian	36	12	7	17	44	51	43
Kilmarnock	36	11	10	15	40	48	43
Partick Thistle	36	10	13	13	40	50	43
Aberdeen	36	10	11	15	43	46	41
Dundee United	*36*	*9*	*9*	*18*	*40*	*56*	*36*

SCOTTISH DIVISION 1 1994-95

Raith Rovers	36	19	12	5	54	32	69
Dunfermline Athletic	36	18	14	4	63	32	68
Dundee	36	20	8	8	65	36	68
Airdrieonians	36	17	10	9	50	33	61
St. Johnstone	36	14	14	8	59	39	56
Hamilton Academical	36	14	7	15	42	48	49
St. Mirren	36	8	12	16	34	50	36
Clydebank	36	8	11	17	33	47	35
Ayr United	*36*	*6*	*11*	*19*	*31*	*58*	*29*
Stranraer	*36*	*4*	*5*	*27*	*25*	*81*	*17*

SCOTTISH DIVISION 2 1994-95

Greenock Morton	36	18	10	8	55	33	64
Dumbarton	36	17	9	10	57	35	60
Stirling Albion	36	17	7	12	54	43	58
Stenhousemuir	36	14	14	8	46	39	56
Berwick Rangers	36	15	10	11	52	46	55
Clyde	36	14	10	12	53	48	52
Queen of the South	36	11	11	14	46	51	44
East Fife	36	11	10	15	48	56	43
Meadowbank Thistle	*36*	*11*	*5*	*20*	*32*	*54*	*35*
Brechin City	*36*	*6*	*6*	*24*	*22*	*60*	*24*

Meadowbank Thistle had 3 points deducted

SCOTTISH DIVISION 3 1994-95

Forfar Athletic	36	25	5	6	67	33	80
Montrose	36	20	7	9	69	32	67
Ross County	36	18	6	12	59	44	60
East Stirlingshire	36	18	5	13	61	50	59
Alloa Athletic	36	15	9	12	50	45	54
Inverness Caledonian Thistle	36	12	9	15	48	61	45
Arbroath	36	13	5	18	51	62	44
Queen's Park	36	12	6	18	46	57	42
Cowdenbeath	36	11	7	18	48	60	40
Albion Rovers	36	5	3	28	27	82	18

1995 Scottish F.A. Cup

Semi-finals

Celtic vs Hibernian	0-0, 3-1
Airdrieonians vs Heart of Midlothian	1-0

Final

Hampden Park, 27th May 1995

Celtic 1 (Van Hooijdonk)
Airdrieonians 0

Attendance 36,915

1994/95 Scottish League Cup

Semi-finals

Airdrieonians vs Raith Rovers	1-1
Raith Rovers won 5-4 on penalties	
Celtic vs Aberdeen	1-0

Final

Ibrox Stadium, 27th November 1994

Raith Rovers 2   (Crawford, Dalziel)
Celtic 2 (aet.)   (Walker, Nicholas)

Raith Rovers won 6-5 on penalties

Attendance 45,384

SCOTTISH PREMIER 1995-96

RANGERS	36	27	6	3	85	25	87
Celtic	36	24	11	1	74	25	83
Aberdeen	36	16	7	13	52	45	55
Heart of Midlothian	36	16	7	13	55	53	55
Hibernian	36	11	10	15	43	57	43
Raith Rovers	36	12	7	17	41	57	43
Kilmarnock	36	11	8	17	39	54	41
Motherwell	36	9	12	15	28	39	39
Partick Thistle	*36*	*8*	*6*	*22*	*29*	*62*	*30*
Falkirk	*36*	*8*	*6*	*24*	*31*	*60*	*24*

SCOTTISH DIVISION 1 1995-96

Dunfermline Athletic	36	21	8	7	73	41	71
Dundee United	36	19	10	7	73	37	67
Greenock Morton	36	20	7	9	57	39	67
St. Johnstone	36	19	8	9	60	36	65
Dundee	36	15	12	9	53	40	57
St. Mirren	36	13	8	15	46	51	47
Clydebank	36	10	10	16	39	58	40
Airdrieonians	36	9	11	16	43	54	38
Hamilton Academical	*36*	*10*	*6*	*20*	*40*	*57*	*36*
Dumbarton	*36*	*3*	*2*	*31*	*23*	*94*	*11*

SCOTTISH DIVISION 2 1995-96

Stirling Albion	36	24	9	3	83	30	81
East Fife	36	19	10	7	50	29	67
Berwick Rangers	36	18	6	12	64	47	60
Stenhousemuir	36	14	7	15	51	49	49
Clyde	36	11	12	13	47	45	45
Ayr United	36	11	12	13	40	45	45
Queen of the South	36	11	10	15	54	67	43
Stranraer	36	8	18	10	38	43	42
Forfar Athletic	*36*	*11*	*7*	*18*	*37*	*61*	*40*
Montrose	*36*	*5*	*5*	*26*	*33*	*86*	*20*

SCOTTISH DIVISION 3 1995-96

Livingston	36	21	9	6	51	24	72
Brechin City	36	18	9	9	41	21	63
Inverness Caledonian Thistle	36	15	12	9	64	38	57
Ross County	36	12	17	7	56	39	53
Arbroath	36	13	13	10	41	41	52
Queen's Park	36	12	12	12	40	43	48
East Stirlingshire	36	11	11	14	58	62	44
Cowdenbeath	36	10	8	18	45	59	38
Alloa Athletic	36	6	11	19	26	58	29
Albion Rovers	36	7	8	21	37	74	29

1996 Scottish F.A. Cup

Semi-finals

Aberdeen vs Heart of Midlothian	1-2
Celtic vs Rangers	1-2

Final

Hampden Park, 18th May 1996

Rangers 5 (Laudrup 2, Durie 3)
Heart of Midlothian 1 (Colquhoun)

Attendance 37,730

1995/96 Scottish League Cup

Semi-finals

Rangers vs Aberdeen	1-2
Dundee vs Airdrieonians	2-1

Final

Hampden Park, 26th November 1995

Aberdeen 2 (Dodds, Shearer)
Dundee 0

Attendance 33,096

SCOTTISH PREMIER 1996-97

RANGERS	36	25	5	6	85	33	80
Celtic	36	23	6	7	78	32	75
Dundee United	36	17	9	10	46	33	60
Heart of Midlothian	36	14	10	12	46	43	52
Dunfermline Athletic	36	12	9	15	52	65	45
Aberdeen	36	10	14	12	45	57	44
Kilmarnock	36	11	6	19	41	61	39
Motherwell	36	9	11	16	44	55	38
Hibernian	36	9	11	16	38	55	38
Raith Rovers	*36*	*6*	*7*	*23*	*29*	*73*	*25*

SCOTTISH DIVISION 1 1996-97

St. Johnstone	36	24	8	4	74	23	80
Airdrieonians	36	15	15	6	56	34	60
Dundee	36	15	13	8	47	33	58
St. Mirren	36	17	7	12	48	41	58
Falkirk	36	15	9	12	42	39	54
Partick Thistle	36	12	12	12	49	48	48
Stirling Albion	36	12	10	14	54	61	46
Greenock Morton	36	12	9	15	42	41	45
Clydebank	*36*	*7*	*7*	*22*	*31*	*59*	*28*
East Fife	*36*	*2*	*8*	*26*	*28*	*92*	*14*

SCOTTISH DIVISION 2 1996-97

Ayr United	36	23	8	5	61	33	77
Hamilton Academical	36	22	8	6	75	28	74
Livingston	36	18	10	8	56	38	64
Clyde	36	14	10	12	42	39	52
Queen of the South	36	13	8	15	55	57	47
Stenhousemuir	36	11	11	14	49	43	44
Brechin City	36	10	11	15	36	49	41
Stranraer	36	9	9	18	29	51	36
Dumbarton	*36*	*9*	*8*	*19*	*44*	*66*	*35*
Berwick Rangers	*36*	*4*	*11*	*21*	*32*	*75*	*23*

SCOTTISH DIVISION 3 1996-97

Inverness Caledonian Thistle	36	23	7	6	70	37	76
Forfar Athletic	36	19	10	7	74	45	67
Ross County	36	20	7	9	58	41	67
Alloa Athletic	36	16	7	13	50	47	55
Albion Rovers	36	13	10	13	50	47	49
Montrose	36	12	7	17	46	62	43
Cowdenbeath	36	10	9	17	38	51	39
Queen's Park	36	9	9	18	46	59	36
East Stirlingshire	36	8	9	19	36	58	33
Arbroath	36	6	13	17	31	52	31

1997 Scottish F.A. Cup

Semi-finals

Celtic vs Falkirk	1-1, 0-1
Kilmarnock vs Dundee United	0-0, 1-0

Final

Ibrox Stadium, 24th May 1997

Kilmarnock 1 (Wright)
Falkirk 0

Attendance 48,953

1996/97 Scottish League Cup

Semi-finals

Dunfermline Athletic vs Rangers	1-6
Heart of Midlothian vs Dundee	3-1

Final

Celtic Park, 24th November 1996

Rangers 4 (McCoist 2, Gascoigne 2)
Heart of Midlothian 3 (Fulton, Robinson, Weir)

Attendance 48,559

SCOTTISH PREMIER 1997-98

CELTIC	36	22	8	6	64	24	74
Rangers	36	21	9	6	76	38	72
Heart of Midlothian	36	19	10	7	70	46	67
Kilmarnock	36	13	11	12	40	52	50
St. Johnstone	36	13	9	14	38	42	48
Aberdeen	36	9	12	15	39	53	39
Dundee United	36	8	13	15	43	51	37
Dunfermline Athletic	36	8	13	15	43	68	37
Motherwell	36	9	7	20	46	64	34
Hibernian	*36*	*6*	*12*	*18*	*38*	*59*	*30*

SCOTTISH DIVISION 1 1997-98

Dundee	36	20	10	6	52	24	70
Falkirk	36	19	8	9	56	41	65
Raith Rovers	36	17	9	10	51	33	60
Airdrieonians	36	16	12	8	42	35	60
Greenock Morton	36	12	10	14	47	48	46
St. Mirren	36	11	8	17	41	53	41
Ayr United	36	10	10	16	40	56	40
Hamilton Academical	36	9	11	16	43	56	38
Partick Thistle	*36*	*8*	*12*	*16*	*45*	*55*	*36*
Stirling Albion	*36*	*8*	*10*	*18*	*40*	*56*	*34*

SCOTTISH DIVISION 2 1997-98

Stranraer	36	18	7	11	62	44	61
Clydebank	36	16	12	8	48	31	60
Livingston	36	16	11	9	56	40	59
Queen of the South	36	15	9	12	57	51	54
Inverness Caledonian Thistle	36	13	10	13	65	51	49
East Fife	36	14	6	16	51	59	48
Forfar Athletic	36	12	10	14	51	61	46
Clyde	36	10	12	14	40	53	42
Stenhousemuir	*36*	*10*	*10*	*16*	*44*	*53*	*40*
Brechin City	*36*	*7*	*11*	*18*	*42*	*73*	*32*

SCOTTISH DIVISION 3 1997-98

Alloa Athletic	36	24	4	8	78	39	76
Arbroath	36	20	8	8	67	39	68
Ross County	36	19	10	7	71	36	67
East Stirlingshire	36	17	6	13	50	48	57
Albion Rovers	36	13	5	18	60	73	44
Berwick Rangers	36	10	12	14	47	55	42
Queen's Park	36	10	11	15	42	55	41
Cowdenbeath	36	12	2	22	33	57	38
Montrose	36	10	8	18	53	80	38
Dumbarton	36	7	10	19	42	61	31

1998 Scottish F.A. Cup

Semi-finals

Falkirk vs Heart of Midlothian	1-3
Rangers vs Celtic	2-1

Final

Celtic Park, 16th May 1998

Heart of Midlothian 2   (Cameron (pen), Adam)

Rangers 1   (McCoist)

Attendance 48,496

1997/98 Scottish League Cup

Semi-finals

Celtic vs Dunfermline Athletic	1-0
Dundee United vs Aberdeen	3-1

Final

Ibrox Stadium, 30th November 1997

Celtic 3   (Rieper, Larsson, Burley)

Dundee United 0

Attendance 49,305

SCOTTISH PREMIER 1998-99

RANGERS	36	23	8	5	78	31	77
Celtic	36	21	8	7	84	35	71
St. Johnstone	36	15	12	9	39	38	57
Kilmarnock	36	14	14	8	47	29	56
Dundee	36	13	7	16	36	56	46
Heart of Midlothian	36	11	9	16	44	50	42
Motherwell	36	10	11	15	35	54	41
Aberdeen	36	10	7	19	43	71	37
Dundee United	36	8	10	18	37	48	34
Dunfermline Athletic	*36*	*4*	*16*	*16*	*28*	*59*	*28*

SCOTTISH DIVISION 1 1998-99

Hibernian	36	28	5	3	84	33	89
Falkirk	36	20	6	10	60	38	66
Ayr United	36	19	5	12	66	42	62
Airdrieonians	36	18	5	13	42	43	59
St. Mirren	36	14	10	12	42	43	52
Greenock Morton	36	14	7	15	45	41	49
Clydebank	36	11	13	12	36	38	46
Raith Rovers	36	8	11	17	37	57	35
Hamilton Academical	*36*	*6*	*10*	*20*	*30*	*62*	*28*
Stranraer	*36*	*5*	*2*	*29*	*29*	*74*	*17*

SCOTTISH DIVISION 2 1998-99

Livingston	36	22	11	3	66	35	77
Inverness Caledonian Thistle	36	21	9	6	80	48	72
Clyde	36	15	8	13	46	42	53
Queen of the South	36	13	9	14	50	45	48
Alloa Athletic	36	13	7	16	65	56	46
Stirling Albion	36	12	8	16	50	63	44
Arbroath	36	12	8	16	37	52	44
Partick Thistle	36	12	7	17	36	45	43
East Fife	*36*	*12*	*6*	*18*	*42*	*64*	*42*
Forfar Athletic	*36*	*8*	*7*	*21*	*48*	*70*	*31*

SCOTTISH DIVISION 3 1998-99

Ross County	36	24	5	7	87	42	77
Stenhousemuir	36	19	7	10	62	42	64
Brechin City	36	17	8	11	47	43	59
Dumbarton	36	16	9	11	50	40	57
Berwick Rangers	36	12	14	10	53	49	50
Queen's Park	36	11	11	14	41	46	44
Albion Rovers	36	12	8	16	43	63	44
East Stirlingshire	36	9	13	14	50	48	40
Cowdenbeath	36	8	7	21	34	65	31
Montrose	36	8	6	22	42	74	30

1999 Scottish F.A. Cup

Semi-finals

Celtic vs Dundee United	2-0
St. Johnstone vs Rangers	0-4

Final

Hampden Park, 29th May 1999

Rangers 1   (Wallace)

Celtic 0

Attendance 52,760

1998/99 Scottish League Cup

Semi-finals

Rangers vs Airdrieonians	5-0
St. Johnstone vs Heart of Midlothian	3-0

Final

Celtic Park, 29th November 1998

Rangers 2   (Guivarc'h, Albertz)

St. Johnstone 1   (Dasovic)

Attendance 45,533

SCOTTISH PREMIER 1999-2000

RANGERS	36	28	6	2	96	26	90
Celtic	36	21	6	9	90	38	69
Heart of Midlothian	36	15	9	12	47	40	54
Motherwell	36	14	10	12	49	63	52
St. Johnstone	36	10	12	14	36	44	42
Hibernian	36	10	11	15	49	61	41
Dundee	36	12	5	19	45	64	41
Dundee United	36	11	6	19	34	57	39
Kilmarnock	36	8	13	15	38	52	37
Aberdeen	36	9	6	21	44	83	33

SCOTTISH DIVISION 1 1999-2000

St. Mirren	36	23	7	6	75	39	76
Dunfermline Athletic	36	20	11	5	66	33	71
Falkirk	36	20	8	8	67	40	68
Livingston	36	19	7	10	60	45	64
Raith Rovers	36	17	8	11	55	40	59
Inverness Caledonian Thistle	36	13	10	13	60	55	49
Ayr United	36	10	8	18	42	52	38
Greenock Morton	36	10	6	20	45	61	36
Airdrieonians	36	7	8	21	29	69	29
Clydebank	*36*	*1*	*7*	*28*	*17*	*82*	*10*

SCOTTISH DIVISION 2 1999-2000

Clyde	36	18	11	7	65	37	65
Alloa Athletic	36	17	13	6	58	38	64
Ross County	36	18	8	10	57	39	62
Arbroath	36	11	14	11	52	55	47
Partick Thistle	36	12	10	14	42	44	46
Stranraer	36	9	18	9	47	46	45
Stirling Albion	36	11	7	18	60	72	40
Stenhousemuir	36	10	8	18	44	59	38
Queen of the South	36	8	9	19	45	75	33
Hamilton Academical	*36*	*10*	*14*	*12*	*39*	*44*	*29**

Hamilton Academical had 15 points deducted

SCOTTISH DIVISION 3 1999-2000

Queen's Park	36	20	9	7	54	37	69
Berwick Rangers	36	19	9	8	53	30	66
Forfar Athletic	36	17	10	9	64	40	61
East Fife	36	17	8	11	45	39	59
Cowdenbeath	36	15	9	12	59	43	54
Dumbarton	36	15	8	13	53	51	53
East Stirlingshire	36	11	7	18	20	50	40
Brechin City	36	10	8	18	42	51	38
Montrose	36	10	7	19	39	54	37
Albion Rovers	36	5	7	24	33	75	22

1999 Scottish F.A. Cup

Semi-finals

Ayr United vs Rangers	0-7
Hibernian vs Aberdeen	1-2

Final

Hampden Park, 27th May 2000

Rangers 4 (Van Bronckhorst, Vidmar, Dodds, Albertz)
Aberdeen 0

Attendance 50,865

1999/2000 Scottish League Cup

Semi-finals

Aberdeen vs Dundee United	1-0
Celtic vs Kilmarnock	1-0

Final

Hampden Park, 19th March 2000

Celtic 2 (Riseth, Johnson)
Aberdeen 0

Attendance 50,073

SCOTTISH PREMIER 2000-2001

CELTIC	38	31	4	3	90	29	97
Rangers	38	26	4	8	76	36	82
Hibernian	38	18	12	8	57	35	66
Kilmarnock	38	15	9	14	44	53	54
Heart of Midlothian	38	14	10	14	56	50	52
Dundee	38	13	8	17	51	49	47
Aberdeen	38	11	12	15	45	52	45
Motherwell	38	12	7	19	42	56	43
Dunfermline Athletic	38	11	9	18	34	54	42
St. Johnstone	38	9	13	16	40	56	40
Dundee United	38	9	8	21	38	63	35
St. Mirren	*38*	*8*	*6*	*24*	*32*	*72*	*30*

With 5 games of the season left, the Division was split into two groups of 6. The top half contended for the Championship while the bottom half decided relegation.

SCOTTISH DIVISION 1 2000-2001

Livingston	36	23	7	6	72	31	76
Ayr United	36	19	12	5	73	41	69
Falkirk	36	16	8	12	57	59	56
Inverness Caledonian Thistle	36	14	12	10	71	54	54
Clyde	36	11	14	11	44	46	47
Ross County	36	11	10	15	48	52	43
Raith Rovers	36	10	8	18	41	55	38
Airdrieonians	36	8	14	14	49	67	38
Greenock Morton	*36*	*9*	*8*	*19*	*34*	*61*	*35*
Alloa Athletic	*36*	*7*	*11*	*18*	*38*	*61*	*32*

SCOTTISH DIVISION 2 2000-2001

Partick Thistle	36	22	9	5	66	32	75
Arbroath	36	15	13	8	54	38	58
Berwick Rangers	36	14	12	10	51	44	54
Stranraer	36	15	9	12	51	50	54
Clydebank	36	12	11	13	42	43	47
Queen of the South	36	13	7	16	52	59	46
Stenhousemuir	36	12	6	18	45	63	42
Forfar Athletic	36	10	10	16	48	52	40
Queen's Park	*36*	*10*	*10*	*16*	*28*	*40*	*40*
Stirling Albion	*36*	*5*	*17*	*14*	*34*	*50*	*32*

SCOTTISH DIVISION 3 2000-2001

Hamilton Academical	36	22	10	4	75	30	76
Cowdenbeath	36	23	7	6	58	31	76
Brechin City	36	22	6	8	71	36	72
East Fife	36	15	8	13	49	46	53
Peterhead	36	13	10	13	46	46	49
Dumbarton	36	13	6	17	46	49	45
Albion Rovers	36	12	9	15	38	43	45
East Stirlingshire	36	10	7	19	37	69	37
Montrose	36	6	8	22	31	65	26
Elgin City	36	5	7	24	29	65	22

2000/2001 Scottish F.A. Cup

Semi-finals

| Hibernian vs Livingston | 3-0 |
| Celtic vs Dundee | 3-1 |

Final

Hampden Park, 26th May 2001

Celtic 3 (McNamara, Larsson 2 (1 pen))
Hibernian 0

Attendance 51,824

2000/2001 Scottish League Cup

Semi-finals

| Celtic vs Rangers | 3-1 |
| St. Mirren vs Kilmarnock | 0-3 |

Final

Hampden Park, 18th March 2001

Celtic 3 (Larsson 3)
Kilmarnock 0

Attendance 48,830

SCOTTISH PREMIER 2001-2002

CELTIC	38	33	4	1	94	18	103
Rangers	38	25	10	3	82	27	85
Livingston	38	16	10	12	50	47	58
Aberdeen	38	16	7	15	51	49	55
Heart of Midlothian	38	14	6	18	52	57	48
Dunfermline Athletic	38	12	9	17	41	64	45
Kilmarnock	38	13	10	15	44	54	49
Dundee United	38	12	10	16	38	59	46
Dundee	38	12	8	18	41	55	44
Hibernian	38	10	11	17	51	56	41
Motherwell	38	11	7	20	49	69	40
St. Johnstone	*38*	*5*	*6*	*27*	*24*	*62*	*21*

With 5 games of the season left, the Division was split into two groups of 6. The top half contended for the Championship while the bottom half decided relegation.

SCOTTISH DIVISION 1 2001-2002

Partick Thistle	**36**	**19**	**9**	**8**	**61**	**38**	**66**
Airdrieonians	36	15	11	10	59	40	56
Ayr United	36	13	13	10	53	44	52
Ross County	36	14	10	12	51	43	52
Clyde	36	13	10	13	51	56	49
Inverness Caledonian Thistle	36	13	9	14	60	51	48
Arbroath	36	14	6	16	42	59	48
St. Mirren	36	11	12	13	43	53	45
Falkirk	36	10	9	17	49	73	39
Raith Rovers	*36*	*8*	*11*	*17*	*50*	*62*	*35*

Airdrieonians went into liquidation and resigned

SCOTTISH DIVISION 2 2001-2002

Queen of the South	36	20	7	9	64	42	67
Alloa Athletic	36	15	14	7	55	33	59
Forfar Athletic	36	15	8	13	51	47	53
Clydebank	36	14	9	13	44	45	51
Hamilton Academical	36	13	9	14	49	44	48
Berwick Rangers	36	12	11	13	44	52	47
Stranraer	36	10	15	11	48	51	45
Cowdenbeath	36	11	11	14	49	51	44
Stenhousemuir	*36*	*8*	*12*	*16*	*33*	*57*	*36*
Greenock Morton	*36*	*7*	*14*	*15*	*48*	*63*	*35*

Clydebank FC was "bought" by fans of Airdrieonians who renamed it Airdrie United FC and took the place of Clydebank

SCOTTISH DIVISION 3 2001-2002

Brechin City	**36**	**22**	**7**	**7**	**67**	**38**	**73**
Dumbarton	**36**	**18**	**7**	**11**	**59**	**48**	**61**
Albion Rovers	36	16	11	9	51	42	59
Peterhead	36	17	5	14	63	52	56
Montrose	36	16	7	13	43	39	55
Elgin City	36	13	8	15	45	47	47
East Stirlingshire	36	12	4	20	51	58	40
East Fife	36	11	7	18	39	56	40
Stirling Albion	36	9	10	17	45	68	37
Queen's Park	36	9	8	19	38	53	35

2001/2002 Scottish F.A. Cup

Semi-finals

| Ayr United vs Celtic | 0-3 |
| Rangers vs Partick Thistle | 3-0 |

Final

Hampden Park, 4th May 2002

Celtic 2 (Hartson, Balde)
Rangers 3 (Lovenkrands 2, Ferguson)

Attendance 51,138

2001/2002 Scottish League Cup

Semi-finals

| Hibernian vs Ayr United | 0-1 (aet) |
| Rangers vs Celtic | 2-1 (aet) |

Final

Hampden Park, 17th March 2002

Ayr United 0
Rangers 4 (Flo, Ferguson, Caniggia 2)

Attendance 50,076

SCOTTISH PREMIER 2002-2003

RANGERS	38	31	4	3	101	28	97
Celtic	38	31	4	3	98	26	97
Heart of Midlothian	38	18	9	11	57	51	63
Kilmarnock	38	16	9	13	47	56	57
Dunfermline Athletic	38	13	7	18	54	71	46
Dundee	38	10	14	14	50	60	44
Hibernian	38	15	6	17	56	64	51
Aberdeen	38	13	10	15	41	54	49
Livingston	38	9	8	21	48	62	35
Partick Thistle	38	8	11	19	37	58	35
Dundee United	38	7	11	20	35	68	32
Motherwell	38	7	7	24	45	71	28

With 5 games of the season left, the Division was split into two groups of 6. The top half contended for the Championship while the bottom half decided relegation.

SCOTTISH DIVISION 1 2002-2003

Falkirk	36	25	6	5	80	32	81
Clyde	36	21	9	6	66	37	72
St. Johnstone	36	20	7	9	49	29	67
Inverness Caledonian Thistle	36	20	5	11	74	45	65
Queen of the South	36	12	12	12	45	48	48
Ayr United	36	12	9	15	34	44	45
St. Mirren	36	9	10	17	42	71	37
Ross County	36	9	8	19	42	46	35
Alloa Athletic	*36*	*9*	*8*	*19*	*39*	*72*	*35*
Arbroath	*36*	*3*	*6*	*27*	*30*	*77*	*15*

SCOTTISH DIVISION 2 2002-2003

Raith Rovers	36	16	11	9	53	36	59
Brechin City	36	16	7	13	63	59	55
Airdrie United	36	14	12	10	51	44	54
Forfar Athletic	36	14	9	13	55	53	51
Berwick Rangers	36	13	10	13	43	48	49
Dumbarton	36	13	9	14	48	47	48
Stenhousemuir	36	12	11	13	49	51	47
Hamilton Academical	36	12	11	13	43	48	47
Stranraer	*36*	*12*	*8*	*16*	*49*	*57*	*44*
Cowdenbeath	*36*	*8*	*12*	*16*	*46*	*57*	*36*

SCOTTISH DIVISION 3 2002-2003

Greenock Morton	36	21	9	6	67	33	72
East Fife	36	20	11	5	73	37	71
Albion Rovers	36	20	10	6	62	36	70
Peterhead	36	20	8	8	76	37	68
Stirling Albion	36	15	11	10	50	44	56
Gretna	36	11	12	13	50	50	45
Montrose	36	7	12	17	35	61	33
Queen's Park	36	7	11	18	39	51	32
Elgin City	36	5	13	18	33	63	28
East Stirlingshire	36	2	7	27	32	105	13

2002/2003 Scottish F.A. Cup

Semi-finals

Inverness Caledonian Thistle vs Dundee	0-1
Rangers vs Motherwell	4-3

Final

Hampden Park, 31st May 2003

Dundee 0

Rangers 1 (Amoruso)

Attendance 47,136

2002/2003 Scottish League Cup

Semi-finals

Celtic vs Dundee United	3-0
Heart of Midlothian vs Rangers	0-1

Final

Hampden Park, 16th March 2003

Celtic 1 (Larsson)

Rangers 2 (Caniggia, Lovenkrands)

Attendance 52,000

SCOTTISH PREMIER 2003-2004

CELTIC	38	31	5	2	105	25	98
Rangers	38	25	6	7	76	33	81
Heart of Midlothian	38	19	11	8	56	40	68
Dunfermline Athletic	38	14	11	13	45	52	53
Dundee United	38	13	10	15	47	60	49
Motherwell	38	12	10	16	42	49	46
Dundee	38	12	10	16	48	57	46
Hibernian	38	11	11	16	41	60	44
Livingston	38	10	13	15	48	57	43
Kilmarnock	38	12	6	20	51	74	42
Aberdeen	38	9	7	22	39	63	34
Partick Thistle	*38*	*6*	*8*	*24*	*39*	*67*	*26*

With 5 games of the season left, the Division was split into two groups of 6. The top half contended for the Championship while the bottom half decided relegation.

SCOTTISH DIVISION 1 2003-2004

Inverness Caledonian Thistle	36	21	7	8	67	33	70
Clyde	36	20	9	7	64	40	69
St. Johnstone	36	15	12	9	59	45	57
Falkirk	36	15	10	11	43	37	55
Queen of the South	36	15	9	12	46	48	54
Ross County	36	12	13	11	49	41	49
St. Mirren	36	9	14	13	39	46	41
Raith Rovers	36	8	10	18	37	57	34
Ayr United	*36*	*6*	*13*	*17*	*37*	*58*	*31*
Brechin City	*36*	*6*	*9*	*21*	*37*	*73*	*27*

SCOTTISH DIVISION 2 2003-2004

Airdrie United	36	20	10	6	64	36	70
Hamilton Academical	36	18	8	10	70	47	62
Dumbarton	36	18	6	12	56	41	60
Greenock Morton	36	16	11	9	66	58	59
Berwick Rangers	36	14	6	16	61	67	48
Forfar Athletic	36	12	11	13	49	57	47
Alloa Athletic	36	12	8	16	55	55	44
Arbroath	36	11	10	15	41	57	43
East Fife	*36*	*11*	*8*	*17*	*38*	*45*	*41*
Stenhousemuir	*36*	*7*	*4*	*25*	*28*	*65*	*25*

SCOTTISH DIVISION 3 2003-2004

Stranraer	36	24	7	5	87	30	79
Stirling Albion	36	23	8	5	78	27	77
Gretna	36	20	8	8	59	39	68
Peterhead	36	18	7	11	67	37	61
Cowdenbeath	36	15	10	11	46	39	55
Montrose	36	12	12	12	52	63	48
Queen's Park	36	10	11	15	41	53	41
Albion Rovers	36	12	4	20	66	75	40
Elgin City	36	6	7	23	48	93	25
East Stirlingshire	36	2	2	32	30	118	8

2003/2004 Scottish F.A. Cup

Semi-finals

Livingston vs Celtic	1-3
Inverness Cal. Thistle vs Dunfermline Athletic	1-1, 2-3

Final

Hampden Park, 22nd May 2004

Dunfermline Athletic 1   (Skerla)

Celtic 3   (Larsson 2, Petrov)

Attendance 50,846

2003/2004 Scottish League Cup

Semi-finals

Hibernian vs Rangers	1-1 (aet)
Hibernian won 4-3 on penalties	
Dundee vs Livingston	0-1

Final

Hampden Park, 14th March 2004

Livingston 2   (Lilley, McAllister)

Hibernian 0

Attendance 45,500

SCOTTISH PREMIER 2004-2005

RANGERS	38	29	6	3	78	22	93
Celtic	38	30	2	6	85	35	92
Hibernian	38	18	7	13	64	57	61
Aberdeen	38	18	7	13	44	39	61
Heart of Midlothian	38	13	11	14	43	41	50
Motherwell	38	13	9	16	46	49	48
Kilmarnock	38	15	4	19	49	55	49
Inverness Caledonian Thistle	38	11	11	16	41	47	44
Dundee United	38	8	12	18	41	59	36
Livingston	38	9	8	21	34	61	35
Dunfermline Athletic	38	8	10	20	34	60	34
Dundee	*38*	*8*	*9*	*21*	*37*	*71*	*33*

With 5 games of the season left, the Division was split into two groups of 6. The top half contended for the Championship while the bottom half decided relegation.

SCOTTISH DIVISION 1 2004-2005

Falkirk	36	22	9	5	66	30	75
St. Mirren	36	15	15	6	41	23	60
Clyde	36	16	12	8	35	29	60
Queen of the South	36	14	9	13	36	38	51
Airdrie United	36	14	8	14	44	48	50
Ross County	36	13	8	15	40	37	47
Hamilton Academical	36	12	11	13	35	36	47
St. Johnstone	36	12	10	14	38	39	46
Partick Thistle	*36*	*10*	*9*	*17*	*38*	*52*	*39*
Raith Rovers	*36*	*3*	*7*	*26*	*26*	*67*	*16*

SCOTTISH DIVISION 2 2004-2005

Brechin City	36	22	6	8	81	43	72
Stranraer	36	18	9	9	48	41	63
Greenock Morton	36	18	8	10	60	37	62
Stirling Albion	36	14	9	13	56	55	51
Forfar Athletic	36	13	8	15	51	45	47
Alloa Athletic	36	12	10	14	66	68	46
Dumbarton	36	11	9	16	43	53	42
Ayr United	36	11	9	16	39	54	42
Arbroath	*36*	*10*	*8*	*18*	*49*	*73*	*38*
Berwick Rangers	*36*	*8*	*10*	*18*	*40*	*64*	*34*

SCOTTISH DIVISION 3 2004-2005

Gretna	36	32	2	2	130	29	98
Peterhead	36	23	9	4	81	38	78
Cowdenbeath	36	14	9	13	54	61	51
Queen's Park	36	13	9	14	51	50	48
Montrose	36	13	7	16	47	53	46
Elgin City	36	12	7	17	39	61	43
Stenhousemuir	36	10	12	14	58	58	42
East Fife	36	10	8	18	40	56	38
Albion Rovers	36	8	10	18	40	78	34
East Stirlingshire	36	5	7	24	32	88	22

2004/2005 Scottish F.A. Cup

Semi-finals

Heart of Midlothian vs Celtic	1-2
Dundee United vs Hibernian	2-1

Final

Hampden Park, 28th May 2005

Celtic 1   (Thompson)
Dundee United 0

Attendance 50,635

2004/2005 Scottish League Cup

Semi-finals

Celtic vs Dundee United	3-0
Heart of Midlothian vs Rangers	0-1

Final

Hampden Park, 20th March 2005

Rangers 5   (Ross, Kyrgiakos 2, Ricksen, Novo)
Motherwell 1   (Partridge)

Attendance 50,182

SCOTTISH PREMIER 2005-2006

CELTIC	38	28	7	3	93	37	91
Hearts	38	22	8	8	71	31	74
Rangers	38	21	10	7	67	37	73
Hibernian	38	17	5	16	61	56	56
Kilmarnock	38	15	10	13	63	64	55
Aberdeen	38	13	15	10	46	40	54
Inverness Caledonian Thistle	38	15	13	10	51	38	58
Motherwell	38	13	10	15	55	61	49
Dundee United	38	7	12	19	41	66	33
Falkirk	38	8	9	21	35	64	33
Dunfermline	38	8	9	21	33	68	33
Livingston	*38*	*4*	*6*	*28*	*25*	*79*	*18*

With 5 games of the season left, the Division was split into two groups of 6. The top half contended for the Championship while the bottom half decided relegation.

SCOTTISH DIVISION 1 2005-2006

St. Mirren	36	23	7	6	52	28	76
St. Johnstone	36	18	12	6	59	34	66
Hamilton Academical	36	15	14	7	53	39	59
Ross County	36	14	14	8	47	40	56
Clyde	36	15	10	11	54	42	55
Airdrie United	36	11	12	13	57	43	45
Dundee	36	9	16	11	43	50	43
Queen of the South	36	7	12	17	31	54	33
Stranraer	*36*	*5*	*14*	*17*	*33*	*53*	*29*
Brechin City	*36*	*2*	*11*	*23*	*28*	*74*	*17*

SCOTTISH DIVISION 2 2005-2006

Gretna	36	28	4	4	97	30	88
Greenock Morton	36	21	7	8	58	33	70
Peterhead	36	17	6	13	53	47	57
Partick Thistle	36	16	9	11	57	56	57
Stirling Albion	36	15	6	15	54	63	51
Ayr United	36	10	12	14	56	61	42
Raith Rovers	36	11	9	16	44	54	42
Forfar Athletic	36	12	4	20	44	55	40
Alloa Athletic	*36*	*8*	*8*	*20*	*36*	*77*	*32*
Dumbarton	*36*	*7*	*5*	*24*	*40*	*63*	*26*

SCOTTISH DIVISION 3 2005-2006

Cowdenbeath	36	24	4	8	81	34	76
Berwick Rangers	36	23	7	6	54	27	76
Stenhousemuir	36	23	4	9	78	38	73
Arbroath	36	16	7	13	57	47	55
Elgin City	36	15	7	14	55	58	52
Queen's Park	36	13	12	11	47	42	51
East Fife	36	13	4	19	48	64	43
Albion Rovers	36	7	8	21	39	60	29
Montrose	36	6	10	20	31	59	28
East Stirlingshire	36	6	5	25	28	89	23

2005/2006 Scottish F.A. Cup

Semi-finals

Gretna vs Dundee	3-0
Hibernian vs Heart of Midlothian	0-4

Final

Hampden Park, 13th May 2006

Heart of Midlothian 1   (Skacel)
Gretna 1   (aet)   (McGuffie)

Attendance 51,232

Heart of Midlothian won 4-2 on penalties

2005/2006 Scottish League Cup

Semi-finals

Dunfermline Athletic vs Livingston	2-1
Motherwell vs Celtic	1-2

Final

Hampden Park, 19th March 2006

Celtic 3   (Zurawski, Maloney, Dublin)
Dunfermline Athletic 0

Attendance 50,090

SCOTTISH PREMIER 2006-2007

CELTIC	38	26	6	6	65	34	84
Rangers	38	21	9	8	61	32	72
Aberdeen	38	19	8	11	55	38	65
Heart of Midlothian	38	17	10	11	47	35	61
Kilmarnock	38	16	7	15	47	54	55
Hibernian	38	13	10	15	56	46	49
Falkirk	38	15	5	18	49	47	50
Inverness Caledonian Thistle	38	11	13	14	42	48	46
Dundee United	38	10	12	16	40	59	42
Motherwell	38	10	8	20	41	61	38
St. Mirren	38	8	12	18	31	51	36
Dunfermline Athletic	*38*	*8*	*8*	*22*	*26*	*55*	*32*

With 5 games of the season left, the Division was split into two groups of 6. The top half contended for the Championship while the bottom half decided relegation.

SCOTTISH DIVISION 1 2006-2007

Gretna	36	19	9	8	70	40	66
St. Johnstone	36	19	8	9	65	42	65
Dundee	36	16	5	15	48	42	53
Hamilton Academical	36	14	11	11	46	47	53
Clyde	36	11	14	11	46	35	47
Livingston	36	11	12	13	41	46	45
Partick Thistle	36	12	9	15	47	63	45
Queen of the South	36	10	11	15	34	54	41
Airdrie United	*36*	*11*	*7*	*18*	*39*	*50*	*40*
Ross County	*36*	*9*	*10*	*17*	*40*	*57*	*37*

SCOTTISH DIVISION 2 2006-2007

Greenock Morton	36	24	5	7	76	32	77
Stirling Albion	36	21	6	9	67	39	69
Raith Rovers	36	18	8	10	50	33	62
Brechin City	36	18	6	12	61	45	60
Ayr United	36	14	8	14	46	47	50
Cowdenbeath	36	13	6	17	59	56	45
Alloa Athletic	36	11	9	16	47	70	42
Peterhead	36	11	8	17	60	62	41
Stranraer	*36*	*10*	*9*	*17*	*45*	*74*	*39*
Forfar Athletic	*36*	*4*	*7*	*25*	*37*	*90*	*19*

SCOTTISH DIVISION 3 2006-2007

Berwick Rangers	36	24	3	9	51	29	75
Arbroath	36	22	4	10	61	33	70
Queen's Park	36	21	5	10	57	28	68
East Fife	36	20	7	9	59	37	67
Dumbarton	36	18	5	13	52	37	59
Albion Rovers	36	14	6	16	56	61	48
Stenhousemuir	36	13	5	18	53	63	44
Montrose	36	11	4	21	42	62	37
Elgin City	36	9	2	25	39	69	29
East Stirlingshire	36	6	3	27	27	78	21

2006/2007 Scottish F.A. Cup

Semi-finals
Hibernian vs Dunfermline Athletic	0-0, 0-1
St. Johnstone vs Celtic	1-2

Final
Hampden Park, 26th May 2007

Celtic 1 (Perrier Doumbe)

Dunfermline Athletic 0

Attendance 49,600

2006/2007 Scottish League Cup

Semi-finals
Kilmarnock vs Falkirk	3-0
St. Johnstone vs Hibernian	1-3 (aet)

Final
Hampden Park, 18th March 2007

Kilmarnock 1 (Greer)

Hibernian 5 (Jones, Benjelloun 2, Fletcher 2)

Attendance 52,000

SCOTTISH PREMIER 2007-2008

CELTIC	38	28	5	5	84	26	89
Rangers	38	27	5	6	84	33	86
Motherwell	38	18	6	14	50	46	60
Aberdeen	38	15	8	15	50	58	53
Dundee United	38	14	10	14	53	47	52
Hibernian	38	14	10	14	49	45	52
Falkirk	38	13	10	15	45	49	49
Heart of Midlothian	38	13	9	16	47	55	48
Inverness Caledonian Thistle	38	13	4	21	51	62	43
St. Mirren	38	10	11	17	26	54	41
Kilmarnock	38	10	10	18	39	52	40
Gretna	*38*	*5*	*8*	*25*	*32*	*83*	*13*

With 5 games of the season left, the Division was split into two groups of 6. The top half contended for the Championship while the bottom half decided relegation.

SCOTTISH DIVISION 1 2007-2008

Hamilton Academical	36	23	7	6	62	27	76
Dundee	36	20	9	7	58	30	69
St. Johnstone	36	15	13	8	60	45	58
Queen of the South	36	14	10	12	47	43	52
Dunfermline Athletic	36	13	12	11	36	41	51
Partick Thistle	36	11	12	13	40	39	45
Livingston	36	10	9	17	55	66	39
Greenock Morton	36	9	10	17	40	58	37
Clyde	36	9	10	17	40	59	37
Stirling Albion	*36*	*4*	*12*	*20*	*41*	*71*	*24*

SCOTTISH DIVISION 2 2007-2008

Ross County	36	22	7	7	78	44	73
Airdrie United	36	20	6	10	64	36	66
Raith Rovers	36	19	3	14	60	50	60
Alloa Athletic	36	16	8	12	57	56	56
Peterhead	36	16	7	13	65	54	55
Brechin City	36	13	13	10	63	43	52
Ayr United	36	13	7	16	51	62	46
Queen's Park	36	13	5	18	48	51	44
Cowdenbeath	*36*	*10*	*7*	*19*	*47*	*73*	*37*
Berwick Rangers	*36*	*3*	*7*	*26*	*40*	*101*	*16*

SCOTTISH DIVISION 3 2007-2008

East Fife	**36**	**28**	**4**	**4**	**77**	**24**	**88**
Stranraer	**36**	**19**	**8**	**9**	**65**	**43**	**65**
Montrose	36	17	8	11	57	35	59
Arbroath	**36**	**14**	**10**	**12**	**54**	**47**	**52**
Stenhousemuir	36	13	9	14	49	57	48
Elgin City	36	13	8	15	56	69	47
Albion Rovers	36	9	10	17	52	69	37
Dumbarton	36	9	10	17	31	48	37
East Stirlingshire	36	10	4	22	48	71	34
Forfar Athletic	36	8	9	19	35	62	33

2007/2008 Scottish F.A. Cup

Semi-finals

Queen of the South vs Aberdeen	4-3
St. Johnstone vs Rangers	1-1 (aet)
Rangers won 4-3 on penalties	

Final

Hampden Park, 24th May 2008

Queen of the South 2   (Tosh, Thomson)

Rangers 3   (Boyd 2, Beasley)

Attendance 48,821

2007/2008 Scottish League Cup

Semi-finals

Rangers vs Heart of Midlothian	2-0
Aberdeen vs Dundee United	1-4

Final

Hampden Park, 16th March 2008

Dundee United 2   (Hunt, de Vries)

Rangers 2 (aet.)   (Boyd 2)

Attendance 50,019

Rangers won 3-2 on penalties

SCOTTISH PREMIER 2008-2009

RANGERS	**38**	**26**	**8**	**4**	**77**	**28**	**86**
Celtic	38	24	10	4	80	33	82
Heart of Midlothian	38	16	11	11	40	37	59
Aberdeen	38	14	11	13	41	40	53
Dundee United	38	13	14	11	47	50	53
Hibernian	38	11	14	13	42	46	47
Motherwell	38	13	9	16	46	51	48
Kilmarnock	38	12	8	18	38	48	44
Hamilton Academical	38	12	5	21	30	53	41
Falkirk	38	9	11	18	37	52	38
St. Mirren	38	9	10	19	33	52	37
Inverness Caledonian Thistle	*38*	*10*	*7*	*21*	*37*	*58*	*37*

With 5 games of the season left, the Division was split into two groups of 6. The top half contended for the Championship while the bottom half decided relegation.

SCOTTISH DIVISION 1 2008-2009

St. Johnstone	**36**	**17**	**14**	**5**	**55**	**35**	**65**
Partick Thistle	36	16	7	13	39	35	55
Dunfermline Athletic	36	14	9	13	51	43	51
Dundee	36	13	11	12	33	32	50
Queen of the South	36	12	11	13	57	50	47
Greenock Morton	36	12	11	13	40	40	47
Livingston	*36*	*13*	*8*	*15*	*56*	*58*	*47*
Ross County	36	13	8	15	42	46	47
Airdrie United	36	10	12	14	29	43	42
Clyde	*36*	*10*	*9*	*17*	*41*	*58*	*39*

Livingston were relegated due to financial irregularities

SCOTTISH DIVISION 2 2008-2009

Raith Rovers	**36**	**22**	**10**	**4**	**60**	**27**	**76**
Ayr United	**36**	**22**	**8**	**6**	**71**	**38**	**74**
Brechin City	36	18	8	10	51	45	62
Peterhead	36	15	11	10	54	39	56
Stirling Albion	36	14	11	11	59	49	53
East Fife	36	13	5	18	39	44	44
Arbroath	36	11	8	17	44	46	41
Alloa Athletic	36	11	8	17	47	59	41
Queen's Park	*36*	*7*	*12*	*17*	*35*	*54*	*33*
Stranraer	*36*	*3*	*7*	*26*	*31*	*90*	*16*

SCOTTISH DIVISION 3 2008-2009

Dumbarton	**36**	**19**	**10**	**7**	**65**	**36**	**67**
Cowdenbeath	**36**	**18**	**9**	**9**	**48**	**34**	**63**
East Stirlingshire	36	19	4	13	57	50	61
Stenhousemuir	**36**	**16**	**8**	**12**	**55**	**46**	**56**
Montrose	36	16	6	14	47	48	54
Forfar Athletic	36	14	9	13	53	51	51
Annan Athletic	36	14	8	14	56	45	50
Albion Rovers	36	11	6	19	39	47	39
Berwick Rangers	36	10	7	19	46	61	37
Elgin City	36	7	5	24	31	79	26

2008/2009 Scottish F.A. Cup

Semi-finals

| Falkirk vs Dunfermline Athletic | 2-0 |
| Rangers vs St. Mirren | 3-0 |

Final

Hampden Park, 30th May 2009

Rangers 1   (Novo)

Falkirk 0

Attendance 50,956

2008/2009 Scottish League Cup

Semi-finals

Celtic vs Dundee United	0-0 (aet)
Celtic won 11-10 on penalties	
Rangers vs Falkirk	3-0

Final

Hampden Park, 15th March 2009

Celtic 2   (O'Dea, McGeady)

Rangers 0 (aet.)

Attendance 51,193

SCOTTISH PREMIER 2009-2010

RANGERS	38	26	9	3	82	28	87
Celtic	38	25	6	7	75	39	81
Dundee United	38	17	12	9	55	47	63
Hibernian	38	15	9	14	58	55	54
Motherwell	38	13	14	11	52	54	53
Heart of Midlothian	38	13	9	16	35	46	48
Hamilton Academical	38	13	10	15	39	46	49
St. Johnstone	38	12	11	15	57	61	47
Aberdeen	38	10	11	17	36	52	41
St. Mirren	38	7	13	18	36	49	34
Kilmarnock	38	8	9	21	29	51	33
Falkirk	*38*	*6*	*13*	*19*	*31*	*57*	*31*

With 5 games of the season left, the Division was split into two groups of 6. The top half contended for the Championship while the bottom half decided relegation.

SCOTTISH DIVISION 1 2009-2010

Inverness Caledonian Thistle	36	21	10	5	72	32	73
Dundee	36	16	13	7	48	34	61
Dunfermline Athletic	36	17	7	12	54	44	58
Queen of the South	36	15	11	10	53	40	56
Ross County	36	15	11	10	46	44	56
Partick Thistle	36	14	6	16	43	40	48
Raith Rovers	36	11	9	16	36	47	42
Greenock Morton	36	11	4	21	40	65	37
Airdrie United	*36*	*8*	*9*	*19*	*41*	*56*	*33*
Ayr United	*36*	*7*	*10*	*19*	*29*	*60*	*31*

SCOTTISH DIVISION 2 2009-2010

Stirling Albion	36	18	11	7	68	48	65
Alloa Athletic	36	19	8	9	49	35	65
Cowdenbeath	36	16	11	9	60	41	59
Brechin City	36	15	9	12	47	42	54
Peterhead	36	15	6	15	45	49	51
Dumbarton	36	14	6	16	49	58	48
East Fife	36	10	11	15	46	53	41
Stenhousemuir	36	9	13	14	38	42	40
Arbroath	*36*	*10*	*10*	*16*	*41*	*55*	*40*
Clyde	*36*	*8*	*7*	*21*	*37*	*57*	*31*

SCOTTISH DIVISION 3 2009-2010

Livingston	36	24	6	6	63	25	78
Forfar Athletic	36	18	9	9	59	44	63
East Stirlingshire	36	19	4	13	50	46	61
Queen's Park	36	15	6	15	42	42	51
Albion Rovers	36	13	11	12	35	35	50
Berwick Rangers	36	14	8	14	46	50	50
Stranraer	36	13	8	15	48	54	47
Annan Athletic	36	11	10	15	41	42	43
Elgin City	36	9	7	20	46	59	34
Montrose	36	5	9	22	30	63	24

2009/2010 Scottish F.A. Cup

Semi-finals

Celtic vs Ross County	0-2
Dundee United vs Raith Rovers	2-0
Rangers won 4-3 on penalties	

Final

Hampden Park, 15th May 2010

Ross County 0

Dundee United 3   (Goodwillie, Conway 2)

Attendance 47,122

2009/2010 Scottish League Cup

Semi-finals

| Heart of Midlothian vs St. Mirren | 0-1 |
| Rangers vs St. Johnstone | 2-0 |

Final

Hampden Park, 21st March 2010

St. Mirren 0

Rangers 1   (Miller)

Attendance 44,538

SCOTTISH PREMIER 2010-2011

RANGERS	38	30	3	5	88	29	93
Celtic	38	29	5	4	85	22	92
Heart of Midlothian	38	18	9	11	53	45	63
Dundee United	38	17	10	11	55	50	61
Kilmarnock	38	13	10	15	53	55	49
Motherwell	38	13	7	18	40	56	46
Inverness Caledonian Thistle	38	14	11	13	51	44	53
St. Johnstone	38	11	11	16	23	43	44
Aberdeen	38	11	5	22	39	59	38
Hibernian	38	10	7	21	39	61	37
St. Mirren	38	8	9	21	33	57	33
Hamilton Academical	*38*	*5*	*11*	*22*	*24*	*59*	*26*

With 5 games of the season left, the Division was split into two groups of 6. The top half contended for the Championship while the bottom half decided relegation.

SCOTTISH DIVISION 1 2010-2011

Dunfermline Athletic	36	20	10	6	66	31	70
Raith Rovers	36	17	9	10	47	35	60
Falkirk	36	17	7	12	57	41	58
Queen of the South	36	14	7	15	54	53	49
Partick Thistle	36	12	11	13	44	39	47
Dundee	36	19	12	5	54	34	44
Greenock Morton	36	11	10	15	39	43	43
Ross County	36	9	14	13	30	34	41
Cowdenbeath	*36*	*9*	*8*	*19*	*41*	*72*	*35*
Stirling Albion	*36*	*4*	*8*	*24*	*32*	*82*	*20*

Dundee were deducted 25 points for entering administration. The deduction was temporarily lifted pending an appeal by the club, but the appeal failed and the deduction was reinstated.

SCOTTISH DIVISION 2 2010-2011

Livingston	36	25	7	4	79	33	82
Ayr United	36	18	5	13	62	55	59
Forfar Athletic	36	17	8	11	50	48	59
Brechin City	36	15	12	9	63	45	57
East Fife	36	14	10	12	77	60	52
Airdrie United	36	13	9	14	52	60	48
Dumbarton	36	11	7	18	52	70	40
Stenhousemuir	36	10	8	18	46	59	38
Alloa Athletic	*36*	*9*	*9*	*18*	*49*	*71*	*36*
Peterhead	*36*	*5*	*11*	*20*	*47*	*76*	*26*

SCOTTISH DIVISION 3 2010-2011

Arbroath	36	20	6	10	80	61	66
Albion Rovers	36	17	10	9	56	40	61
Queen's Park	36	18	5	13	57	43	59
Annan Athletic	36	16	11	9	58	45	59
Stranraer	36	15	12	9	72	57	57
Berwick Rangers	36	12	13	11	62	56	49
Elgin City	36	13	6	17	53	63	45
Montrose	36	10	7	19	47	61	37
East Stirlingshire	36	10	4	22	33	62	34
Clyde	36	8	8	20	37	67	32

2010/2011 Scottish F.A. Cup

Semi-finals

Motherwell vs St. Johnstone	3-0
Celtic vs Aberdeen	4-0

Final

Hampden Park, 21st May 2011

Motherwell 0

Celtic 3   (Ki Sung-Yeung, Wilson, Mulgrew)

Attendance 49,618

2010/2011 Scottish League Cup

Semi-finals

Aberdeen vs Celtic	1-4
Rangers vs Motherwell	2-1

Final

Hampden Park, 20th March 2011

Celtic 1   (Ledley)

Rangers 2 (aet.)   (Davis, Jelavic)

Attendance 51,181

SCOTTISH PREMIER 2011-2012

CELTIC	38	30	3	5	84	21	93
Rangers	38	26	5	7	77	28	73
Motherwell	38	18	8	12	49	44	62
Dundee United	38	16	11	11	62	50	59
Heart of Midlothian	38	15	7	16	45	43	52
St. Johnstone	38	14	8	16	43	50	50
Kilmarnock	38	11	14	13	44	61	47
St. Mirren	38	9	16	13	39	51	43
Aberdeen	38	9	14	15	36	44	41
Inverness Caledonian Thistle	38	10	9	19	42	60	39
Hibernian	38	8	9	21	40	67	33
Dunfermline Athletic	*38*	*5*	*10*	*23*	*40*	*82*	*25*

Rangers were deducted 10 points for entering administration. With 5 games of the season left, the Division was split into two groups of 6. The top half contended for the Championship while the bottom half decided relegation.

SCOTTISH DIVISION 1 2011-2012

Ross County	36	22	13	1	72	32	79
Dundee	36	15	10	11	53	43	55
Falkirk	36	13	13	10	53	48	52
Hamilton Academical	36	14	7	15	55	56	49
Livingston	36	13	9	14	56	54	48
Partick Thistle	36	12	11	13	50	39	47
Raith Rovers	36	11	11	14	46	49	44
Greenock Morton	36	10	12	14	40	55	42
Ayr United	*36*	*9*	*11*	*16*	*44*	*67*	*38*
Queen of the South	*36*	*7*	*11*	*18*	*38*	*64*	*32*

SCOTTISH DIVISION 2 2011-2012

Cowdenbeath	36	20	11	5	68	29	71
Arbroath	36	17	12	7	76	51	63
Dumbarton	36	17	7	12	61	61	58
Airdrie United	36	14	10	12	68	60	52
Stenhousemuir	36	15	6	15	54	49	51
East Fife	36	14	6	16	55	57	48
Forfar Athletic	36	11	9	16	59	72	42
Brechin City	36	10	11	15	47	62	41
Albion Rovers	36	10	7	19	43	66	37
Stirling Albion	*36*	*9*	*7*	*20*	*46*	*70*	*34*

SCOTTISH DIVISION 3 2011-2012

Alloa Athletic	36	23	8	5	70	39	77
Queen's Park	36	19	6	11	70	48	63
Stranraer	36	17	7	12	77	57	58
Elgin City	36	16	9	11	68	60	57
Peterhead	36	15	6	15	51	53	51
Annan Athletic	36	13	10	13	53	53	49
Berwick Rangers	36	12	12	12	61	58	48
Montrose	36	11	5	20	58	75	38
Clyde	36	8	11	17	35	50	35
East Stirlingshire	36	6	6	24	38	88	24

2011/2012 Scottish F.A. Cup

Semi-finals

Aberdeen vs Hibernian	1-2
Celtic vs Heart of Midlothian	1-2

Final

Hampden Park, 19th May 2012

Hibernian 1 (McPake)

Heart of Midlothian 5 (Barr, Skácel 2, Grainger (pen), McGowan)

Attendance 51,041

2011/2012 Scottish League Cup

Semi-finals

Ayr United vs Kilmarnock	0-1 (aet)
Falkirk vs Celtic	1-3

Final

Hampden Park, 18th March 2012

Celtic 0

Kilmarnock 1 (Aet.) (Van Tournhout)

Attendance 49,572

SCOTTISH PREMIER 2012-2013

CELTIC	38	24	7	7	92	35	79
Motherwell	38	18	9	11	67	51	63
St. Johnstone	38	14	14	10	45	44	56
Inverness Caledonian Thistle	38	13	15	10	64	60	54
Ross County	38	13	14	11	47	48	53
Dundee United	38	11	14	13	51	62	47
Hibernian	38	13	12	13	49	52	51
Aberdeen	38	11	15	12	41	43	48
Kilmarnock	38	11	12	15	52	53	45
Heart of Midlothian	38	11	11	16	40	49	44
St. Mirren	38	9	14	15	47	60	41
Dundee	*38*	*7*	*9*	*22*	*28*	*66*	*30*

With 5 games of the season left, the Division was split into two groups of 6. The top half contended for the Championship while the bottom half decided relegation.
Teams in the bottom half at the time of the split may not overtake a team in the top 6 at the time of the split, hence the positioning of Hibernian and Aberdeen below Dundee United.

SCOTTISH DIVISION 1 2012-2013

Partick Thistle	36	23	9	4	76	28	78
Greenock Morton	36	20	7	9	73	47	67
Falkirk	36	15	8	13	52	48	53
Livingston	36	14	10	12	58	56	52
Hamilton Academical	36	14	9	13	52	45	51
Raith Rovers	36	11	13	12	45	48	46
Dumbarton	36	13	4	19	58	83	43
Cowdenbeath	36	8	12	16	51	65	36
Dunfermline Athletic	*36*	*14*	*7*	*15*	*62*	*59*	*34*
Airdrie United	*36*	*5*	*7*	*24*	*41*	*89*	*22*

Dunfermline Athletic had 15 points deducted after entering administration.

SCOTTISH DIVISION 2 2012-2013

Queen of the South	36	29	5	2	92	23	92
Alloa Athletic	36	20	7	9	62	35	67
Brechin City	36	19	4	13	72	59	61
Forfar Athletic	36	17	3	16	67	74	54
Arbroath	36	15	7	14	47	57	52
Stenhousemuir	36	12	13	11	59	59	49
Ayr United	36	12	5	19	53	65	41
Stranraer	36	10	7	19	43	71	37
East Fife	36	8	8	20	50	65	32
Albion Rovers	*36*	*7*	*3*	*26*	*45*	*82*	*24*

SCOTTISH DIVISION 3 2012-2013

Rangers	36	25	8	3	87	29	83
Peterhead	36	17	8	11	52	28	59
Queen's Park	36	16	8	12	60	54	56
Berwick Rangers	36	14	7	15	59	55	49
Elgin City	36	13	10	13	67	69	49
Montrose	36	12	11	13	60	68	47
Stirling Albion	36	12	9	15	59	58	45
Annan Athletic	36	11	10	15	54	65	43
Clyde	36	12	4	20	42	66	40
East Stirlingshire	36	8	5	23	49	97	29

2012/2013 Scottish F.A. Cup

Semi-finals

Hibernian vs Falkirk	4-3 (aet)
Dundee United vs Celtic	3-4 (aet)

Final

Hampden Park, 26th May 2013

Hibernian 0

Celtic 3   (Hooper 2, Ledley)

Attendance 51,254

2012/2013 Scottish League Cup

Semi-finals

Inverness Caled. Thistle vs Heart of Midlothian	1-1 (aet)
Heart of Midlothian won 5-4 on penalties	
St. Mirren vs Celtic	3-2

Final

Hampden Park, 17th March 2013

St. Mirren 3   (Gonçalves, Thompson, Newton)

Heart of Midlothian 2

Attendance 44,036

SCOTTISH PREMIERSHIP 2013-2014

CELTIC	38	31	6	1	102	25	99
Motherwell	38	22	4	12	64	60	70
Aberdeen	38	20	8	10	53	38	68
Dundee United	38	16	10	12	65	50	58
Inverness Caledonian Thistle	38	16	9	13	44	44	57
St. Johnstone	38	15	8	15	48	42	53
Ross County	38	11	7	20	44	62	40
St Mirren	38	10	9	19	39	58	39
Kilmarnock	38	11	6	21	45	66	39
Partick Thistle	38	8	14	16	46	65	38
Hibernian	*38*	*8*	*11*	*19*	*31*	*51*	*35*
Heart of Midlothian	*38*	*10*	*8*	*20*	*45*	*65*	*23*

Heart of Midlothian had 15 points deducted after entering administration.

With 5 games of the season left, the Division was split into two groups of 6. The top half contended for the Championship while the bottom half decided relegation.

SCOTTISH CHAMPIONSHIP 2013-14

Dundee	36	21	6	9	54	26	69
Hamilton Academical	36	19	10	7	68	41	67
Falkirk	36	19	9	8	59	33	66
Queen of the South	36	16	7	13	53	39	55
Dumbarton	36	15	6	15	65	64	51
Livingston	36	13	7	16	51	56	46
Raith Rovers	36	11	9	16	48	61	42
Alloa Athletic	36	11	7	18	34	51	40
Cowdenbeath	36	11	7	18	50	72	40
Greenock Morton	*36*	*6*	*8*	*22*	*32*	*71*	*26*

SCOTTISH LEAGUE ONE 2013-2014

Rangers	36	33	3	0	106	18	102
Dunfermline Athletic	36	19	6	11	68	54	63
Stranraer	36	14	9	13	57	57	51
Ayr United	36	14	7	15	65	66	49
Stenhousemuir	36	12	12	12	57	66	48
Airdrieonians	36	12	9	15	47	57	45
Forfar Athletic	36	12	7	17	55	62	43
Brechin City	36	12	6	18	57	71	42
East Fife	*36*	*9*	*5*	*22*	*31*	*69*	*32*
Arbroath	*36*	*9*	*4*	*23*	*52*	*75*	*31*

SCOTTISH LEAGUE TWO 2013-2014

Peterhead	36	23	7	6	74	38	76
Annan Athletic	36	19	6	11	69	49	63
Stirling Albion	36	16	10	10	60	50	58
Clyde	36	17	6	13	50	48	57
Berwick Rangers	36	15	7	14	63	49	52
Montrose	36	12	10	14	44	56	46
Albion Rovers	36	12	8	16	41	54	44
East Stirlingshire	36	12	8	16	45	59	44
Elgin City	36	9	9	18	62	73	36
Queen's Park	36	5	9	22	36	68	24

2013/2014 Scottish F.A. Cup

Semi-finals

Rangers vs Dundee United	1-3
St. Johnstone vs Aberdeen	2-1

Final

Hampden Park, 17th May 2014

Dundee United 0

St. Johnstone 2   (Anderson, MacLean)

Attendance 47,345

2013/2014 Scottish League Cup

Semi-finals

Aberdeen vs St. Johnstone	4-0
Heart of Midlothian vs Inverness Cal. Thistle	2-2 (aet)
Inverness Caledonian Thistle won 4-2 on penalties	

Final

Hampden Park, 16th March 2014

Aberdeen 0

Inverness Caledonian Thistle 0 (aet.)

Attendance 51,143

Aberdeen won 4-2 on penalties

SCOTTISH PREMIERSHIP 2014-2015

CELTIC	38	29	5	4	84	17	92
Aberdeen	38	23	6	9	57	33	75
Inverness Caledonian Thistle	38	19	8	11	52	42	65
St. Johnstone	38	16	9	13	34	34	57
Dundee United	38	17	5	16	58	56	56
Dundee	38	11	12	15	46	57	45
Hamilton Academical	38	15	8	15	50	53	53
Partick Thistle	38	12	10	16	48	44	46
Ross County	38	12	8	18	46	63	44
Kilmarnock	38	11	8	19	44	59	41
Motherwell	38	10	6	22	38	63	36
St. Mirren	*38*	*9*	*3*	*26*	*30*	*66*	*30*

With 5 games of the season left, the Division was split into two groups of 6. The top half contended for the Championship while the bottom half decided relegation.
Teams in the bottom half at the time of the split may not overtake a team in the top 6 at the time of the split, hence the positioning of Hamilton Academical and Partick Thistle below Dundee.

SCOTTISH CHAMPIONSHIP 2014-15

Heart of Midlothian	36	29	4	3	96	26	91
Hibernian	36	21	7	8	70	32	70
Rangers	36	19	10	7	69	39	67
Queen of the South	36	17	9	10	58	41	60
Falkirk	36	14	11	11	48	48	53
Raith	36	12	7	17	42	65	43
Dumbarton	36	9	7	20	36	79	34
Livingston	36	8	8	20	41	53	27
Alloa Athletic	36	6	9	21	34	56	27
Cowdenbeath	*36*	*7*	*4*	*25*	*31*	*86*	*25*

Livingston had 5 points deducted after failing to make tax payments.

SCOTTISH LEAGUE ONE 2014-2015

Greenock Morton	36	22	3	11	65	40	69
Stranraer	36	20	7	9	59	38	67
Forfar Athletic	36	20	6	10	59	41	66
Brechin City	36	15	14	7	58	46	59
Airdrieonians	36	16	10	10	53	39	58
Peterhead	36	14	9	13	51	54	51
Dunfermline Athletic	36	13	9	14	46	48	48
Ayr United	36	9	7	20	45	60	34
Stenhousemuir	36	8	5	23	42	63	29
Stirling Albion	*36*	*4*	*8*	*24*	*35*	*84*	*20*

SCOTTISH LEAGUE TWO 2014-2015

Albion Rovers	36	22	5	9	61	33	71
Queen's Park	36	17	10	9	51	34	61
Arbroath	36	16	8	12	65	46	56
East Fife	36	15	8	13	56	48	53
Annan Athletic	36	14	8	14	56	56	50
Clyde	36	13	8	15	40	50	47
Elgin City	36	12	9	15	55	58	45
Berwick Rangers	36	11	10	15	60	57	43
East Stirlingshire	35	13	4	18	40	66	43
Montrose	36	9	6	21	42	78	33

2014/2015 Scottish F.A. Cup

Semi-finals

Hibernian vs Falkirk	0-1
Inverness Caledonian Thistle vs Celtic	3-2 (aet)

Final

Hampden Park, 30th May 2015

Inverness Caledonian Thistle 2   (Watkins, Vincent)

Falkirk 1   (Grant)

Attendance 37,149

2014/2015 Scottish League Cup

Semi-finals

Aberdeen vs Dundee United	1-2
Celtic vs Rangers	2-0

Final

Hampden Park, 15th March 2015

Dundee United 0

Celtic 2   (Commons, Forrest)

Attendance 49,259

SCOTTISH PREMIERSHIP 2015-2016

CELTIC	38	26	8	4	93	31	86
Aberdeen	38	22	5	11	62	48	71
Heart of Midlothian	38	18	11	9	59	40	65
St Johnstone	38	16	8	14	58	55	56
Motherwell	38	15	5	18	47	63	50
Ross County	38	14	6	18	55	61	48
Inverness Caledonian Thistle	38	14	10	14	54	48	52
Dundee	38	11	15	12	53	57	48
Partick Thistle	38	12	10	16	41	50	46
Hamilton Academical	38	11	10	17	42	63	43
Kilmarnock	38	9	9	20	41	64	36
Dundee United	*38*	*8*	*7*	*23*	*45*	*70*	*28*

Dundee United had 3 points deducted for fielding an ineligible player.

With 5 games of the season left, the Division was split into two groups of 6. The top half contended for the Championship while the bottom half decided relegation.
Teams in the bottom half at the time of the split may not overtake a team in the top 6 at the time of the split, hence the positioning of Inverness Caledonian Thistle below Ross County.

SCOTTISH CHAMPIONSHIP 2015-16

Rangers	36	25	6	5	88	34	81
Falkirk	36	19	13	4	61	34	70
Hibernian	36	21	7	8	59	34	70
Raith Rovers	36	18	8	10	52	46	62
Greenock Morton	36	11	10	15	39	42	43
St. Mirren	36	11	9	16	44	53	42
Queen of the South	36	12	6	18	46	56	42
Dumbarton	36	10	7	19	35	66	37
Livingston	*36*	*8*	*7*	*21*	*37*	*51*	*31*
Alloa Athletic	*36*	*4*	*9*	*23*	*22*	*67*	*21*

SCOTTISH LEAGUE ONE 2015-2016

Dunfermline Athletic	36	24	7	5	83	30	79
Ayr United	36	19	4	13	65	47	61
Peterhead	36	16	11	9	72	47	59
Stranraer	36	15	6	15	43	49	51
Airdrieonians	36	14	7	15	48	50	49
Albion Rovers	36	13	10	13	40	44	49
Brechin City	36	12	6	18	47	59	42
Stenhousemuir	36	11	7	18	46	80	40
Cowdenbeath	*36*	*11*	*6*	*19*	*46*	*72*	*39*
Forfar Athletic	*36*	*8*	*10*	*18*	*48*	*60*	*34*

SCOTTISH LEAGUE TWO 2015-2016

East Fife	36	18	8	10	62	41	62
Elgin City	36	17	8	11	59	46	59
Clyde	36	17	6	13	56	45	57
Queen's Park	36	15	11	10	46	32	56
Annan Athletic	36	16	8	12	69	57	56
Berwick Rangers	36	14	7	15	45	50	49
Stirling Albion	36	13	9	14	47	46	48
Montrose	36	11	10	15	50	70	43
Arbroath	36	11	6	19	42	51	39
East Stirlingshire	*36*	*9*	*5*	*22*	*41*	*79*	*32*

2015/2016 Scottish F.A. Cup

Semi-finals

Hibernian vs Dundee United	0-0 (aet)

Hibernian won 4-2 on penalties

Rangers vs Celtic	2-2 (aet)

Rangers won 5-4 on penalties

Final

Hampden Park, 21st May 2016

Rangers 2 (Miller, Halliday)
Hibernian 3 (Stokes 2, Gray)

Attendance 50,701

2015/2016 Scottish League Cup

Semi-finals

Hibernian vs St. Johnstone	2-1
Ross County vs Celtic	3-1

Final

Hampden Park, 13th March 2016

Hibernian 1 (Fontaine)
Ross County 2 (Gardyne, Schalk)

Attendance 38,296

SCOTTISH PREMIERSHIP 2016-2017

CELTIC	38	34	4	0	106	25	106
Aberdeen	38	24	4	10	74	35	76
Rangers	38	19	10	9	56	44	67
St Johnstone	38	17	7	14	50	46	58
Heart of Midlothian	38	12	10	16	55	52	46
Partick Thistle	38	10	12	16	38	54	42
Ross County	38	11	13	14	48	58	46
Kilmarnock	38	9	14	15	36	56	41
Motherwell	38	10	8	20	46	69	38
Dundee	38	10	7	21	38	62	37
Hamilton Academical	38	7	14	17	37	56	35
Inverness Caledonian Thistle	*38*	*7*	*13*	*18*	*44*	*71*	*34*

With 5 games of the season left, the Division was split into two groups of 6. The top half contended for the Championship while the bottom half decided relegation.
Teams in the bottom half at the time of the split may not overtake a team in the top 6 at the time of the split, hence the positioning of Ross County below Partick Thistle.

SCOTTISH CHAMPIONSHIP 2016-17

Hibernian	36	19	14	3	59	25	71
Falkirk	36	16	12	8	58	40	60
Dundee United	36	15	12	9	50	42	57
Greenock Morton	36	13	13	10	44	41	52
Dunfermline Athletic	36	12	12	12	46	43	48
Queen of the South	36	11	10	15	46	52	43
St Mirren	36	9	12	15	52	56	39
Dumbarton	36	9	12	15	46	56	39
Raith Rovers	*36*	*10*	*9*	*17*	*35*	*52*	*39*
Ayr United	*36*	*7*	*12*	*17*	*33*	*62*	*33*

SCOTTISH LEAGUE ONE 2016-2017

Livingston	36	26	3	7	80	32	81
Alloa Athletic	36	17	11	8	69	44	62
Airdrieonians	36	16	4	16	61	66	52
Brechin City	36	15	5	16	43	49	50
East Fife	36	12	10	14	41	44	46
Queen's Park	36	12	10	14	37	51	46
Stranraer	36	12	8	16	46	50	44
Albion Rovers	36	11	9	16	41	48	42
Peterhead	*36*	*10*	*10*	*16*	*44*	*59*	*40*
Stenhousemuir	*36*	*11*	*6*	*19*	*45*	*64*	*39*

SCOTTISH LEAGUE TWO 2016-2017

Arbroath	36	18	12	6	63	36	66
Forfar Athletic	36	18	10	8	69	49	64
Annan Athletic	36	18	4	14	61	58	58
Montrose	36	14	10	12	44	53	52
Elgin City	36	14	9	13	67	47	51
Stirling Albion	36	12	11	13	50	59	47
Edinburgh City	36	11	10	15	38	45	43
Berwick Rangers	36	10	10	16	50	65	40
Clyde	36	10	8	18	49	64	38
Cowdenbeath	36	9	8	19	40	55	35

2016/2017 Scottish F.A. Cup

Semi-finals

Hibernian vs Aberdeen	2-3
Celtic vs Rangers	2-0

Final

Hampden Park, 27th May 2017

Celtic 2 (Armstrong, Rogic)
Aberdeen 1 (Hayes)

Attendance 48,713

2016/2017 Scottish League Cup

Semi-finals

Greenock Morton vs Aberdeen	0-2
Rangers vs Celtic	0-1

Final

Hampden Park, 27th November 2016

Aberdeen 0
Celtic 3 (Rogic, Forrest, Dembélé)

Attendance 49,629

SCOTTISH PREMIERSHIP 2017-2018

CELTIC	38	24	10	4	73	25	82
Aberdeen	38	22	7	9	56	37	73
Rangers	38	21	7	10	76	50	70
Hibernian	38	18	13	7	62	46	67
Kilmarnock	38	16	11	11	49	47	59
Heart of Midlothian	38	12	13	13	39	39	49
Motherwell	38	13	9	16	43	49	48
St. Johnstone	38	12	10	16	42	53	46
Dundee	38	11	6	21	36	57	39
Hamilton Academical	38	9	6	23	47	68	33
Partick Thistle	*38*	*8*	*9*	*21*	*31*	*61*	*33*
Ross County	*38*	*6*	*11*	*21*	*40*	*62*	*29*

With 5 games of the season left, the Division was split into two groups of 6. The top half contended for the Championship while the bottom half decided relegation.

SCOTTISH CHAMPIONSHIP 2017-18

St. Mirren	36	23	5	8	63	36	74
Livingston	36	17	11	8	56	37	62
Dundee United	36	18	7	11	52	42	61
Dunfermline Athletic	36	16	11	9	60	35	59
Inverness Caledonian Thistle	36	16	9	11	53	37	57
Queen of the South	36	14	10	12	59	53	52
Greenock Morton	36	13	11	12	47	40	50
Falkirk	36	12	11	13	45	49	47
Dumbarton	*36*	*7*	*9*	*20*	*27*	*63*	*30*
Brechin City	*36*	*0*	*4*	*32*	*20*	*90*	*4*

SCOTTISH LEAGUE ONE 2017-2018

Ayr United	36	24	4	8	92	42	76
Raith Rovers	36	22	9	5	68	32	75
Alloa Athletic	**36**	**17**	**9**	**10**	**56**	**43**	**60**
Arbroath	36	17	8	11	70	51	59
Stranraer	36	16	5	15	58	66	53
East Fife	36	13	3	20	49	67	42
Airdrieonians	36	10	11	15	46	60	41
Forfar Athletic	36	11	5	20	40	65	38
Queen's Park	*36*	*7*	*10*	*19*	*42*	*72*	*31*
Albion Rovers	*36*	*8*	*6*	*22*	*57*	*80*	*30*

SCOTTISH LEAGUE TWO 2017-2018

Montrose	36	23	8	5	60	35	77
Peterhead	36	24	4	8	79	39	76
Stirling Albion	36	16	7	13	61	52	55
Stenhousemuir	**36**	**15**	**9**	**12**	**56**	**47**	**54**
Clyde	36	14	9	13	52	50	51
Elgin City	36	14	7	15	54	61	49
Annan Athletic	36	12	11	13	49	41	47
Berwick Rangers	36	9	10	17	31	59	37
Edinburgh City	36	7	9	20	37	62	30
Cowdenbeath	36	4	10	22	23	56	22

2017/2018 Scottish F.A. Cup

Semi-finals

Motherwell vs Aberdeen	3-0
Celtic vs Rangers	4-0

Final

Hampden Park, 19th May 2018

Celtic 2 (McGregor, Ntcham)

Motherwell 0

Attendance 49,967

2017/2018 Scottish League Cup

Semi-finals

Hibernian vs Celtic	2-4
Rangers vs Motherwell	0-2

Final

Hampden Park, 26th November 2017

Motherwell 0

Celtic 2 (Forrest, Dembélé (pen))

Attendance 49,483

SCOTTISH PREMIERSHIP 2018-2019

CELTIC	38	27	6	5	77	20	87
Rangers	38	23	9	6	82	27	78
Kilmarnock	38	19	10	9	50	31	67
Aberdeen	38	20	7	11	57	44	67
Hibernian	38	14	12	12	51	39	54
Heart of Midlothian	38	15	6	17	42	50	51
St. Johnstone	38	15	7	16	38	48	52
Motherwell	38	15	6	17	46	56	51
Livingston	38	11	11	16	42	44	44
Hamilton Academical	38	9	6	23	28	75	33
St. Mirren	38	8	8	22	34	66	32
Dundee	*38*	*5*	*6*	*27*	*31*	*78*	*21*

With 5 games of the season left, the Division was split into two groups of 6. The top half contended for the Championship while the bottom half decided relegation.

SCOTTISH CHAMPIONSHIP 2018-19

Ross County	36	21	8	7	63	34	71
Dundee United	36	19	8	9	49	40	65
Inverness Caledonian Thistle	36	14	14	8	48	40	56
Ayr United	36	15	9	12	50	38	54
Greenock Morton	36	11	13	12	36	45	46
Partick Thistle	36	12	7	17	43	52	43
Dunfermline Athletic	36	11	8	17	33	40	41
Alloa Athletic	36	10	9	17	39	53	39
Queen of the South	36	9	11	16	41	48	38
Falkirk	*36*	*9*	*11*	*16*	*37*	*49*	*38*

SCOTTISH LEAGUE ONE 2018-2019

Arbroath	36	20	10	6	63	38	70
Forfar Athletic	36	19	6	11	54	47	63
Raith Rovers	36	16	12	8	74	48	60
Montrose	36	15	6	15	49	50	51
Airdrieonians	36	14	6	16	51	44	48
Dumbarton	36	12	10	14	60	60	46
East Fife	36	13	7	16	49	56	46
Stranraer	36	11	9	16	45	57	42
Stenhousemuir	*36*	*10*	*7*	*19*	*35*	*61*	*37*
Brechin City	*36*	*9*	*9*	*18*	*42*	*61*	*36*

SCOTTISH LEAGUE TWO 2018-2019

Peterhead	36	24	7	5	65	29	79
Clyde	36	23	5	8	63	35	74
Edinburgh City	36	20	7	9	58	31	67
Annan Athletic	36	20	6	10	70	39	66
Stirling Albion	36	13	8	15	44	45	47
Cowdenbeath	36	12	7	17	46	46	43
Queen's Park	36	11	10	15	44	47	43
Elgin City	36	13	4	19	52	67	43
Albion Rovers	36	7	6	23	32	71	27
Berwick Rangers	*36*	*5*	*4*	*27*	*27*	*91*	*19*

Albion Rovers and Queen's Park were each awarded 3-0 technical victories against Clyde in February 2019 after it was discovered that Clyde had fielded an ineligible player. The original matches had finished 1-0 to Clyde and 1-1 respectively.

2018/2019 Scottish F.A. Cup

Semi-finals

Heart of Midlothian vs Inverness Caledonian Thistle	3-0
Aberdeen vs Celtic	0-3

Final

Hampden Park, 25th May 2019

Heart of Midlothian 1   (Edwards)
Celtic 2   (Édouard 2 (1 pen))

Attendance 49,434

2018/2019 Scottish League Cup

Semi-finals

Heart of Midlothian vs Celtic	0-3
Aberdeen vs Rangers	1-0

Final

Hampden Park, 2nd December 2018

Celtic 1   (Christie)
Aberdeen 0

Attendance 50,936

SCOTTISH PREMIERSHIP 2019-2020

CELTIC	30	26	2	2	89	19	80	2.67
Rangers	29	21	4	4	64	19	67	2.31
Motherwell	30	14	4	12	41	38	46	1.53
Aberdeen	30	12	9	9	40	36	45	1.50
Livingston	30	10	9	11	41	39	39	1.30
St. Johnstone	29	8	12	9	28	46	36	1.24
Hibernian	30	9	10	11	42	49	37	1.23
Kilmarnock	30	9	6	15	31	41	33	1.10
St. Mirren	30	7	8	15	24	41	29	0.97
Ross County	30	7	8	15	29	60	29	0.97
Hamilton Academical	30	6	9	15	30	50	27	0.90
Heart of Midlothian	*30*	*4*	*11*	*15*	*31*	*52*	*23*	*0.77*

Play was suspended in March 2020 due to the effects of the Covid-19 pandemic. SPFL clubs later voted to curtail the season with final league placings decided on a points per game basis. Celtic were duly declared champions and Heart of Midlothian were relegated. Heart of Midlothian instigated legal action against the SPFL to challenge this decision but their appeal against relegation was denied.

SCOTTISH CHAMPIONSHIP 2019-20

Dundee United	28	18	5	5	52	22	59	2.11
Inverness Cal. Thistle	27	14	3	10	39	32	45	1.67
Dundee	27	11	8	8	32	31	41	1.52
Ayr United	27	12	4	11	38	35	40	1.48
Arbroath	26	10	6	10	24	26	36	1.38
Dunfermline Athletic	28	10	7	11	41	36	37	1.32
Greenock Morton	28	10	6	12	45	52	36	1.29
Alloa Athletic	28	7	10	11	33	43	31	1.11
Queen of the South	28	7	7	14	28	40	28	1.00
Partick Thistle	*27*	*6*	*8*	*13*	*32*	*47*	*26*	*0.96*

Due to the curtailment of the season, Dundee United won promotion after topping the table on a points per game basis and Partick Thistle were relegated. Partick Thistle instigated legal action against the SPFL to challenge this decision but their appeal against relegation was denied.

SCOTTISH LEAGUE ONE 2019-2020

Raith Rovers	28	15	8	5	49	33	53	1.89
Falkirk	28	14	10	4	54	18	52	1.86
Airdrieonians	28	14	6	8	38	27	48	1.71
Montrose	28	15	2	11	48	38	47	1.68
East Fife	28	12	9	7	44	36	45	1.61
Dumbarton	28	11	5	12	35	44	38	1.36
Clyde	28	9	7	12	35	43	34	1.21
Peterhead	27	7	5	15	30	44	26	0.96
Forfar Athletic	28	6	6	16	26	47	24	0.86
Stranraer	*27*	*2*	*10*	*15*	*28*	*57*	*16*	*0.59*

Due to the curtailment of the season, Raith Rovers won promotion after topping the table on a points per game basis and Stranraer were relegated.

SCOTTISH LEAGUE TWO 2019-2020

Cove Rangers	28	22	2	4	76	34	68	2.43
Edinburgh City	27	17	4	6	49	28	55	2.04
Elgin City	28	12	7	9	48	34	43	1.54
Cowdenbeath	27	12	5	10	37	35	41	1.52
Queen's Park	28	11	7	10	37	35	40	1.43
Stirling Albion	28	10	6	12	34	35	36	1.29
Annan Athletic	27	9	4	14	33	54	31	1.15
Stenhousemuir	28	7	8	13	32	48	29	1.04
Albion Rovers	26	6	6	14	37	51	24	0.92
Brechin City	27	4	5	18	31	60	17	0.63

Due to the curtailment of the season, Cove Rangers won promotion after topping the table on a points per game basis. As the play-offs were cancelled, there was no relegation from the SPFL this season.

2019/2020 Scottish League Cup

Semi-finals

Hibernian vs Celtic	2-5
Rangers vs Heart of Midlothian	3-0

Final

Hampden Park, 8th December 2019

Rangers 0
Celtic 1   (Jullien)

Attendance 51,117

THE HIGHLAND FOOTBALL LEAGUE

Table errors

The Highland League tables as published contained a number of errors. Additional research has succeeded in correcting several of these, leaving those noted below.

1893-94   Total goals scored – 1 more than total goals conceded.
1899-00   Total goals scored – 2 less than total goals conceded.
1902-03   Total goals scored – 1 less than total goals conceded.
1906-07   Total goals scored – 2 less than total goals conceded.
1908-09   Total goals scored – 1 more than total goals conceded.
1911-12   Total goals scored – 3 more than total goals conceded.
1913-14   Total goals scored – 8 more than total goals conceded.
1921-22   Total goals scored – 6 more than total goals conceded.
1939-40   Total goals scored – 12 more than total goals conceded.
1949-50   Total goals scored – 4 less than total goals conceded.

HIGHLAND LEAGUE 1893-94

Inverness Thistle	12	10	1	1	59	16	21
Inverness Caledonian	12	7	3	2	39	20	17
Clachnacuddin	12	7	1	4	26	22	15
Forres Mechanics	11	4	1	6	35	32	11
Inverness Union	11	4	1	6	19	31	9
Inverness Citadel	12	3	2	7	23	34	8
Cameron Highlanders	12	1	1	10	11	56	3
					212	*211*	

Forres Mechanics were awarded 2 points against Inverness Union, who did not play.
Ross County resigned from the league in November 1893 after playing just 3 games.

HIGHLAND LEAGUE 1894-95

Clachnacuddin	10	8	2	0	44	20	18
Inverness Thistle	10	5	4	1	31	25	14
Inverness Caledonian	9	4	4	1	23	16	12
Inverness Citadel	10	3	1	6	20	24	7
Forres Mechanics	9	2	0	7	17	33	4
Inverness Union	10	1	1	8	14	31	3

HIGHLAND LEAGUE 1895-96

Inverness Caledonian	10	7	1	2	29	16	15
Inverness Thistle	10	7	1	2	26	11	15
Clachnacuddin	10	5	2	3	32	19	12
Elgin City	10	3	2	5	26	24	8
Inverness Citadel	9	2	0	7	11	26	6
Inverness Union	9	2	0	7	8	36	4

Inverness Citadel were awarded 2 points against Union, who did not play.
A Championship play-off was held at Grant Street Park, Inverness on 30th May 1895:

Play-off
Inverness Caledonian 1-0 Inverness Thistle

HIGHLAND LEAGUE 1896-97

Clachnacuddin	6	3	3	0	16	7	9
Inverness Caledonian	6	3	2	1	13	8	8
Inverness Thistle	6	1	2	3	13	15	4
Inverness Citadel	6	1	1	4	7	19	3

Forres Mechanics were unable to complete their fixtures after April 1897 and their record was deleted.

HIGHLAND LEAGUE 1897-98

Clachnacuddin	16	15	1	0	74	8	31
Inverness Caledonian	16	13	1	2	49	20	27
Elgin City	13	8	2	3	44	30	18
Inverness Thistle	15	5	3	7	40	35	13
Inverness Celtic	15	4	4	7	29	36	12
Inverness Citadel	15	4	4	7	23	37	12
Forres Mechanics	15	3	3	9	39	40	9
Inverness Union	14	2	5	7	18	33	9
Cameron Highlanders	15	1	1	13	13	90	3

HIGHLAND LEAGUE 1898-99

Inverness Caledonian	14	11	2	1	39	14	24
Clachnacuddin	14	9	3	2	48	25	21
Elgin City	12	7	2	3	44	19	16
Inverness Citadel	14	4	4	6	22	36	12
Inverness Celtic	13	4	1	8	22	30	11
Forres Mechanics	14	4	4	6	34	41	8
Inverness Thistle	14	3	2	9	25	46	8
Inverness Union	13	2	2	9	14	37	8

Inverness Celtic and Inverness Union were both awarded 2 points due to Elgin City not fulfilling their fixtures.
Forres Mechanics were penalised 4 points for a breach of the Rules.

HIGHLAND LEAGUE 1899-1900

Inverness Caledonian	10	9	0	1	29	7	18
Clachnacuddin	10	6	2	2	26	12	14
Inverness Thistle	10	6	2	2	24	10	14
Inverness Citadel	10	3	1	6	14	37	7
Forres Mechanics	10	3	1	6	27	27	7
Elgin City	10	0	0	10	9	38	0

129131

HIGHLAND LEAGUE 1900-01

Clachnacuddin	10	6	2	2	22	7	14
Inverness Caledonian	10	5	2	3	33	16	12
Inverness Citadel	9	3	4	2	26	15	10
Inverness Thistle	9	4	2	3	21	15	10
Forres Mechanics	9	3	2	4	13	29	8
Elgin Caledonian	7	0	0	7	9	42	0

HIGHLAND LEAGUE 1901-02

Inverness Caledonian	6	4	1	1	16	6	9
Inverness Thistle	6	2	1	3	10	13	5
Clachnacuddin	6	1	3	2	9	8	5
Inverness Citadel	6	1	3	2	8	16	5

HIGHLAND LEAGUE 1902-03

Clachnacuddin	10	7	2	1	30	9	16
Inverness Thistle	10	7	1	2	20	18	15
Inverness Citadel	10	5	0	5	25	18	10
Inverness Caledonian	10	4	1	5	17	19	9
Forres Mechanics	10	2	1	7	14	27	5
Elgin City United	10	1	1	8	9	25	3

115116

HIGHLAND LEAGUE 1903-04

Clachnacuddin	12	11	0	1	51	10	22
Inverness Citadel	12	6	3	3	26	26	15
Inverness Thistle	11	6	0	5	30	17	14
Cameron Highlanders	11	5	2	4	22	26	12
Inverness Caledonian	12	4	1	7	24	20	9
Elgin City	12	2	2	8	19	44	6
Forres Mechanics	12	2	2	8	14	43	6

Inverness Thistle were awarded 2 points when Cameron Highlanders failed to appear for a fixture.

HIGHLAND LEAGUE 1904-05

Clachnacuddin	12	8	1	3	41	16	17
Black Watch	12	6	5	1	19	10	17
Inverness Thistle	12	7	2	3	19	12	16
Inverness Caledonian	12	6	3	3	24	15	15
Inverness Citadel	12	4	3	5	20	25	7
Forres Mechanics	12	2	1	9	16	31	5
Elgin City	12	0	3	9	8	38	3

Clachnacuddin were awarded the Championship after Black Watch refused to play-off on 12th May 1905 due to a disagreement about the referee appointed by the League. Inverness Citadel had 4 points deducted for fielding ineligible players.

HIGHLAND LEAGUE 1905-06

Inverness Caledonian	12	7	2	3	31	9	16
Inverness Thistle	12	6	4	2	28	11	16
Clachnacuddin	12	7	2	3	22	17	16
Inverness Citadel	12	5	5	2	21	13	15
Forres Mechanics	12	6	2	4	20	16	14
Black Watch	12	3	1	8	14	27	7
Elgin City	12	0	0	12	7	50	0

Championship play-offs
Semi final – Clachnacuddin 3   Inverness Thistle 1
Final – Clachnacuddin 2   Inverness Caledonian 0

HIGHLAND LEAGUE 1906-07

Inverness Thistle	10	8	1	1	31	13	17
Inverness Caledonian	9	3	5	1	18	15	11
Inverness Citadel	10	3	4	3	18	17	10
Elgin City	9	4	1	4	16	21	9
Clachnacuddin	10	4	1	5	18	20	9
Forres Mechanics	10	0	2	8	10	27	2

111113

Inverness Caledonian vs Elgin City was not played.

HIGHLAND LEAGUE 1907-08

Clachnacuddin	12	10	1	1	30	15	21
Highland Light Infantry	11	6	3	2	29	16	15
Inverness Citadel	12	5	4	3	19	18	14
Inverness Caledonian	12	3	4	5	17	17	10
Inverness Thistle	11	3	2	6	13	19	8
Elgin City	10	1	3	6	15	26	5
Forres Mechanics	10	2	1	7	10	22	5

Three matches were not played.

HIGHLAND LEAGUE 1908-09

Inverness Citadel	12	7	3	2	20	9	17
Clachnacuddin	12	7	2	3	25	17	16
Forres Mechanics	12	5	3	4	20	19	13
Inverness Caledonian	10	3	5	2	15	15	11
Inverness Thistle	10	3	2	5	13	14	8
Elgin City	11	3	1	7	16	24	7
Highland Light Infantry	11	2	2	7	15	25	6

124123

Three matches were not played.

HIGHLAND LEAGUE 1909-10

Elgin City	14	9	2	3	41	20	20
Inverness Thistle	14	9	2	3	38	23	20
Inverness Citadel	14	9	1	4	35	19	19
Clachnacuddin	14	7	2	5	26	23	16
Inverness Caledonian	13	7	1	5	33	20	15
Buckie Thistle	13	2	5	6	17	35	9
Seaforth Highlanders	14	2	2	10	16	47	6
Forres Mechanics	14	2	1	11	11	30	5

Inverness Caledonian vs Buckie Thistle was not played.

Championship play-off
Inverness Thistle vs Elgin City   1-1, 2-1

HIGHLAND LEAGUE 1910-11

Inverness Caledonian	14	8	5	1	38	15	21
Buckie Thistle	14	10	0	4	32	19	20
Inverness Citadel	14	6	5	3	28	18	17
Clachnacuddin	14	7	3	4	23	21	17
Forres Mechanics	14	5	3	6	24	23	13
Inverness Thistle	14	5	3	6	25	31	13
Seaforth Highlanders	14	3	2	9	31	51	8
Elgin City	14	1	1	12	15	38	3

HIGHLAND LEAGUE 1911-12

Inverness Caledonian	12	7	3	2	25	10	17
Clachnacuddin	12	7	3	2	27	14	17
Inverness Thistle	12	8	1	3	32	20	17
Forres Mechanics	12	5	2	5	22	21	12
Elgin City	12	5	1	6	25	32	11
Buckie Thistle	12	3	1	8	11	27	7
Inverness Citadel	12	0	3	9	8	23	3

150147

Championship play-off
Semi final –   Clachnacuddin 3   Inverness Thistle 2
Final –   Clachnacuddin 2   Inverness Caledonian 1

HIGHLAND LEAGUE 1912-13

Aberdeen 'A'	16	13	3	0	53	18	29
Buckie Thistle	16	9	1	6	20	19	19
Inverness Caledonian	16	8	1	7	34	36	17
Inverness Thistle	16	7	3	6	27	26	17
Clachnacuddin	15	7	1	7	32	25	15
Elgin City	16	5	5	6	27	32	15
93rd Highlanders	15	4	4	7	23	29	12
Inverness Citadel	14	3	2	9	22	37	8
Forres Mechanics	16	4	0	12	23	39	8

HIGHLAND LEAGUE 1913-14

Inverness Caledonian	16	9	7	0	29	13	25
Aberdeen 'A'	16	11	1	4	43	28	23
Elgin City	16	8	2	6	30	23	18
Forres Mechanics	16	8	2	6	26	23	18
Inverness Citadel	16	5	8	3	31	33	18
Clachnacuddin	16	5	4	7	31	29	14
Inverness Thistle	16	5	3	8	30	28	13
93rd Highlanders	16	3	3	10	16	32	9
Buckie Thistle	16	1	4	11	19	38	6

255247

HIGHLAND LEAGUE 1914-15

Clachnacuddin	6	5	0	1	19	5	10
Inverness Caledonian	6	2	2	2	10	5	6
Aberdeen 'A'	3	2	1	0	10	4	5
Elgin City	4	1	1	2	4	12	3
Inverness Thistle	6	0	3	3	4	13	3
Forres Mechanics	4	0	2	2	4	12	2
Buckie Thistle	1	0	1	0	2	2	1

The competition was abandoned in February 1915 following the outbreak of the Great War.

HIGHLAND LEAGUE 1919-20

Buckie Thistle	18	14	3	1	52	22	31
Clachnacuddin	18	14	1	3	59	25	29
Inverness Caledonian	18	11	2	5	52	31	24
Elgin City	18	10	3	5	56	31	23
Inverness Thistle	18	7	2	9	37	41	16
Forres Mechanics	18	7	2	9	34	48	16
Inverness Citadel	18	4	3	11	25	39	11
Nairn County	18	4	3	11	25	45	11
Seaforth Highlanders	18	5	1	12	31	63	11
Cameron Highlanders	18	2	4	12	26	52	8

HIGHLAND LEAGUE 1920-21

Clachnacuddin	14	10	2	2	38	16	22
Inverness Thistle	14	9	1	4	41	22	19
Inverness Caledonian	14	7	3	4	28	18	17
Buckie Thistle	14	6	3	5	26	22	15
Inverness Citadel	13	4	3	6	21	29	11
Elgin City	12	4	2	6	12	25	10
Nairn County	14	5	1	8	19	29	11
Forres Mechanics	13	1	1	11	13	37	3

It is believed that two games featuring Elgin City which are missing from the above table were not played.

HIGHLAND LEAGUE 1921-22

Clachnacuddin	14	10	3	1	29	11	23
Buckie Thistle	14	8	3	3	26	18	19
Inverness Citadel	14	6	3	5	30	26	15
Inverness Thistle	14	7	1	6	22	23	15
Inverness Caledonian	14	5	4	5	25	28	14
Elgin City	14	4	2	8	22	25	10
Nairn County	14	3	3	8	14	20	9
Forres Mechanics	14	2	3	9	15	34	7

183185

HIGHLAND LEAGUE 1922-23

Clachnacuddin	16	11	2	3	47	21	24
Elgin City	16	10	3	3	33	16	23
Buckie Thistle	16	9	3	4	31	14	21
Fraserburgh	16	7	2	7	36	26	16
Inverness Caledonian	15	7	1	7	20	26	15
Inverness Citadel	16	7	0	9	30	34	14
Inverness Thistle	15	5	2	8	12	34	12
Nairn County	16	4	2	10	14	26	10
Forres Mechanics	16	1	5	10	19	39	7

242236

HIGHLAND LEAGUE 1923-24

Clachnacuddin	16	12	2	2	32	10	26
Buckie Thistle	16	9	3	4	36	30	21
Elgin City	16	8	4	4	26	13	20
Inverness Caledonian	16	7	3	6	34	28	17
Fraserburgh	16	5	6	5	18	20	16
Inverness Thistle	16	5	4	7	22	23	14
Forres Mechanics	16	4	5	7	26	24	13
Inverness Citadel	16	5	3	8	32	33	13
Nairn County	16	1	2	13	8	53	4

HIGHLAND LEAGUE 1924-25

Aberdeen 'A'	20	16	3	1	57	11	35
Inverness Caledonian	20	12	3	5	41	18	27
Elgin City	20	10	4	6	48	30	24
Buckie Thistle	20	11	2	7	45	30	24
Inverness Thistle	20	11	2	7	38	31	24
Inverness Citadel	20	9	3	8	35	43	21
Fraserburgh	20	7	3	10	30	37	17
Keith	20	4	7	9	28	51	15
Clachnacuddin	20	5	3	12	28	38	13
Forres Mechanics	20	4	4	12	32	55	12
Nairn County	20	3	2	15	19	57	8

HIGHLAND LEAGUE 1925-26

Inverness Caledonian	18	14	2	2	69	27	30
Inverness Thistle	18	13	1	4	59	22	27
Elgin City	18	12	1	5	48	39	25
Buckie Thistle	18	10	3	5	55	32	23
Clachnacuddin	18	9	4	5	48	37	22
Fraserburgh	18	7	2	9	43	54	16
Forres Mechanics	18	6	2	10	43	49	14
Nairn County	18	3	3	12	29	54	9
Inverness Citadel	18	4	0	14	25	51	8
Keith	18	2	2	14	24	78	6

HIGHLAND LEAGUE 1926-27

Buckie Thistle	18	13	1	4	50	35	27
Clachnacuddin	18	12	2	4	57	26	26
Inverness Caledonian	18	11	3	4	42	36	25
Forres Mechanics	18	7	5	6	52	44	19
Elgin City	18	8	2	8	49	42	18
Inverness Citadel	18	7	4	7	44	49	18
Keith	18	7	3	8	47	40	17
Black Watch	18	5	3	10	37	59	13
Inverness Thistle	18	5	3	10	40	46	13
Nairn County	18	1	2	15	29	70	4

HIGHLAND LEAGUE 1927-28

Buckie Thistle	18	12	4	2	49	21	28
Clachnacuddin	18	12	2	4	40	28	26
Forres Mechanics	18	12	1	5	65	40	25
Inverness Caledonian	18	10	2	6	46	32	22
Keith	18	8	2	8	46	37	18
Black Watch	18	5	4	9	38	39	14
Elgin City	18	5	4	9	25	35	14
Inverness Thistle	18	5	3	10	34	43	13
Inverness Citadel	18	4	4	10	36	69	12
Nairn County	18	2	4	12	23	58	8

HIGHLAND LEAGUE 1928-29

Inverness Thistle	22	14	4	4	54	25	32
Elgin City	22	13	3	6	49	36	29
Clachnacuddin	22	12	5	5	60	32	29
Inverness Citadel	21	10	7	4	47	28	27
Buckie Thistle	22	10	4	8	50	38	24
Forres Mechanics	22	8	6	8	52	57	22
Huntly	22	8	5	9	47	49	21
Inverness Caledonian	22	8	2	12	40	53	18
Fraserburgh	22	6	6	10	39	45	18
Keith	21	6	5	10	54	57	17
Nairn County	22	6	2	14	33	70	14
Black Watch	22	4	3	15	28	63	11
Inverness Citadel vs Keith was not played							

HIGHLAND LEAGUE 1929-30

Huntly	22	17	1	4	65	31	35
Elgin City	22	15	3	4	72	38	33
Inverness Thistle	22	15	3	4	70	37	33
Buckie Thistle	22	12	7	3	48	26	31
Fraserburgh	22	10	2	10	37	51	22
Inverness Citadel	22	8	3	11	55	49	19
Ross County	22	7	3	12	44	54	17
Forres Mechanics	22	8	1	13	57	75	17
Keith	22	6	3	13	58	65	15
Clachnacuddin	22	5	4	13	46	55	14
Inverness Caledonian	22	5	4	13	40	66	14
Nairn County	22	5	4	13	38	83	14

HIGHLAND LEAGUE 1930-31

Inverness Caledonian	22	12	8	2	62	36	32
Buckie Thistle	22	15	1	6	55	34	31
Forres Mechanics	22	10	6	6	55	53	26
Ross County	22	9	5	8	59	40	23
Huntly	22	9	5	8	70	48	23
Inverness Citadel	22	9	5	8	56	54	23
Elgin City	21	10	3	8	46	38	23
Inverness Thistle	22	8	6	8	59	54	22
Clachnacuddin	21	7	4	10	44	57	18
Nairn County	22	6	3	13	46	73	15
Fraserburgh	22	5	4	13	47	66	14
Keith	22	5	2	15	46	92	12
Clachnacuddin vs Elgin City was not played.							

HIGHLAND LEAGUE 1931-32

Elgin City	26	16	6	4	71	25	38
Keith	26	17	3	6	92	53	37
Inverness Citadel	26	15	6	5	59	39	36
Buckie Thistle	26	16	3	7	62	35	35
Inverness Thistle	26	14	3	9	73	53	31
Huntly	26	11	5	10	57	54	27
Inverness Caledonian	26	11	4	11	53	54	26
Ross County	26	10	6	10	67	75	26
Peterhead	26	10	6	10	52	48	26
Forres Mechanics	26	7	7	12	76	90	21
Fraserburgh	26	9	2	15	53	54	20
King's Own Scottish Borderers	26	5	5	16	40	78	15
Nairn County	26	6	2	18	37	86	14
Clachnacuddin	26	4	4	18	40	88	12

HIGHLAND LEAGUE 1932-33

Fraserburgh	26	21	1	4	72	33	43
Elgin City	26	15	4	7	76	59	34
Buckie Thistle	26	12	6	8	78	58	30
Huntly	26	13	4	9	79	63	30
Inverness Thistle	26	12	6	8	55	45	30
Keith	26	11	6	9	70	65	28
Peterhead	26	12	3	11	47	42	27
Inverness Citadel	26	9	7	10	51	25	25
Forres Mechanics	26	11	2	13	71	78	24
Ross County	26	10	4	12	50	56	22
Clachnacuddin	26	7	4	15	56	75	18
Nairn County	26	7	4	15	60	75	18
Inverness Caledonian	26	7	3	16	46	71	17
King's Own Scottish Borderers	26	6	4	16	52	86	16
Ross County had 2 points deducted for fielding ineligible players.							

HIGHLAND LEAGUE 1933-34

Buckie Thistle	26	22	3	1	95	36	47
Forres Mechanics	26	15	3	8	78	57	33
Keith	26	15	3	8	73	57	33
Inverness Thistle	26	14	2	10	73	61	30
Fraserburgh	26	14	2	10	51	50	30
Elgin City	26	11	6	9	53	58	28
Ross County	26	13	2	11	76	67	28
Huntly	26	13	2	11	68	66	28
Nairn County	26	9	3	14	59	86	21
Peterhead	26	9	2	15	52	56	20
Clachnacuddin	26	8	4	14	52	63	20
Inverness Citadel	26	8	3	15	53	70	19
Inverness Caledonian	26	8	0	18	57	77	16
King's Own Scottish Borderers	26	4	3	19	37	73	11

HIGHLAND LEAGUE 1934-35

Elgin City	24	16	4	4	72	33	36
Huntly	24	15	4	5	71	48	34
Inverness Thistle	24	14	4	6	84	57	32
Fraserburgh	24	12	3	9	66	53	27
Inverness Caledonian	24	11	5	8	66	62	27
Buckie Thistle	24	11	4	9	58	45	26
Peterhead	24	10	6	8	51	48	26
Forres Mechanics	24	11	3	10	85	73	25
Clachnacuddin	24	9	3	12	56	61	21
Ross County	24	7	3	14	53	80	17
Inverness Citadel	24	6	4	14	52	87	16
Keith	24	6	3	15	54	69	15
Nairn County	24	4	2	18	46	98	10

HIGHLAND LEAGUE 1935-36

Inverness Thistle	22	18	1	3	79	32	37
Peterhead	22	14	1	7	68	50	29
Forres Mechanics	22	13	2	7	62	47	28
Inverness Caledonian	22	12	3	7	59	46	27
Elgin City	22	11	2	9	63	55	24
Buckie Thistle	22	9	5	8	49	45	23
Ross County	22	7	6	9	49	58	20
Fraserburgh	22	5	8	9	42	50	18
Clachnacuddin	22	8	2	12	56	65	18
Keith	22	7	3	12	47	76	17
Huntly	22	6	2	14	46	68	14
Nairn County	22	4	1	17	54	82	9

HIGHLAND LEAGUE 1936-37

Buckie Thistle	22	16	3	3	65	30	35
Peterhead	22	12	4	6	69	44	28
Elgin City	22	11	5	6	78	47	27
Inverness Thistle	22	10	7	5	64	44	27
Huntly	22	8	6	8	47	49	22
Inverness Caledonian	22	8	5	9	47	64	21
Keith	22	8	3	11	50	57	19
Nairn County	22	7	4	11	57	83	18
Fraserburgh	22	8	1	13	66	66	17
Clachnacuddin	22	6	5	11	56	72	17
Forres Mechanics	22	6	5	11	46	64	17
Ross County	22	7	2	13	47	72	16

HIGHLAND LEAGUE 1937-38

Fraserburgh	22	16	3	3	78	43	35
Clachnacuddin	22	16	2	4	74	48	34
Elgin City	22	16	1	5	93	36	33
Ross County	22	12	2	8	64	61	26
Inverness Thistle	22	10	4	8	53	47	24
Buckie Thistle	22	9	4	9	49	49	22
Keith	22	11	3	8	57	49	21
Peterhead	22	8	3	11	57	72	19
Inverness Caledonian	22	7	3	12	40	58	17
Nairn County	22	5	2	15	56	70	12
Forres Mechanics	22	4	1	17	56	93	9
Huntly	22	3	2	17	36	87	8

Keith had 4 points deducted for fielding ineligible players.

HIGHLAND LEAGUE 1938-39

Clachnacuddin	26	18	3	5	88	46	39
Buckie Thistle	26	17	2	7	82	47	36
Elgin City	26	14	3	9	75	57	31
Nairn County	26	13	4	9	71	56	30
Ross County	26	12	3	11	74	80	27
Inverness Thistle	26	10	7	9	56	59	27
Keith	26	11	4	11	61	73	26
Inverness Caledonian	26	11	3	12	60	69	25
Fraserburgh	26	12	1	13	65	68	25
Peterhead	26	11	2	13	60	57	24
Forres Mechanics	26	8	7	11	44	62	23
Rothes	26	9	2	15	66	64	20
Huntly	26	8	3	15	54	67	19
Deveronvale	26	4	4	18	31	82	12

HIGHLAND LEAGUE 1939-40

Keith	4	4	0	0	12	4	8
Buckie Thistle	4	2	1	1	8	6	5
Deveronvale	3	2	0	1	12	7	4
Nairn County	2	2	0	0	7	3	4
Fraserburgh	3	2	0	1	12	8	4
Rothes	3	2	0	1	11	8	4
Inverness Caledonian	4	2	0	2	15	15	4
Peterhead	4	1	1	2	10	10	3
Ross County	2	0	2	0	4	4	2
Huntly	3	1	0	2	8	10	2
Forres Mechanics	2	1	0	1	3	4	2
Inverness Thistle	3	0	2	1	4	11	2
Elgin City	2	0	1	1	4	5	1
Royal Air Force Kinloss	4	0	1	3	10	21	1
Clachnacuddin	3	0	0	3	4	8	0

The championship was abandoned in October 1939 following the outbreak of the Second World War.

Two emergency leagues were started.

1939-40 HIGHLAND EMERGENCY LEAGUE

Inverness Thistle	14	10	4	0	36	29	24
Clachnacuddin	13	6	3	4	46	34	15
Army XI	12	6	2	4	45	29	14
Evanton RAF / Service XI	12	4	4	4	27	31	12
Ross County	11	4	2	5	28	28	10
Nairn County	12	5	0	7	25	31	10
Forres Mechanics	11	4	1	6	28	46	9
Inverness Caledonian	14	1	4	9	23	50	6

258278

1939-40   CENTRAL HIGHLAND LEAGUE 1

Rothes	10	10	0	0	42	12	20
Elgin City	10	7	0	3	38	19	14
Buckie Thistle	9	5	0	4	31	23	10
Royal Air Force Kinloss	10	4	1	5	32	34	9
Lossiemouth	9	1	1	7	22	43	3
Keith	10	1	0	9	18	40	2

183171

Buckie Thistle vs Lossiemouth was not played.

1939-40   CENTRAL HIGHLAND LEAGUE 2

Lossiemouth	4	3	1	0	19	9	7
Rothes	4	2	0	2	12	14	4
Elgin City	4	2	1	1	9	9	5
Army XI	5	1	1	3	8	13	3
Royal Air Force Kinloss	3	0	1	2	7	10	1

HIGHLAND LEAGUE 1946-47

Peterhead	30	22	5	3	89	38	49
Huntly	30	22	3	5	111	68	47
Clachnacuddin	30	21	4	5	100	41	46
Inverness Caledonian	30	19	3	8	99	52	41
Forres Mechanics	30	16	4	10	80	57	36
Ross County	30	16	2	12	76	60	34
Inverness Thistle	30	14	4	12	86	67	32
Buckie Thistle	30	13	4	13	81	75	30
Deveronvale	30	12	6	12	83	82	30
Fraserburgh	30	11	4	15	80	92	26
Elgin City	30	9	5	16	59	79	23
Lossiemouth	30	9	5	16	62	99	23
Nairn County	30	7	5	18	42	91	19
Keith	30	7	4	19	50	94	18
Rothes	30	6	5	19	54	89	17
30th TB	30	3	3	24	62	130	9

HIGHLAND LEAGUE 1947-48

Clachnacuddin	30	21	6	3	99	41	48
Peterhead	30	22	3	5	98	43	47
Buckie Thistle	30	18	4	8	86	66	40
Inverness Thistle	30	17	4	9	107	76	38
Elgin City	30	16	6	8	117	78	38
Inverness Caledonian	30	16	4	10	74	62	36
Deveronvale	30	16	2	12	100	78	34
Fraserburgh	30	13	7	10	83	65	33
Ross County	30	15	3	12	103	98	33
Keith	30	12	4	14	77	82	28
Lossiemouth	30	9	6	15	66	80	24
Forres Mechanics	30	10	4	16	66	90	24
Huntly	30	9	4	17	79	102	22
Nairn County	30	7	5	18	61	96	19
Rothes	30	3	4	23	46	108	10
Royal Air Force	30	1	4	25	48	145	6

HIGHLAND LEAGUE 1948-49

Peterhead	30	24	3	3	120	35	51
Clachnacuddin	30	20	3	7	80	39	43
Elgin City	30	20	3	7	101	55	43
Buckie Thistle	30	19	4	7	84	56	42
Inverness Caledonian	30	17	3	10	84	60	37
Ross County	30	15	5	10	92	74	35
Huntly	30	12	9	9	63	62	33
Fraserburgh	30	14	5	11	72	56	33
Deveronvale	30	13	3	14	92	69	29
Inverness Thistle	30	11	7	12	66	61	29
Forres Mechanics	30	13	3	14	82	94	29
Keith	30	12	1	17	63	85	25
Lossiemouth	30	7	3	20	45	100	17
Rothes	30	7	2	21	40	97	16
HGTB	30	5	1	24	43	124	11
Nairn County	30	2	3	25	36	96	7

HIGHLAND LEAGUE 1949-50

Peterhead	30	21	4	5	85	42	46
Inverness Caledonian	30	19	2	9	88	45	40
Deveronvale	30	18	4	8	90	48	40
Fraserburgh	30	17	5	8	90	55	39
Elgin City	30	16	6	8	72	55	38
Huntly	30	15	7	8	96	61	37
Buckie Thistle	30	17	3	10	87	54	37
Clachnacuddin	30	16	2	12	70	57	34
Ross County	30	12	4	14	66	73	28
Inverness Thistle	30	10	7	13	56	61	27
Lossiemouth	30	9	5	16	56	86	23
Nairn County	30	9	3	18	47	82	21
Keith	30	7	6	17	61	89	20
Forres Mechanics	30	8	3	19	50	83	19
Rothes	30	6	7	17	48	85	19
1st Batallion HLI	30	4	4	22	48	128	12

11101104

HIGHLAND LEAGUE 1950-51

Inverness Caledonian	28	22	4	2	93	32	48
Buckie Thistle	28	17	5	6	99	56	39
Fraserburgh	28	14	6	8	72	50	34
Peterhead	28	15	2	11	76	49	32
Forres Mechanics	28	15	2	11	85	90	32
Elgin City	28	14	3	11	72	58	31
Clachnacuddin	28	14	2	12	80	58	30
Deveronvale	28	13	4	11	75	71	30
Rothes	28	10	7	11	61	59	27
Ross County	28	11	5	12	79	82	27
Huntly	28	11	2	15	65	75	24
Lossiemouth	28	10	2	16	60	82	22
Inverness Thistle	28	7	4	17	65	95	18
Nairn County	28	7	1	20	46	101	15
Keith	28	5	1	22	51	121	11

HIGHLAND LEAGUE 1951-52

Inverness Caledonian	28	23	3	2	111	35	49
Huntly	28	16	6	6	92	64	38
Buckie Thistle	28	18	2	8	84	56	38
Clachnacuddin	28	14	3	11	74	51	31
Rothes	28	12	7	9	59	68	31
Fraserburgh	28	13	4	11	70	60	30
Lossiemouth	28	11	6	11	61	56	28
Elgin City	28	12	3	13	79	66	27
Deveronvale	28	9	9	10	71	62	27
Forres Mechanics	28	10	6	12	64	82	26
Ross County	28	8	7	13	60	69	23
Inverness Thistle	28	9	5	14	61	90	23
Peterhead	28	8	4	16	39	66	20
Keith	28	7	3	18	57	95	17
Nairn County	28	6	0	22	34	96	12

HIGHLAND LEAGUE 1952-53

Elgin City	28	23	1	4	84	37	47
Buckie Thistle	28	18	5	5	88	36	41
Inverness Caledonian	28	19	3	6	86	44	41
Clachnacuddin	28	14	3	11	66	54	31
Ross County	28	14	1	13	81	64	29
Lossiemouth	28	11	5	12	58	70	27
Rothes	28	10	6	12	55	61	26
Inverness Thistle	28	10	5	13	49	53	25
Huntly	28	10	5	13	66	84	25
Deveronvale	28	10	4	14	66	60	24
Nairn County	28	10	4	14	49	70	24
Forres Mechanics	28	9	5	14	81	81	23
Peterhead	28	10	3	15	52	73	23
Fraserburgh	28	8	3	17	59	92	19
Keith	28	6	3	19	43	104	15

HIGHLAND LEAGUE 1953-54

Buckie Thistle	28	21	4	3	93	38	46
Elgin City	28	17	4	7	77	49	38
Inverness Caledonian	28	15	4	9	79	64	34
Huntly	28	14	5	9	73	65	33
Peterhead	28	14	4	10	83	69	32
Deveronvale	28	13	5	10	78	62	31
Inverness Thistle	28	13	4	11	62	74	30
Clachnacuddin	28	13	3	12	64	56	29
Fraserburgh	28	13	2	13	61	66	28
Rothes	28	11	4	13	77	74	26
Forres Mechanics	28	10	4	14	55	71	24
Nairn County	28	9	6	13	49	65	24
Ross County	28	7	3	18	52	91	17
Lossiemouth	28	6	4	18	47	77	16
Keith	28	4	4	20	61	90	12

HIGHLAND LEAGUE 1954-55

Fraserburgh	25	18	2	5	91	55	38
Clachnacuddin	26	18	2	6	70	31	38
Buckie Thistle	25	18	1	6	96	34	37
Inverness Thistle	24	15	3	3	73	56	33
Elgin City	27	15	3	9	72	54	33
Nairn County	28	13	4	11	54	71	30
Forres Mechanics	24	13	2	9	65	50	28
Deveronvale	26	13	2	11	79	67	28
Inverness Caledonian	25	11	2	12	60	50	24
Lossiemouth	27	9	3	15	42	75	21
Ross County	28	8	4	16	52	60	20
Peterhead	27	8	4	15	55	75	20
Huntly	28	9	1	18	51	73	19
Rothes	27	5	2	20	39	81	12
Keith	28	4	3	21	32	99	11

The season was abandoned with no Championship awarded.

HIGHLAND LEAGUE 1955-56

Elgin City	28	22	1	5	92	44	45
Buckie Thistle	28	22	1	5	94	34	45
Inverness Thistle	27	18	2	7	108	52	38
Clachnacuddin	28	14	8	6	71	48	36
Inverness Caledonian	28	15	5	8	63	45	35
Fraserburgh	28	13	6	9	71	59	32
Forres Mechanics	28	13	4	11	73	73	30
Lossiemouth	28	9	5	14	32	57	23
Ross County	27	10	2	15	36	58	22
Huntly	28	7	6	15	40	72	20
Deveronvale	28	8	4	16	55	77	20
Peterhead	28	8	4	16	63	88	20
Rothes	28	9	0	19	55	95	18
Keith	28	7	4	17	49	66	18
Nairn County	28	6	4	18	48	82	16

Ross County vs Inverness Thistle was not played.

Championship play-off
Elgin City 3   Buckie Thistle 2

HIGHLAND LEAGUE 1956-57

Buckie Thistle	28	20	5	3	78	32	45
Inverness Caledonian	28	18	5	5	106	58	41
Elgin City	28	16	5	7	75	48	37
Huntly	28	17	3	8	92	68	37
Clachnacuddin	28	17	2	9	82	63	36
Fraserburgh	28	14	2	12	93	76	30
Nairn County	28	12	5	11	68	56	29
Peterhead	28	12	5	11	64	62	29
Forres Mechanics	28	13	2	13	68	71	28
Lossiemouth	28	10	4	14	60	89	24
Inverness Thistle	28	10	2	16	71	77	22
Ross County	28	8	5	15	58	79	21
Keith	28	5	6	17	55	93	16
Deveronvale	28	6	2	20	41	75	14
Rothes	28	4	3	21	48	112	11

HIGHLAND LEAGUE 1957-58

Buckie Thistle	28	22	2	4	102	23	46
Elgin City	28	19	2	7	77	45	40
Peterhead	28	14	5	9	57	52	33
Clachnacuddin	28	15	2	11	75	55	32
Forres Mechanics	28	15	2	11	66	61	32
Inverness Caledonian	28	14	3	11	74	65	31
Fraserburgh	28	13	3	12	68	67	29
Keith	28	12	4	12	53	44	28
Huntly	28	10	7	11	70	78	27
Inverness Thistle	28	12	3	13	65	83	27
Nairn County	28	11	3	14	58	58	25
Ross County	28	10	3	15	54	71	23
Lossiemouth	28	7	6	15	41	64	20
Rothes	28	5	5	18	61	106	15
Deveronvale	28	4	4	20	42	91	12

HIGHLAND LEAGUE 1958-59

Rothes	28	18	5	5	87	49	41
Fraserburgh	28	18	5	5	93	54	41
Elgin City	28	15	6	7	85	49	36
Peterhead	28	15	3	10	74	65	33
Keith	28	13	6	9	59	48	32
Buckie Thistle	28	12	7	9	64	55	31
Inverness Thistle	27	12	4	11	67	59	28
Forres Mechanics	27	10	6	11	74	65	26
Inverness Caledonian	28	12	2	14	59	65	26
Ross County	28	12	2	14	54	62	26
Lossiemouth	28	8	7	13	60	75	23
Clachnacuddin	28	8	6	14	46	60	22
Deveronvale	28	9	1	18	44	88	19
Nairn County	28	6	7	15	57	91	19
Huntly	28	6	3	19	55	93	15

Inverness Thistle vs Forres Mechanics was not played.

Championship play-off
Rothes 1   Fraserburgh 0

HIGHLAND LEAGUE 1959-60

Elgin City	28	19	4	5	90	54	42
Inverness Caledonian	28	17	6	5	96	61	40
Keith	28	18	3	7	66	35	39
Ross County	28	16	4	8	65	46	36
Lossiemouth	28	13	8	7	74	53	34
Deveronvale	28	14	6	8	72	52	34
Inverness Thistle	28	15	4	9	72	68	34
Buckie Thistle	28	12	2	14	70	68	26
Peterhead	28	10	5	13	65	67	25
Huntly	28	10	4	14	63	76	24
Forres Mechanics	28	10	3	15	52	72	23
Clachnacuddin	28	8	4	16	47	68	20
Rothes	28	7	4	17	55	83	18
Nairn County	28	7	2	19	55	97	16
Fraserburgh	28	2	5	21	36	78	9

HIGHLAND LEAGUE 1960-61

Elgin City	28	19	6	3	85	39	44
Keith	28	19	6	3	75	47	44
Buckie Thistle	28	17	4	7	78	46	38
Peterhead	28	14	5	9	74	57	33
Deveronvale	28	13	5	10	67	44	31
Rothes	28	12	5	11	69	67	29
Nairn County	28	11	6	11	60	62	28
Clachnacuddin	28	10	7	11	50	55	27
Huntly	28	11	5	12	72	82	27
Inverness Thistle	28	10	5	13	63	77	25
Inverness Caledonian	28	8	8	12	56	60	24
Fraserburgh	28	8	7	13	58	80	23
Lossiemouth	28	9	2	17	50	75	20
Ross County	28	3	8	17	41	68	14
Forres Mechanics	28	5	3	20	36	75	13

Championship play-off
Victoria Park, Buckie on 6th May 1961
Elgin City 3   Keith 1

HIGHLAND LEAGUE 1961-62

Keith	28	22	2	4	93	29	46
Elgin City	28	18	4	6	91	46	40
Deveronvale	28	16	4	8	87	48	36
Clachnacuddin	28	16	4	8	59	52	36
Peterhead	28	17	1	10	87	61	35
Buckie Thistle	28	14	4	10	95	49	32
Ross County	28	12	7	9	54	51	31
Forres Mechanics	28	11	7	10	60	54	29
Fraserburgh	28	12	4	12	51	60	28
Inverness Caledonian	28	13	0	15	58	82	26
Rothes	28	8	6	14	57	84	22
Lossiemouth	28	7	4	17	49	86	18
Inverness Thistle	28	5	6	17	53	75	16
Nairn County	28	7	1	20	47	101	15
Huntly	28	5	1	22	43	106	11

HIGHLAND LEAGUE 1962-63

Elgin City	28	22	1	5	105	47	45
Inverness Caledonian	28	19	4	5	56	48	42
Clachnacuddin	28	14	4	10	65	45	32
Forres Mechanics	28	13	6	9	74	55	32
Nairn County	27	14	4	9	65	53	32
Rothes	28	12	6	10	67	58	30
Keith	26	12	5	9	68	55	29
Huntly	28	9	9	10	54	67	27
Peterhead	28	11	3	14	75	71	25
Buckie Thistle	28	11	3	14	51	55	25
Ross County	26	9	4	13	58	56	22
Inverness Thistle	28	9	4	15	46	71	22
Deveronvale	27	7	7	13	46	69	21
Lossiemouth	28	10	1	17	54	75	21
Fraserburgh	28	3	3	22	34	93	9

Nairn County vs Deveronvale was not played.
Keith vs Ross County was not played.
Ross County vs Keith was not played.

HIGHLAND LEAGUE 1963-64

Inverness Caledonian	30	20	4	6	90	47	44
Nairn County	30	19	5	6	92	53	43
Huntly	30	16	6	8	78	54	38
Keith	30	16	6	8	83	61	38
Elgin City	30	17	3	10	90	59	37
Forres Mechanics	30	15	6	9	93	64	36
Clachnacuddin	30	15	2	13	79	59	32
Deveronvale	30	14	2	14	58	73	30
Buckie Thistle	30	13	4	13	62	69	30
Lossiemouth	30	11	7	12	73	83	29
Ross County	30	13	2	15	76	83	28
Brora Rangers	30	9	3	18	41	74	21
Fraserburgh	30	8	4	18	52	90	20
Peterhead	30	8	3	19	70	85	19
Rothes	30	8	2	20	49	88	18
Inverness Thistle	30	7	3	20	58	102	17

HIGHLAND LEAGUE 1964-65

Elgin City	30	21	4	5	109	52	46
Nairn County	30	21	3	6	99	64	45
Inverness Caledonian	30	18	5	7	104	68	41
Ross County	30	17	5	8	109	68	39
Buckie Thistle	29	15	8	6	92	62	38
Forres Mechanics	30	16	3	11	113	89	35
Clachnacuddin	29	15	4	10	94	60	34
Peterhead	30	16	2	12	94	83	34
Deveronvale	30	12	6	12	92	78	30
Keith	30	12	3	15	78	81	27
Brora Rangers	30	11	4	15	83	88	26
Lossiemouth	30	8	7	15	61	88	23
Rothes	30	8	3	19	62	116	19
Inverness Thistle	30	8	3	19	69	101	19
Huntly	30	4	4	22	52	142	12
Fraserburgh	30	3	4	23	67	138	10

Clachnacuddin vs Buckie Thistle was not played.

HIGHLAND LEAGUE 1967-68

Elgin City	30	26	3	1	117	28	55
Ross County	30	22	5	3	82	35	49
Inverness Caledonian	30	22	3	5	120	45	47
Peterhead	30	19	2	9	98	57	40
Inverness Thistle	30	15	4	11	66	66	34
Nairn County	30	13	6	11	76	64	32
Huntly	30	15	2	13	72	85	32
Keith	30	15	0	15	68	63	30
Clachnacuddin	30	14	2	14	63	75	30
Lossiemouth	30	12	3	15	70	74	27
Brora Rangers	30	11	3	16	69	67	25
Deveronvale	30	10	3	17	62	84	23
Buckie Thistle	30	5	6	19	53	112	16
Forres Mechanics	30	6	3	21	52	99	15
Fraserburgh	30	6	2	22	51	99	14
Rothes	30	4	3	23	47	113	11

HIGHLAND LEAGUE 1965-66

Elgin City	30	24	5	1	96	35	53
Inverness Caledonian	30	21	5	4	111	46	47
Ross County	29	19	2	8	92	50	40
Clachnacuddin	30	17	3	10	85	61	37
Keith	29	15	5	9	82	67	35
Nairn County	30	17	1	12	93	66	35
Peterhead	30	14	5	11	78	67	33
Forres Mechanics	30	13	4	13	89	82	30
Rothes	30	12	5	13	79	81	29
Lossiemouth	30	12	2	16	68	81	26
Deveronvale	30	10	5	15	61	70	25
Buckie Thistle	30	12	0	18	75	90	24
Brora Rangers	30	9	6	15	57	72	24
Fraserburgh	30	8	3	19	58	93	19
Huntly	30	4	3	23	44	147	11
Inverness Thistle	30	3	4	23	52	112	10

Keith vs Ross County was not played.

HIGHLAND LEAGUE 1968-69

Elgin City	30	24	4	2	100	32	52
Inverness Thistle	30	20	3	7	106	53	43
Ross County	30	17	9	4	83	46	43
Peterhead	30	19	3	8	93	45	41
Inverness Caledonian	30	17	5	8	98	61	39
Nairn County	30	16	6	8	74	51	38
Keith	30	17	3	10	81	54	37
Brora Rangers	30	16	5	9	82	61	37
Forres Mechanics	30	11	2	17	58	69	24
Deveronvale	30	10	4	16	53	81	24
Lossiemouth	30	10	3	17	52	83	23
Fraserburgh	30	9	3	18	48	79	21
Clachnacuddin	30	5	8	17	56	74	18
Huntly	30	5	4	21	37	102	14
Buckie Thistle	30	6	1	23	46	100	13
Rothes	30	4	5	21	53	129	13

HIGHLAND LEAGUE 1966-67

Ross County	30	24	4	2	107	32	52
Elgin City	30	19	9	2	111	37	47
Inverness Caledonian	30	21	3	6	101	54	45
Peterhead	30	18	2	10	94	60	38
Nairn County	30	14	9	7	76	48	37
Lossiemouth	30	13	6	11	70	60	32
Fraserburgh	30	12	5	13	55	56	29
Brora Rangers	30	13	2	15	85	92	28
Forres Mechanics	30	11	5	14	64	79	27
Deveronvale	30	11	4	15	63	81	26
Clachnacuddin	30	11	4	15	64	84	26
Keith	30	8	6	16	53	81	22
Inverness Thistle	30	9	2	19	49	85	20
Buckie Thistle	30	7	5	18	55	90	19
Rothes	30	6	7	17	53	104	19
Huntly	30	4	5	21	38	95	13

HIGHLAND LEAGUE 1969-70

Elgin City	30	24	1	5	101	28	49
Inverness Caledonian	30	22	3	5	101	37	47
Ross County	30	21	4	5	95	33	46
Inverness Thistle	30	20	4	6	124	52	44
Keith	30	18	5	7	89	56	41
Peterhead	30	16	5	9	83	52	37
Clachnacuddin	30	16	3	11	81	62	35
Brora Rangers	30	16	2	12	78	59	34
Forres Mechanics	30	14	4	12	70	60	32
Lossiemouth	30	11	4	15	61	69	26
Nairn County	30	9	5	16	55	60	23
Fraserburgh	30	7	6	17	47	87	20
Rothes	30	6	5	19	51	134	17
Deveronvale	30	5	3	22	52	105	13
Huntly	30	4	3	23	51	121	11
Buckie Thistle	30	0	5	25	22	146	5

HIGHLAND LEAGUE 1970-71

	P	W	D	L	F	A	Pts
Inverness Caledonian	30	23	5	2	92	32	51
Inverness Thistle	30	20	6	4	115	41	46
Peterhead	30	19	7	4	98	45	45
Elgin City	30	19	6	5	90	37	44
Ross County	30	15	7	8	71	49	37
Keith	30	14	6	10	67	56	34
Nairn County	30	14	4	12	58	54	32
Huntly	30	14	3	13	63	64	31
Forres Mechanics	30	10	6	14	53	65	26
Brora Rangers	30	10	4	16	64	67	24
Clachnacuddin	30	7	10	13	44	67	24
Fraserburgh	30	7	6	17	47	77	20
Deveronvale	30	6	8	16	47	84	20
Lossiemouth	30	7	3	20	43	91	17
Rothes	30	8	0	22	72	118	16
Buckie Thistle	30	4	5	21	43	120	13

HIGHLAND LEAGUE 1973-74

	P	W	D	L	F	A	Pts
Elgin City	30	19	7	4	71	30	45
Inverness Thistle	30	14	12	4	66	39	40
Fraserburgh	30	16	7	7	72	43	39
Keith	30	15	8	7	64	34	38
Nairn County	30	15	7	8	60	52	37
Clachnacuddin	30	15	6	9	71	35	36
Ross County	30	15	4	11	81	42	34
Huntly	30	13	6	11	45	56	32
Inverness Caledonian	30	12	8	10	57	49	32
Rothes	30	12	6	12	48	58	30
Deveronvale	30	8	9	13	49	69	25
Forres Mechanics	30	8	5	17	51	76	21
Peterhead	30	5	10	15	33	61	20
Lossiemouth	30	6	6	18	44	72	18
Buckie Thistle	30	6	5	19	45	93	17
Brora Rangers	30	5	6	19	37	85	16

HIGHLAND LEAGUE 1971-72

	P	W	D	L	F	A	Pts
Inverness Thistle	30	25	2	3	114	38	52
Elgin City	30	25	1	4	99	32	51
Inverness Caledonian	30	21	4	5	107	38	46
Keith	30	22	0	8	70	54	44
Peterhead	30	19	5	6	62	31	43
Ross County	30	12	7	11	61	56	31
Buckie Thistle	30	14	2	14	65	51	30
Fraserburgh	30	14	2	14	69	63	30
Brora Rangers	30	12	4	14	72	79	28
Clachnacuddin	30	8	6	16	57	73	22
Forres Mechanics	30	9	4	17	44	80	22
Nairn County	30	7	8	15	49	84	22
Huntly	30	7	7	16	55	71	21
Lossiemouth	30	5	5	20	47	87	15
Rothes	30	6	2	22	49	116	14
Deveronvale	30	4	1	25	25	92	9

HIGHLAND LEAGUE 1974-75

	P	W	D	L	F	A	Pts
Clachnacuddin	30	19	8	3	72	32	46
Keith	30	20	5	5	90	41	45
Fraserburgh	30	18	5	7	86	48	41
Inverness Caledonian	30	15	9	6	60	45	39
Elgin City	30	15	6	9	64	46	36
Nairn County	30	13	9	8	67	61	35
Ross County	30	14	6	10	66	59	34
Buckie Thistle	30	13	6	11	62	63	32
Huntly	30	12	7	11	66	58	31
Inverness Thistle	30	11	7	12	69	49	29
Peterhead	30	11	6	13	54	58	28
Rothes	30	9	5	16	54	64	23
Deveronvale	30	9	4	17	58	88	22
Lossiemouth	30	6	3	21	31	77	15
Forres Mechanics	30	5	4	21	38	85	14
Brora Rangers	30	3	4	23	41	104	10

HIGHLAND LEAGUE 1972-73

	P	W	D	L	F	A	Pts
Inverness Thistle	30	22	3	5	106	44	47
Ross County	30	20	7	3	72	34	47
Huntly	30	20	4	6	69	32	44
Elgin City	30	18	5	7	75	39	41
Forres Mechanics	30	14	5	11	59	60	33
Buckie Thistle	30	11	10	9	58	59	32
Peterhead	30	13	4	13	51	40	30
Inverness Caledonian	30	11	8	11	59	55	30
Clachnacuddin	30	11	7	12	65	52	29
Keith	30	10	8	12	57	58	28
Fraserburgh	30	11	5	14	46	53	27
Rothes	30	7	8	15	57	72	22
Brora Rangers	30	8	6	16	49	68	22
Lossiemouth	30	6	7	17	31	74	19
Nairn County	30	4	7	19	46	95	15
Deveronvale	30	5	4	21	38	103	14

HIGHLAND LEAGUE 1975-76

	P	W	D	L	F	A	Pts
Nairn County	30	19	6	5	75	35	44
Fraserburgh	30	20	4	6	67	35	44
Keith	30	19	5	6	65	30	43
Peterhead	30	19	5	6	85	42	43
Inverness Thistle	30	15	7	8	69	41	37
Inverness Caledonian	30	15	7	8	52	49	37
Elgin City	30	11	11	8	57	48	33
Ross County	30	12	9	9	64	62	33
Rothes	30	13	3	14	57	57	29
Clachnacuddin	30	8	10	12	38	43	26
Buckie Thistle	30	9	6	15	31	48	24
Brora Rangers	30	9	5	16	39	57	23
Huntly	30	8	7	15	31	46	23
Lossiemouth	30	4	8	18	34	74	16
Forres Mechanics	30	4	7	19	53	74	15
Deveronvale	30	3	4	23	29	105	10

Championship play-off

Inverness Thistle 2　Ross County 1

Championship play-off

Nairn County 2　Fraserburgh 1 (aet)

HIGHLAND LEAGUE 1976-77

Inverness Caledonian	30	21	4	5	80	31	46
Peterhead	30	21	4	5	77	35	46
Nairn County	30	19	3	8	64	39	41
Brora Rangers	30	16	7	7	69	66	39
Inverness Thistle	30	16	5	9	66	44	37
Keith	30	13	8	9	71	45	34
Fraserburgh	30	13	8	9	58	49	34
Buckie Thistle	30	13	7	10	57	44	33
Clachnacuddin	30	11	9	10	53	44	31
Rothes	30	13	5	12	61	55	31
Elgin City	30	9	7	14	33	53	25
Ross County	30	9	3	18	52	66	21
Huntly	30	7	6	17	45	65	20
Lossiemouth	30	4	9	17	37	69	17
Deveronvale	30	6	5	19	43	82	17
Forres Mechanics	30	2	4	24	34	113	8

HIGHLAND LEAGUE 1979-80

Keith	30	24	4	2	82	20	52
Brora Rangers	30	15	10	5	60	27	40
Inverness Thistle	30	17	4	9	74	43	38
Ross County	30	14	9	7	65	57	37
Buckie Thistle	30	13	11	6	56	48	37
Inverness Caledonian	30	14	8	8	70	47	36
Rothes	30	15	5	10	65	50	35
Peterhead	30	13	7	10	43	30	33
Elgin City	30	11	11	8	39	42	33
Nairn County	30	10	6	14	53	57	26
Huntly	30	10	4	16	57	66	24
Deveronvale	30	6	11	13	40	58	23
Fraserburgh	30	7	7	16	39	53	21
Clachnacuddin	30	6	7	17	37	63	19
Forres Mechanics	30	6	4	20	37	92	16
Lossiemouth	30	2	6	22	21	85	10

HIGHLAND LEAGUE 1977-78

Inverness Caledonian	30	23	3	4	85	40	49
Peterhead	30	22	3	5	85	33	47
Ross County	30	19	7	4	73	41	45
Inverness Thistle	30	15	9	6	78	47	39
Elgin City	30	15	8	7	56	44	38
Keith	30	12	11	7	65	40	35
Buckie Thistle	30	13	9	8	61	40	35
Nairn County	30	15	5	10	71	61	35
Fraserburgh	30	9	6	15	55	65	24
Huntly	30	9	6	15	46	60	24
Deveronvale	30	8	7	15	50	71	23
Rothes	30	8	6	16	50	69	22
Clachnacuddin	30	7	7	16	49	66	21
Lossiemouth	30	6	7	17	42	70	19
Brora Rangers	30	6	4	20	39	89	16
Forres Mechanics	30	4	0	26	42	111	8

HIGHLAND LEAGUE 1980-81

Keith	30	17	8	5	52	26	42
Fraserburgh	30	17	7	6	55	31	41
Elgin City	30	17	6	7	63	32	40
Clachnacuddin	30	14	9	7	55	42	37
Buckie Thistle	30	15	6	9	63	43	36
Peterhead	30	14	8	8	50	35	36
Rothes	30	14	7	9	55	40	35
Inverness Thistle	30	15	4	11	62	42	34
Inverness Caledonian	30	11	8	11	48	44	30
Brora Rangers	30	12	6	12	49	47	30
Ross County	30	13	3	14	51	59	29
Huntly	30	10	8	12	63	65	28
Deveronvale	30	6	10	14	40	68	22
Nairn County	30	6	8	16	49	74	20
Lossiemouth	30	2	6	22	30	70	10
Forres Mechanics	30	3	4	23	31	98	10

HIGHLAND LEAGUE 1978-79

Keith	30	21	6	3	67	25	48
Inverness Caledonian	30	20	5	5	59	26	45
Peterhead	30	19	5	6	62	32	43
Inverness Thistle	30	18	2	10	91	43	38
Ross County	30	17	4	9	52	33	38
Elgin City	30	14	7	9	64	49	35
Buckie Thistle	30	14	6	10	61	49	34
Deveronvale	30	14	6	10	63	57	34
Rothes	30	9	10	11	47	60	28
Fraserburgh	30	10	7	13	45	50	27
Nairn County	30	9	6	15	47	56	24
Brora Rangers	30	9	4	17	45	51	22
Clachnacuddin	30	8	3	19	45	75	19
Huntly	30	7	4	19	51	66	18
Forres Mechanics	30	7	3	20	52	94	17
Lossiemouth	30	3	4	23	24	109	10

HIGHLAND LEAGUE 1981-82

Inverness Caledonian	30	22	5	3	76	28	49
Peterhead	30	17	7	6	67	39	41
Keith	30	17	6	7	69	28	40
Elgin City	30	15	7	8	55	37	37
Brora Rangers	30	13	8	9	49	38	34
Ross County	30	12	9	9	61	52	33
Fraserburgh	30	15	3	12	56	48	33
Inverness Thistle	30	11	9	10	56	55	31
Huntly	30	9	11	10	62	71	29
Rothes	30	13	2	15	52	55	28
Deveronvale	30	9	9	12	47	47	27
Clachnacuddin	30	10	6	14	49	59	26
Forres Mechanics	30	9	5	16	53	84	23
Buckie Thistle	30	5	9	16	33	62	19
Nairn County	30	5	6	19	46	85	16
Lossiemouth	30	6	2	22	31	74	14

HIGHLAND LEAGUE 1982-83

Inverness Caledonian	30	23	7	0	92	21	76
Elgin City	30	19	4	7	65	30	61
Keith	30	16	10	4	57	34	58
Brora Rangers	30	17	7	6	68	32	58
Peterhead	30	15	7	8	68	49	52
Fraserburgh	30	14	9	7	58	39	51
Inverness Thistle	30	14	5	11	61	55	47
Clachnacuddin	30	12	8	10	75	72	44
Ross County	30	12	4	14	68	68	40
Nairn County	30	10	5	15	56	64	35
Forres Mechanics	30	10	3	17	45	81	33
Huntly	30	9	4	17	55	81	31
Buckie Thistle	30	7	9	14	52	69	30
Deveronvale	30	4	11	15	46	66	23
Rothes	30	4	5	21	38	81	17
Lossiemouth	30	2	6	22	29	91	12

3 points were awarded for a win from this season.

HIGHLAND LEAGUE 1985-86

Forres Mechanics	32	22	6	4	77	27	72
Elgin City	32	21	7	4	67	33	70
Peterhead	32	22	3	7	50	25	69
Inverness Caledonian	32	19	9	4	70	32	66
Keith	32	17	5	10	66	40	56
Huntly	32	15	8	9	58	45	53
Buckie Thistle	32	14	8	10	48	36	50
Inverness Thistle	32	12	9	11	56	53	45
Nairn County	32	11	6	15	47	60	39
Ross County	32	11	4	17	65	66	37
Rothes	32	9	8	15	51	62	35
Fort William	32	10	5	17	40	73	35
Clachnacuddin	32	8	7	17	43	72	31
Fraserburgh	32	8	6	18	40	60	30
Lossiemouth	32	6	8	18	38	63	26
Brora Rangers	32	6	5	21	39	74	23
Deveronvale	32	4	10	18	31	65	22

HIGHLAND LEAGUE 1983-84

Inverness Caledonian	30	21	5	4	85	28	68
Keith	30	20	6	4	62	30	66
Peterhead	30	17	6	7	45	21	57
Elgin City	30	17	5	8	59	31	56
Buckie Thistle	30	14	8	8	74	65	50
Inverness Thistle	30	15	3	12	60	51	48
Brora Rangers	30	10	10	10	55	42	40
Fraserburgh	30	11	7	12	55	55	40
Forres Mechanics	30	12	4	14	53	60	40
Huntly	30	9	7	14	45	51	34
Clachnacuddin	30	9	7	14	55	63	34
Nairn County	30	8	9	13	57	57	33
Ross County	30	7	9	14	51	63	30
Deveronvale	30	8	5	17	38	67	29
Rothes	30	6	5	19	43	97	23
Lossiemouth	30	6	4	20	26	82	22

HIGHLAND LEAGUE 1986-87

Inverness Thistle	34	27	6	1	96	30	87
Inverness Caledonian	34	25	6	3	114	31	81
Elgin City	34	21	7	6	93	33	70
Keith	34	21	6	7	89	39	69
Buckie Thistle	34	20	8	6	84	37	68
Forres Mechanics	34	18	9	7	53	34	63
Peterhead	34	18	7	9	67	45	61
Cove Rangers	34	17	6	11	79	58	57
Huntly	34	16	6	12	60	63	54
Lossiemouth	34	10	7	17	54	77	37
Fort William	34	9	6	19	44	76	33
Nairn County	34	9	6	19	48	92	33
Fraserburgh	34	9	5	20	48	63	32
Rothes	34	10	2	22	54	99	32
Brora Rangers	34	7	6	21	43	86	27
Clachnacuddin	34	6	4	24	42	84	22
Deveronvale	34	6	4	24	36	96	22
Ross County	34	5	3	26	31	92	18

HIGHLAND LEAGUE 1984-85

Keith	30	19	6	5	70	30	63
Inverness Caledonian	30	18	4	8	59	31	58
Brora Rangers	30	15	4	11	52	50	49
Forres Mechanics	30	15	3	12	51	37	48
Buckie Thistle	30	14	6	10	56	50	48
Ross County	30	14	6	10	53	47	48
Elgin City	30	13	8	9	55	37	47
Peterhead	30	14	5	11	45	41	47
Huntly	30	15	1	14	44	41	46
Nairn County	30	13	5	12	47	50	44
Inverness Thistle	30	12	4	14	57	41	40
Clachnacuddin	30	11	2	17	47	60	35
Fraserburgh	30	10	5	15	39	54	35
Deveronvale	30	9	4	17	46	70	31
Rothes	30	8	4	18	38	70	28
Lossiemouth	30	5	3	22	33	83	18

HIGHLAND LEAGUE 1987-88

Inverness Caledonian	34	23	5	6	97	40	74
Buckie Thistle	34	22	6	6	80	30	72
Peterhead	34	22	5	7	68	40	71
Inverness Thistle	34	19	7	8	69	42	64
Keith	34	20	2	12	81	49	62
Forres Mechanics	34	20	2	12	70	40	62
Elgin City	34	17	8	9	69	41	59
Ross County	34	19	2	13	67	39	59
Huntly	34	16	9	9	60	44	57
Cove Rangers	34	14	10	10	67	54	52
Deveronvale	34	12	10	12	64	70	46
Brora Rangers	34	12	5	17	49	69	41
Fraserburgh	34	9	6	19	37	71	33
Clachnacuddin	34	8	5	21	53	93	29
Rothes	34	8	5	21	51	94	29
Lossiemouth	34	8	4	22	38	78	28
Fort William	34	6	3	25	43	89	21
Nairn County	34	1	6	27	30	110	9

HIGHLAND LEAGUE 1988-89

Team	P	W	D	L	F	A	Pts
Peterhead	34	22	8	4	79	35	74
Cove Rangers	34	21	6	7	71	38	69
Huntly	34	20	6	8	82	40	66
Inverness Thistle	34	19	9	6	70	29	66
Elgin City	34	19	9	6	73	37	66
Keith	34	19	8	7	61	32	65
Forres Mechanics	34	19	8	7	66	34	65
Ross County	34	18	3	13	61	51	57
Buckie Thistle	34	16	6	12	66	53	54
Inverness Caledonian	34	14	11	9	70	42	53
Fraserburgh	34	15	8	11	52	43	53
Lossiemouth	34	10	8	16	54	66	38
Deveronvale	34	8	7	19	44	80	31
Brora Rangers	34	8	2	24	42	67	26
Nairn County	34	5	8	21	49	102	23
Clachnacuddin	34	5	5	24	34	89	20
Rothes	34	5	4	25	44	104	19
Fort William	34	3	4	27	24	100	13

HIGHLAND LEAGUE 1991-92

Team	P	W	D	L	F	A	Pts
Ross County	34	24	3	7	95	43	75
Inverness Caledonian	34	23	6	5	93	33	75
Huntly	34	21	7	6	70	43	70
Cove Rangers	34	18	9	7	62	35	63
Keith	34	18	6	10	67	45	60
Lossiemouth	34	17	7	10	62	42	58
Buckie Thistle	34	17	6	11	46	58	57
Elgin City	34	16	6	12	76	51	54
Peterhead	34	16	6	12	61	59	54
Inverness Thistle	34	14	8	12	54	57	50
Forres Mechanics	34	13	8	13	66	62	47
Clachnacuddin	34	11	6	17	43	51	39
Deveronvale	34	12	3	19	40	58	39
Brora Rangers	34	11	5	18	67	52	38
Fraserburgh	34	11	3	20	43	67	36
Fort William	34	8	4	22	48	63	28
Rothes	34	4	4	26	35	99	16
Nairn County	34	3	3	28	24	111	12

HIGHLAND LEAGUE 1989-90

Team	P	W	D	L	F	A	Pts
Elgin City	34	26	3	5	103	33	81
Inverness Caledonian	34	23	7	4	103	35	76
Peterhead	34	23	4	7	77	35	73
Inverness Thistle	34	23	4	7	69	31	73
Forres Mechanics	34	20	5	9	79	53	65
Cove Rangers	34	17	8	9	72	59	59
Fraserburgh	34	17	6	11	58	51	57
Huntly	34	17	5	12	72	46	56
Lossiemouth	34	15	5	14	77	67	50
Buckie Thistle	34	14	7	13	63	53	49
Ross County	34	13	5	16	54	54	44
Keith	34	11	8	15	49	45	41
Fort William	34	12	4	18	59	73	40
Brora Rangers	34	9	6	19	52	80	33
Nairn County	34	9	6	19	51	90	33
Deveronvale	34	6	2	26	42	102	20
Rothes	34	4	6	24	36	84	18
Clachnacuddin	34	0	3	31	26	151	3

HIGHLAND LEAGUE 1992-93

Team	P	W	D	L	F	A	Pts
Elgin City	34	24	5	5	110	35	77
Cove Rangers	34	23	4	7	78	37	73
Lossiemouth	34	21	6	7	104	54	69
Inverness Caledonian	34	21	6	7	76	41	69
Ross County	34	19	7	8	87	49	64
Huntly	34	19	5	10	96	55	62
Clachnacuddin	34	17	7	10	47	34	58
Inverness Thistle	34	17	6	11	55	50	57
Buckie Thistle	34	17	4	13	62	55	55
Fraserburgh	34	15	7	12	63	52	52
Deveronvale	34	14	4	16	57	71	46
Keith	34	12	9	13	46	59	45
Brora Rangers	34	11	8	15	72	74	41
Peterhead	34	8	10	16	61	80	34
Rothes	34	4	8	22	42	104	20
Fort William	34	5	4	25	37	89	19
Forres Mechanics	34	4	6	24	40	94	18
Nairn County	34	1	2	31	26	126	5

The Championship was withheld.

HIGHLAND LEAGUE 1990-91

Team	P	W	D	L	F	A	Pts
Ross County	34	24	4	6	91	37	76
Inverness Caledonian	34	23	4	7	87	40	73
Cove Rangers	34	23	2	9	95	52	71
Forres Mechanics	34	22	3	9	77	49	69
Inverness Thistle	34	20	5	9	55	39	65
Huntly	34	17	10	7	79	52	61
Elgin City	34	17	6	11	84	53	57
Peterhead	34	13	11	10	50	45	50
Brora Rangers	34	13	10	11	66	54	49
Lossiemouth	34	14	5	15	69	61	47
Buckie Thistle	34	12	7	15	47	52	43
Fort William	34	11	10	13	76	85	43
Fraserburgh	34	11	8	15	54	56	41
Keith	34	11	4	19	37	55	37
Deveronvale	34	7	9	18	38	91	30
Clachnacuddin	34	8	2	24	42	92	26
Nairn County	34	4	3	27	36	104	15
Rothes	34	2	5	27	36	102	11

Elgin City had applied to have their last game of the season brought forward by 24 hours to 23rd April, claiming this would give their players extra time to rest their players before a friendly game against Dundee on the Sunday. Elgin duly beat Forres 6-0 to claim the Championship, but it was subsequently discovered that had the game gone ahead on the scheduled date, two of their players would have been ineligible through being suspended by the Scottish FA.

At a League meeting on 29th April, it was agreed that Elgin City had brought the game into disrepute by not informing them of the impending suspensions. The League duly stripped Elgin of the title.

HIGHLAND LEAGUE 1993-94

	P	W	D	L	F	A	Pts
Huntly	34	27	4	3	95	21	85
Inverness Caledonian	34	20	7	7	80	44	67
Ross County	34	21	4	9	80	51	67
Cove Rangers	34	20	4	10	89	46	64
Lossiemouth	34	19	6	9	74	45	63
Elgin City	34	19	6	9	60	33	63
Keith	34	16	6	12	57	40	54
Buckie Thistle	34	16	6	12	54	48	54
Fraserburgh	34	15	8	11	52	36	53
Brora Rangers	34	13	9	12	60	61	48
Peterhead	34	12	8	14	55	56	44
Inverness Clachnacuddin	34	11	7	16	49	60	40
Forres Mechanics	34	11	6	17	56	67	39
Deveronvale	34	7	8	19	46	84	29
Inverness Thistle	34	6	9	19	38	62	27
Fort William	34	8	3	23	26	78	27
Nairn County	34	6	3	25	30	114	21
Rothes	34	4	6	24	42	97	18

HIGHLAND LEAGUE 1996-97

	P	W	D	L	F	A	Pts
Huntly	30	23	4	3	86	26	73
Keith	30	21	3	6	76	36	66
Peterhead	30	17	7	6	77	30	58
Lossiemouth	30	18	4	8	66	31	58
Inverness Clachnacuddin	30	16	5	9	59	46	53
Fraserburgh	30	15	7	8	56	38	52
Cove Rangers	30	15	5	10	84	47	50
Deveronvale	30	16	2	12	55	54	50
Elgin City	30	13	4	13	64	66	43
Wick Academy	30	9	8	13	41	46	35
Rothes	30	9	8	13	44	52	35
Forres Mechanics	30	8	5	17	40	60	29
Buckie Thistle	30	8	4	18	41	55	28
Brora Rangers	30	5	10	15	43	88	25
Nairn County	30	4	3	23	21	93	15
Fort William	30	2	3	25	31	116	9

HIGHLAND LEAGUE 1994-95

	P	W	D	L	F	A	Pts
Huntly	30	24	2	4	102	30	74
Cove Rangers	30	18	3	9	69	38	57
Lossiemouth	30	17	3	10	75	53	54
Keith	30	16	5	9	59	32	53
Brora Rangers	30	15	7	8	63	41	52
Peterhead	30	15	7	8	64	43	52
Fraserburgh	30	16	4	10	56	43	52
Elgin City	30	15	3	12	52	42	48
Deveronvale	30	14	5	11	58	49	47
Buckie Thistle	30	12	8	10	50	52	44
Forres Mechanics	30	12	5	13	46	56	41
Fort William	30	11	4	15	46	57	37
Clachnacuddin	30	7	5	18	37	61	26
Wick Academy	30	7	4	19	32	77	25
Rothes	30	2	5	23	27	77	11
Nairn County	30	3	2	25	20	105	11

HIGHLAND LEAGUE 1997-98

	P	W	D	L	F	A	Pts
Huntly	30	22	5	3	92	32	71
Fraserburgh	30	21	4	5	69	31	67
Peterhead	30	20	5	5	88	34	65
Cove Rangers	30	19	4	7	100	39	61
Elgin City	30	16	7	7	59	33	55
Keith	30	15	6	9	65	54	51
Forres Mechanics	30	13	6	11	64	58	45
Clachnacuddin	30	14	3	13	59	57	45
Deveronvale	30	11	6	13	59	61	39
Buckie Thistle	30	11	6	13	42	47	39
Brora Rangers	30	10	4	16	54	66	34
Lossiemouth	30	9	6	15	39	66	33
Rothes	30	7	8	15	41	56	29
Wick Academy	30	5	5	20	40	74	20
Fort William	30	3	4	23	31	130	13
Nairn County	30	3	3	24	30	94	12

HIGHLAND LEAGUE 1995-96

	P	W	D	L	F	A	Pts
Huntly	30	27	0	3	103	34	81
Cove Rangers	30	20	5	5	74	35	65
Lossiemouth	30	18	3	9	55	37	57
Peterhead	30	16	7	7	74	51	55
Fraserburgh	30	14	9	7	85	46	51
Keith	30	14	6	10	59	40	48
Elgin City	30	15	3	12	59	55	48
Brora Rangers	30	12	5	13	40	50	41
Deveronvale	30	12	3	15	47	53	39
Wick Academy	30	11	5	14	42	63	39
Clachnacuddin	30	9	7	14	45	51	34
Buckie Thistle	30	8	8	14	45	61	32
Forres Mechanics	30	6	8	18	38	51	26
Fort William	30	8	2	20	27	72	26
Rothes	30	4	8	18	39	74	20
Nairn County	30	4	5	21	26	85	17

HIGHLAND LEAGUE 1998-99

	P	W	D	L	F	A	Pts
Peterhead	30	24	4	2	89	19	76
Huntly	30	23	3	4	86	38	72
Keith	30	22	4	4	92	41	70
Elgin City	30	21	1	8	71	39	64
Fraserburgh	30	18	6	6	86	39	60
Clachnacuddin	30	16	8	6	80	45	56
Cove Rangers	30	16	5	9	88	48	53
Forres Mechanics	30	11	6	13	60	60	39
Brora Rangers	30	11	5	14	61	63	38
Deveronvale	30	11	4	15	57	72	37
Rothes	30	8	5	17	46	64	29
Buckie Thistle	30	8	4	18	36	60	28
Lossiemouth	30	8	4	18	40	67	28
Wick Academy	30	7	2	21	33	85	23
Nairn County	30	3	2	25	32	114	11
Fort William	30	1	1	28	24	127	4

HIGHLAND LEAGUE 1999-2000

Keith	30	21	3	6	76	38	66
Fraserburgh	30	17	10	3	75	32	61
Buckie Thistle	30	18	7	5	58	31	61
Peterhead	30	18	4	8	66	39	58
Huntly	30	16	6	8	69	45	54
Forres Mechanics	30	15	7	8	60	42	52
Clachnacuddin	30	14	6	10	55	37	48
Cove Rangers	30	12	6	12	81	54	42
Elgin City	30	12	6	12	45	44	42
Lossiemouth	30	12	6	12	51	54	42
Deveronvale	30	11	5	14	51	63	38
Brora Rangers	30	9	6	15	53	61	33
Rothes	30	8	5	17	41	52	29
Wick Academy	30	6	4	20	35	84	22
Nairn County	30	3	8	19	24	91	17
Fort William	30	1	5	24	34	107	8

HIGHLAND LEAGUE 2000-01

Cove Rangers	26	20	3	3	74	32	63
Huntly	26	19	2	5	61	29	59
Buckie Thistle	26	13	7	6	46	33	46
Clachnacuddin	26	13	5	8	47	35	44
Keith	26	11	9	6	54	43	42
Deveronvale	26	11	8	7	40	32	41
Forres Mechanics	26	10	10	6	44	39	40
Fraserburgh	26	12	3	11	47	38	39
Nairn County	26	8	7	11	44	58	31
Wick Academy	26	8	5	13	39	43	29
Rothes	26	6	5	15	30	45	23
Lossiemouth	26	6	4	16	27	60	22
Brora Rangers	26	4	3	19	42	78	15
Fort William	26	3	5	18	27	57	14

HIGHLAND LEAGUE 2001-02

Fraserburgh	28	20	4	4	71	36	64
Deveronvale	28	19	4	5	68	27	61
Buckie Thistle	28	15	8	5	51	27	53
Clachnacuddin	28	13	10	5	60	39	49
Keith	28	14	5	9	57	37	47
Cove Rangers	28	12	7	9	72	60	43
Inverurie Loco Works	28	12	4	12	48	43	40
Brora Rangers	28	12	4	12	47	55	40
Huntly	28	11	6	11	46	36	39
Forres Mechanics	28	9	10	9	49	46	37
Lossiemouth	28	9	6	13	23	40	33
Nairn County	28	6	8	14	45	61	26
Fort William	28	7	2	19	30	62	23
Wick Academy	28	5	4	19	20	59	19
Rothes	28	2	6	20	24	83	12

HIGHLAND LEAGUE 2002-03

Deveronvale	28	21	6	1	90	24	69
Keith	28	17	1	10	66	35	52
Buckie Thistle	28	15	6	7	63	36	51
Cove Rangers	28	14	7	7	69	46	49
Nairn County	28	13	7	8	67	47	46
Fraserburgh	28	14	4	10	61	45	46
Clachnacuddin	28	13	4	11	45	50	43
Huntly	28	12	5	11	53	42	41
Inverurie Loco Works	28	11	7	10	50	50	40
Lossiemouth	28	12	4	12	41	52	40
Forres Mechanics	28	12	2	14	59	61	38
Rothes	28	8	5	15	26	50	29
Wick Academy	28	8	2	18	33	68	26
Brora Rangers	28	3	6	19	30	77	15
Fort William	28	2	4	22	20	90	10

HIGHLAND LEAGUE 2003-04

Clachnacuddin	28	21	3	4	61	25	66
Buckie Thistle	28	18	7	3	56	32	61
Fraserburgh	28	18	5	5	81	36	59
Deveronvale	28	18	1	9	77	41	55
Keith	28	17	2	9	70	36	53
Huntly	28	16	5	7	73	47	53
Inverurie Loco Works	28	13	10	5	76	51	49
Forres Mechanics	28	13	4	11	63	49	43
Nairn County	28	9	5	14	40	60	32
Cove Rangers	28	7	6	15	45	61	27
Wick Academy	28	6	5	17	42	65	23
Brora Rangers	28	5	6	17	34	70	21
Lossiemouth	28	4	8	16	41	74	20
Rothes	28	2	9	17	19	62	15
Fort William	28	3	4	21	20	89	13

HIGHLAND LEAGUE 2004-05

Huntly	28	20	5	3	79	32	65
Inverurie Loco Works	28	20	3	5	81	25	63
Fraserburgh	28	19	2	7	75	35	59
Deveronvale	28	19	2	7	75	40	59
Buckie Thistle	28	16	4	8	51	26	52
Cove Rangers	28	16	4	8	59	44	52
Clachnacuddin	28	14	3	11	60	37	45
Keith	28	14	3	11	56	45	45
Forres Mechanics	28	10	9	9	49	44	39
Nairn County	28	11	3	14	54	58	36
Lossiemouth	28	10	1	17	49	60	31
Wick Academy	28	6	1	21	30	71	19
Fort William	28	5	1	22	22	89	16
Rothes	28	4	2	22	30	78	14
Brora Rangers	28	2	5	21	26	96	11

HIGHLAND LEAGUE 2005-06

Deveronvale	28	20	4	4	77	29	64
Inverurie Loco Works	28	19	3	6	72	26	60
Buckie Thistle	28	16	8	4	48	23	56
Forres Mechanics	28	17	3	8	76	37	54
Keith	28	16	4	8	63	41	52
Huntly	28	15	6	7	66	41	51
Fraserburgh	28	13	6	9	68	45	45
Cove Rangers	28	12	6	10	55	46	42
Clachnacuddin	28	12	5	11	56	57	41
Nairn County	28	12	4	12	57	46	40
Rothes	28	9	1	18	48	75	28
Wick Academy	28	7	4	17	41	67	25
Lossiemouth	28	7	4	17	40	97	25
Brora Rangers	28	4	1	23	31	82	13
Fort William	28	1	1	26	18	104	4

HIGHLAND LEAGUE 2006-07

Keith	28	20	4	4	67	26	64
Inverurie Loco Works	28	20	4	4	62	33	64
Buckie Thistle	28	17	8	3	54	28	59
Deveronvale	28	17	4	7	77	35	55
Huntly	28	17	4	7	67	39	55
Cove Rangers	28	13	6	9	52	36	45
Nairn County	28	13	4	11	57	42	43
Fraserburgh	28	11	8	9	48	42	41
Clachnacuddin	28	9	6	13	43	42	33
Rothes	28	10	2	16	42	57	32
Wick Academy	28	10	2	16	44	61	32
Forres Mechanics	28	7	7	14	54	60	28
Brora Rangers	28	8	2	18	38	84	26
Lossiemouth	28	3	5	20	25	64	14
Fort William	28	3	0	25	26	107	9

HIGHLAND LEAGUE 2007-08

Cove Rangers	28	19	7	2	85	33	64
Keith	28	18	7	3	80	27	61
Deveronvale	28	17	7	4	85	33	58
Buckie Thistle	28	17	6	5	54	24	57
Fraserburgh	28	16	3	9	65	43	51
Inverurie Loco Works	28	15	4	9	67	39	49
Huntly	28	13	6	9	60	44	45
Forres Mechanics	28	13	5	10	67	46	44
Nairn County	28	12	4	12	44	49	40
Clachnacuddin	28	10	7	11	49	50	37
Wick Academy	28	9	5	14	49	60	32
Rothes	28	5	4	19	49	75	19
Lossiemouth	28	4	5	19	22	66	17
Brora Rangers	28	4	4	20	29	74	16
Fort William	28	1	0	27	16	158	3

HIGHLAND LEAGUE 2010-11

Buckie Thistle	34	24	5	5	84	42	77
Deveronvale	34	23	3	8	100	45	72
Cove Rangers	34	22	5	7	100	43	71
Keith	34	22	4	8	93	54	70
Nairn County	34	18	9	7	86	49	63
Forres Mechanics	34	19	6	9	72	56	63
Inverurie Loco Works	34	19	5	10	81	50	62
Turriff United	34	15	8	11	89	60	53
Formartine United	34	15	3	16	71	68	48
Huntly	34	13	6	15	63	72	45
Brora Rangers	34	13	6	15	51	64	45
Lossiemouth	34	12	8	14	52	63	44
Fraserburgh	34	11	9	14	69	65	42
Wick Academy	34	12	3	19	75	78	39
Clachnacuddin	34	9	7	18	68	89	34
Rothes	34	6	4	24	43	92	22
Strathspey Thistle	34	2	4	28	36	131	10
Fort William	34	2	3	29	36	148	9

HIGHLAND LEAGUE 2008-09

Cove Rangers	28	22	4	2	96	26	70
Deveronvale	28	18	7	3	78	31	61
Inverurie Loco Works	28	18	3	7	72	33	57
Keith	28	18	2	8	62	35	56
Wick Academy	28	16	3	9	54	46	51
Buckie Thistle	28	15	4	9	60	39	49
Fraserburgh	28	13	8	7	62	47	47
Huntly	28	14	4	10	51	40	46
Forres Mechanics	28	12	7	9	64	42	43
Nairn County	28	12	5	11	44	45	41
Clachnacuddin	28	8	7	13	53	58	31
Lossiemouth	28	7	4	17	31	54	25
Rothes	28	2	4	22	24	80	10
Brora Rangers	28	2	3	23	21	91	9
Fort William	28	0	1	27	16	121	1

HIGHLAND LEAGUE 2011-12

Forres Mechanics	34	24	5	5	85	35	77
Cove Rangers	34	23	7	4	93	33	76
Nairn County	34	19	9	6	92	44	66
Inverurie Loco Works	34	20	5	9	71	35	65
Buckie Thistle	34	18	7	9	79	45	61
Fraserburgh	34	17	8	9	79	63	59
Deveronvale	34	17	4	13	75	50	55
Wick Academy	34	16	7	11	77	55	55
Keith	34	16	6	12	85	57	54
Clachnacuddin	34	14	8	12	79	65	50
Formartine United	34	14	7	13	62	60	49
Lossiemouth	34	15	4	15	51	52	49
Huntly	34	14	4	16	50	67	46
Turriff United	34	13	4	17	61	64	43
Rothes	34	7	5	22	31	80	26
Brora Rangers	34	6	2	26	33	115	20
Strathspey Thistle	34	3	2	29	27	102	11
Fort William	34	1	4	29	14	122	7

HIGHLAND LEAGUE 2009-10

Buckie Thistle	34	26	5	3	83	26	83
Cove Rangers	34	23	6	5	97	42	75
Deveronvale	34	21	5	8	91	47	68
Fraserburgh	34	21	5	8	75	48	68
Forres Mechanics	34	20	5	9	72	42	65
Formartine United	34	18	6	10	75	47	60
Huntly	34	19	3	12	66	49	60
Keith	34	17	6	11	77	54	57
Wick Academy	34	16	6	12	79	64	54
Inverurie Loco Works	34	15	6	13	60	47	51
Nairn County	34	15	5	14	61	59	50
Clachnacuddin	34	12	7	15	73	73	43
Turriff United	34	9	4	21	60	86	31
Lossiemouth	34	7	6	21	52	74	27
Brora Rangers	34	6	6	22	32	81	24
Rothes	34	7	3	24	39	102	24
Fort William	34	6	2	26	37	98	20
Strathspey Thistle	34	3	4	27	30	120	13

HIGHLAND LEAGUE 2012-13

Cove Rangers	34	25	5	4	101	26	80
Formartine United	34	25	3	6	106	39	78
Wick Academy	34	25	1	8	101	48	76
Nairn County	34	22	5	7	80	43	71
Clachnacuddin	34	21	3	10	68	49	66
Fraserburgh	34	18	5	11	83	47	59
Deveronvale	34	17	7	10	66	45	58
Brora Rangers	34	17	4	13	83	52	55
Forres Mechanics	34	16	7	11	78	49	55
Inverurie Loco Works	34	16	5	13	71	60	53
Turriff United	34	16	4	14	68	67	52
Buckie Thistle	34	13	7	14	58	62	46
Huntly	34	14	3	17	66	68	45
Keith	34	12	7	15	56	65	43
Strathspey Thistle	34	5	0	29	23	112	15
Rothes	34	4	2	28	29	126	14
Lossiemouth	34	3	1	30	35	108	10
Fort William	34	1	3	30	20	126	6

HIGHLAND LEAGUE 2013-14

Team	P	W	D	L	F	A	Pts
Brora Rangers	34	31	2	1	123	16	95
Inverurie Loco Works	34	23	6	5	97	39	75
Nairn County	34	24	3	7	86	39	75
Formartine United	34	22	6	6	88	36	72
Fraserburgh	34	23	2	9	89	44	71
Deveronvale	34	20	5	9	64	43	65
Cove Rangers	34	16	7	11	91	62	55
Wick Academy	34	15	8	11	83	51	53
Forres Mechanics	34	15	7	12	68	50	52
Buckie Thistle	34	13	10	11	54	48	49
Clachnacuddin	34	13	7	14	67	64	46
Turriff United	34	13	5	16	60	57	44
Huntly	34	9	8	17	55	82	35
Keith	34	9	2	23	50	98	29
Lossiemouth	34	4	8	22	34	93	20
Strathspey Thistle	34	3	3	28	28	116	12
Rothes	34	3	3	28	36	136	12
Fort William	34	1	6	27	35	131	9

HIGHLAND LEAGUE 2014-15

Team	P	W	D	L	F	A	Pts
Brora Rangers	34	30	4	0	134	13	94
Turriff United	34	27	2	5	90	40	80
Cove Rangers	34	22	7	5	103	40	73
Wick Academy	34	23	3	8	94	43	72
Fraserburgh	34	19	8	7	91	48	65
Formartine United	34	19	7	8	85	59	64
Inverurie Loco Works	34	20	3	11	93	51	63
Nairn County	34	18	3	13	88	43	57
Forres Mechanics	34	18	3	13	71	59	57
Buckie Thistle	34	15	5	14	71	66	50
Clachnacuddin	34	14	3	17	63	74	45
Deveronvale	34	9	9	16	53	82	36
Fort William	34	8	3	23	52	98	27
Keith	34	7	3	24	42	97	24
Lossiemouth	34	7	2	25	50	105	23
Huntly	34	5	5	24	37	100	20
Strathspey Thistle	34	3	5	26	36	125	14
Rothes	34	2	5	27	32	142	11

Turriff United had 3 points deducted after fielding an ineligible player.

HIGHLAND LEAGUE 2015-16

Team	P	W	D	L	F	A	Pts
Cove Rangers	34	29	2	3	98	28	89
Formartine United	34	27	4	3	137	35	85
Brora Rangers	34	27	4	3	128	35	85
Turriff United	34	20	8	6	88	31	68
Wick Academy	34	18	6	10	76	42	60
Inverurie Loco Works	34	18	4	12	71	43	58
Buckie Thistle	34	18	4	12	80	77	58
Nairn County	34	17	6	11	75	55	57
Fraserburgh	34	15	8	11	63	49	53
Keith	34	17	1	16	70	76	52
Forres Mechanics	34	15	4	15	60	65	49
Lossiemouth	34	12	2	20	46	70	38
Deveronvale	34	8	8	18	46	64	32
Clachnacuddin	34	10	2	22	59	80	32
Huntly	34	7	5	22	49	89	26
Strathspey Thistle	34	6	2	26	38	118	20
Fort William	34	5	1	28	38	116	16
Rothes	34	1	1	32	16	165	4

HIGHLAND LEAGUE 2016-17

Team	P	W	D	L	F	A	Pts
Buckie Thistle	34	26	4	4	130	36	82
Cove Rangers	34	25	7	2	109	30	82
Brora Rangers	34	26	3	5	116	36	81
Formartine United	34	22	7	5	82	47	73
Fraserburgh	34	19	6	9	77	48	63
Forres Mechanics	34	17	7	10	84	63	58
Turriff United	34	18	4	12	56	42	58
Wick Academy	34	15	8	11	75	52	53
Inverurie Loco Works	34	14	8	12	71	53	50
Keith	34	15	2	17	74	88	47
Clachnacuddin	34	11	8	15	53	77	41
Lossiemouth	34	11	5	18	52	70	38
Nairn County	34	9	7	18	57	74	34
Huntly	34	9	7	18	54	97	34
Deveronvale	34	9	3	22	51	75	30
Rothes	34	7	5	22	37	106	26
Fort William	34	3	2	29	44	136	11
Strathspey Thistle	34	2	3	29	28	120	9

HIGHLAND LEAGUE 2017-18

Team	P	W	D	L	F	A	Pts
Cove Rangers	34	29	3	2	127	22	90
Formartine United	34	26	1	7	124	41	79
Inverurie Loco Works	34	25	3	6	104	37	78
Fraserburgh	34	23	4	7	101	38	73
Forres Mechanics	34	23	4	7	88	45	73
Brora Rangers	34	20	3	11	87	39	63
Buckie Thistle	34	15	6	13	80	56	51
Deveronvale	34	16	3	15	73	76	51
Nairn County	34	16	3	15	61	71	51
Rothes	34	15	4	15	77	70	49
Huntly	34	15	4	15	66	81	49
Wick Academy	34	12	10	12	67	54	46
Clachnacuddin	34	11	8	15	54	69	41
Turriff United	34	11	4	19	54	70	37
Keith	34	4	4	26	45	104	16
Lossiemouth	34	4	3	27	41	125	15
Strathspey Thistle	34	4	2	28	26	124	14
Fort William	34	0	5	29	31	184	5

HIGHLAND LEAGUE 2018-19

Team	P	W	D	L	F	A	Pts
Cove Rangers	34	30	3	1	100	12	93
Brora Rangers	34	27	4	3	99	12	85
Fraserburgh	34	26	1	7	125	37	79
Formartine United	34	22	6	6	97	37	72
Inverurie Loco Works	34	20	6	8	96	48	66
Forres Mechanics	34	21	3	10	79	40	66
Wick Academy	34	15	7	12	69	54	52
Buckie Thistle	34	14	7	13	72	54	49
Huntly	34	14	7	13	57	65	49
Rothes	34	13	8	13	73	57	44
Nairn County	34	13	3	18	61	67	42
Deveronvale	34	13	2	19	55	65	41
Keith	34	10	7	17	62	68	37
Strathspey Thistle	34	10	3	21	47	90	33
Turriff United	34	9	5	20	74	91	32
Clachnacuddin	34	6	6	22	44	79	24
Lossiemouth	34	2	2	30	29	139	8
Fort William	34	0	2	32	21	245	-7

Rothes had 3 points deducted for fielding an ineligible player.
Fort William had 9 points deducted for fielding an ineligible player in 3 games.

HIGHLAND LEAGUE 2019-20

Brora Rangers	26	24	0	2	96	14	72
Inverurie Loco Works	28	19	2	7	80	40	59
Fraserburgh	23	17	4	2	79	23	55
Rothes	23	17	2	4	53	22	53
Buckie Thistle	24	17	2	5	64	35	53
Formartine United	23	14	2	7	62	21	44
Forres Mechanics	27	13	4	10	67	49	43
Nairn County	22	12	3	7	39	41	39
Keith	27	10	4	13	50	65	34
Wick Academy	25	9	5	11	38	47	32
Deveronvale	27	9	4	14	42	56	31
Huntly	27	6	6	15	35	73	24
Strathspey Thistle	22	6	1	15	29	54	19
Turriff United	27	5	3	19	33	83	18
Clachnacuddin	27	4	4	19	27	63	16
Lossiemouth	28	4	1	23	22	87	13
Fort William	20	3	1	16	18	61	10

Play was suspended during March 2020 due to the effects of the Covid-19 pandemic. The competition was subsequently curtailed and Brora Rangers were declared champions following a vote by members of the league.

THE LOWLAND FOOTBALL LEAGUE

LOWLAND LEAGUE 2013-14

Spartans	22	15	4	3	57	16	49
Stirling University	22	14	3	5	48	26	45
Dalbeattie Star	22	11	7	4	59	34	40
Whitehill Welfare	22	12	3	7	54	36	39
Edinburgh City	22	12	1	9	49	32	37
Vale of Leithen	22	11	3	8	41	43	36
Gretna 2008	22	8	7	7	40	33	31
East Kilbride	22	8	4	10	28	31	28
Preston Athletic	22	7	3	12	40	53	24
Gala Fairydean Rovers	22	7	2	13	46	63	23
Threave Rovers	22	4	5	13	22	53	17
Selkirk	22	1	2	19	20	85	5

LOWLAND LEAGUE 2014-15

Edinburgh City	26	22	3	1	65	14	69
East Kilbride	26	15	5	6	63	25	50
Gretna 2008	26	13	6	7	62	32	45
Dalbeattie Star	26	11	9	6	51	39	42
Spartans	26	11	9	6	45	34	42
Stirling University	26	12	6	8	46	38	42
Whitehill Welfare	26	11	7	8	57	38	40
Gala Fairydean Rovers	26	9	7	10	48	54	34
BSC Glasgow	25	7	9	9	39	51	30
Vale of Leithen	25	8	6	11	38	53	30
Edinburgh University	26	8	4	14	40	52	28
Selkirk	26	6	5	15	53	74	23
Preston Athletic	26	3	5	18	31	75	14
Threave Rovers	26	2	5	19	21	80	11

LOWLAND LEAGUE 2015-16

Edinburgh City	**28**	**24**	**1**	**3**	**74**	**28**	**73**
Spartans	28	18	4	6	74	36	58
Stirling University	28	17	5	6	65	32	56
Cumbernauld Colts	28	15	6	7	60	42	51
East Kilbride	28	14	7	7	68	44	49
Edinburgh University	28	13	3	12	51	46	42
BSC Glasgow	28	12	5	11	54	51	41
Whitehill Welfare	28	12	4	12	47	43	40
Dalbeattie Star	28	10	6	12	54	50	36
Gretna 2008	28	11	3	14	38	50	36
Gala Fairydean Rovers	28	10	2	16	53	61	32
Selkirk	28	9	2	17	52	70	29
Vale of Leithen	28	7	5	16	38	67	26
Preston Athletic	28	6	4	18	28	70	22
Threave Rovers	28	3	1	24	30	96	10

LOWLAND LEAGUE 2016-17

East Kilbride	30	24	3	3	89	21	75
East Stirlingshire	30	21	5	4	107	43	68
Spartans	30	17	5	8	69	30	56
Stirling University	30	16	5	9	60	53	53
Dalbeattie Star	30	14	5	11	60	50	47
Cumbernauld Colts	30	13	8	9	51	43	47
BSC Glasgow	30	12	6	12	63	56	42
Whitehill Welfare	30	13	1	16	53	64	40
Gretna 2008	30	12	4	14	44	65	40
Gala Fairydean Rovers	30	11	7	12	55	77	40
Edinburgh University	30	10	7	13	40	42	37
Civil Service Strollers	30	10	7	13	59	68	37
Vale of Leithen	30	11	4	15	52	66	37
Hawick Royal Albert	30	8	1	21	58	93	25
Selkirk	30	6	5	19	58	86	23
Preston Athletic	30	5	1	24	41	102	16

LOWLAND LEAGUE 2017-18

Spartans	30	23	4	3	64	17	73
East Kilbride	30	22	5	3	76	23	71
BSC Glasgow	30	20	5	5	71	27	65
East Stirlingshire	30	19	7	4	67	31	64
Selkirk	30	15	3	12	63	50	48
Cumbernauld Colts	30	11	8	11	50	51	41
Civil Service Strollers	30	11	7	12	47	44	40
Gretna 2008	30	12	4	14	50	56	40
Stirling University	30	11	5	14	45	49	38
Edusport Academy	30	9	7	14	46	49	34
Edinburgh University	30	9	7	14	40	45	34
Whitehill Welfare	30	11	1	18	50	66	34
Gala Fairydean Rovers	30	8	7	15	43	63	31
Dalbeattie Star	30	7	8	15	46	65	29
Vale of Leithen	30	8	5	17	44	76	29
Hawick Royal Albert	30	1	3	26	11	108	6

LOWLAND LEAGUE 2018-19

East Kilbride	28	23	3	2	66	12	72
BSC Glasgow	28	18	7	3	67	29	61
Kelty Hearts	28	16	6	6	61	32	54
Spartans	28	14	9	5	63	31	51
Civil Service Strollers	28	15	4	9	51	38	49
East Stirlingshire	28	11	6	11	57	47	39
Cumbernauld Colts	28	11	6	11	40	47	39
Gala Fairydean Rovers	28	10	4	14	43	48	34
Edusport Academy	28	9	6	13	43	52	33
Stirling University	28	7	10	11	43	50	31
Edinburgh University	28	7	9	12	38	54	30
Gretna 2008	28	9	2	17	42	67	29
Vale of Leithen	28	8	5	15	43	74	29
Dalbeattie Star	28	5	7	16	33	63	22
Whitehill Welfare	*28*	*2*	*6*	*20*	*24*	*70*	*12*

After failing to fulfil three fixtures due to financial difficulties, Selkirk resigned from the league on 28th August 2018. Their record was expunged and the club later folded.

LOWLAND LEAGUE 2019-20

Kelty Hearts	25	22	2	1	95	17	68	2.72
Bonnyrigg Rose Athletic	24	20	2	2	70	22	62	2.58
BSC Glasgow[a]	22	16	3	3	58	21	51	2.32
East Stirlingshire	26	17	2	7	77	29	53	2.04
The Spartans	25	16	1	8	49	32	49	1.96
Civil Service Strollers	23	12	3	8	40	38	39	1.70
East Kilbride	23	11	4	8	43	24	37	1.61
Caledonian Braves	26	11	3	12	57	55	36	1.38
Cumbernauld Colts	27	10	6	11	49	50	36	1.33
Stirling University	25	9	4	12	28	44	31	1.24
Gala Fairydean Rovers	25	7	6	12	39	55	27	1.08
Berwick Rangers	24	6	6	12	32	41	24	1.00
Gretna 2008	24	2	6	16	21	62	12	0.50
Edinburgh University	25	2	6	17	18	66	12	0.48
Dalbeattie Star	23	3	2	18	19	68	11	0.48
Vale of Leithen	23	2	2	19	18	89	8	0.35

Play was suspended during March 2020 due to the Covid-19 pandemic. With the season not being fully completed, a points per game formula was subsequently used to determine the final standings, with Kelty Hearts declared champions on 13th April.

EAST OF SCOTLAND FOOTBALL LEAGUE

1923-24

Coldstream	12	7	3	2	28	15	17
Berwick Rangers	12	6	4	2	25	12	16
Gala Fairydean	12	6	1	5	25	19	13
Leith Amateurs	12	5	1	6	18	24	11
Civil Service Strollers	12	3	4	5	18	14	10
Vale of Leithen	12	3	4	5	23	37	10
Selkirk	12	1	5	6	14	30	7

Leith Amateurs replaced Edinburgh Civil Service after six matches had been played, continuing with their record.

1924-25

Vale of Leithen	12	8	3	1	49	17	19
Civil Service Strollers	12	8	1	3	23	15	17
Berwick Rangers	12	4	4	4	26	25	12
Coldstream	10	4	3	3	20	19	11
Leith Amateurs	9	4	0	5	13	18	8
Selkirk	12	2	3	7	14	24	7
Gala Fairydean	11	1	2	8	13	40	4

1925-26

Civil Service Strollers	11	8	1	2	29	13	17
Gala Fairydean	12	8	0	4	39	31	16
Leith Amateurs	12	7	1	4	40	28	15
Coldstream	11	5	3	3	24	20	13
Berwick Rangers	12	5	1	6	29	23	11
Vale of Leithen	12	2	3	7	18	32	7
Selkirk	12	1	1	10	14	44	3

1926-27

Civil Service Strollers	16	8	5	3	49	24	21
Selkirk	16	8	3	5	33	24	19
Gala Fairydean	16	9	1	6	55	48	19
Coldstream	16	8	3	5	38	30	19
Berwick Rangers	16	8	2	6	40	33	18
Vale of Leithen	16	7	2	7	51	55	16
Leith Amateurs	16	5	4	7	39	39	14
Edinburgh University	16	4	3	9	33	43	11
Hawick United	16	2	3	11	37	79	7

1927-28

Berwick Rangers	14	13	1	0	54	12	27
Civil Service Strollers	14	7	4	3	30	21	18
Leith Amateurs	14	8	1	5	38	27	17
Gala Fairydean	13	6	2	5	34	25	14
Coldstream	13	6	1	6	39	35	13
Edinburgh University	14	5	2	7	36	32	12
Selkirk	14	2	1	11	21	43	5
Hawick United	14	2	0	12	20	77	4

1928-29

Peebles Rovers	28	17	5	6	81	45	39
Berwick Rangers	28	16	6	6	88	51	38
Corstorpine Amateurs	27	14	4	9	89	54	32
Clerwood Amateurs	27	14	2	11	71	60	30
Gala Fairydean	25	12	6	7	70	57	30
Civil Service Strollers	23	13	3	7	53	36	29
Murrayfield Amateurs	17	13	2	2	51	30	28
Edinburgh City	27	11	5	11	64	60	27
Coldstream	23	10	5	8	73	54	25
Vale of Leithen	28	8	8	12	59	69	24
Edinburgh University	25	8	4	13	62	80	20
Duns	21	7	3	11	49	52	17
Selkirk	26	6	5	15	38	62	17
Leith Amateurs	25	6	3	16	50	87	15
Hawick United	24	1	1	22	37	138	3

Clerwood Amateurs and Corstorphine Amateurs merged under the Clerwood Amateurs name before the start of the next season.

1929-30

Bathgate	27	22	4	1	88	29	48
Edinburgh City	30	19	5	6	86	34	43
Cameron Highlanders	28	19	1	8	92	60	39
Murrayfield Amateurs	22	18	1	3	75	25	37
Berwick Rangers	28	12	6	10	74	59	30
Peebles Rovers	28	14	1	13	60	57	29
Gala Fairydean	28	13	3	12	63	72	29
Vale of Leithen	27	12	4	11	55	59	28
Clerwood Amateurs	22	10	6	6	67	44	26
Leith Amateurs	27	7	7	13	59	63	21
Civil Service Strollers	26	7	6	13	38	73	20
Selkirk	27	7	5	15	47	80	19
Hawick United	29	8	1	20	55	94	17
Coldstream	30	6	4	20	63	102	16
Duns	28	5	2	21	51	99	12
Edinburgh University	17	4	2	11	37	60	10

1930-31

Bathgate	20	15	2	3	50	18	32
Penicuik Athletic	20	14	4	2	69	32	32
Berwick Rangers	20	12	1	7	54	35	25
Selkirk	20	8	5	7	50	49	21
Vale of Leithen	20	8	4	8	48	54	20
Clerwood Amateurs	20	7	5	8	47	50	19
Peebles Rovers	20	8	2	10	51	53	18
Duns	20	7	2	11	56	67	16
Gala Fairydean	20	5	6	9	39	53	16
Coldstream	20	6	2	12	44	51	14
Jedburgh Artisans	20	1	5	14	27	70	7

Hawick United resigned from the league after 8 matches and their record was expunged. They subsequently joined the Border Amateur League. Their record at the time of their resignation stood as follows:

	8	1	0	7	11	31	2

1931-32

Penicuik Athletic	20	15	2	3	79	31	32
Selkirk	20	14	2	4	59	39	30
Berwick Rangers	20	10	2	8	44	53	22
Chirnside United	20	8	5	7	63	48	21
Peebles Rovers	20	9	2	9	45	38	20
Clerwood Amateurs	20	9	2	9	50	48	20
Vale of Leithen	20	8	4	8	35	41	20
Duns	20	8	3	9	39	35	19
Jedburgh Artisans	20	6	3	11	28	43	15
Coldstream	20	6	3	11	37	58	15
Gala Fairydean	20	1	4	15	34	72	6

1932-33

Peebles Rovers	20	18	0	2	83	27	36
Penicuik Athletic	20	17	1	2	83	22	35
Berwick Rangers	18	11	3	4	69	43	24
Clerwood Amateurs	18	8	3	7	46	45	19
Duns	20	8	3	9	57	57	19
Chirnside United	20	6	4	10	46	54	16
Selkirk	20	7	1	12	43	65	15
Jeburgh Artisans	20	7	1	12	39	68	15
Vale of Leithen	18	6	2	10	25	35	14
Coldstream	20	4	3	13	32	63	11
Gala Fairydean	20	2	5	13	38	82	9

Berwick Rangers had 1 point deducted after fielding an ineligible player.

An alternate table has also been found which contains a number of differences and this is shown below.
If this alternative table is correct then Penicuik Athletic would almost certainly be champions and not Peebles, due to their superior goal average. However, it is not known which is accurate.

1932-33   Alternative Table

Penicuik Athletic	20	17	1	2	83	22	36
Peebles Rovers	19	17	0	2	83	27	34
Berwick Rangers	18	11	3	4	68	43	24
Clerwood Amateurs	17	8	3	6	45	40	19
Duns	20	8	3	9	57	57	19
Chirnside United	20	6	4	10	46	54	16
Selkirk	19	7	1	11	43	65	15
Vale of Leithen	18	6	2	10	25	35	14
Jedburgh Artisans	20	6	2	12	39	68	14
Coldstream	20	4	3	13	32	63	11
Gala Fairydean	20	2	5	13	38	82	9

Penicuik Athletic had 1 point added to their total.
Berwick Rangers had 1 point deducted after fielding an ineligible player.

1933-34

Peebles Rovers	18	13	2	3	60	21	28
Vale of Leithen	18	11	3	4	49	25	25
Berwick Rangers	18	11	3	4	46	41	25
Gala Fairydean	18	8	5	5	46	38	21
Coldstream	18	8	4	6	34	38	20
Duns	18	6	3	9	40	44	15
Selkirk	18	6	2	10	43	48	14
Chirnside United	18	5	1	12	32	44	11
Peebles YMCA	18	5	1	12	44	61	11
Jedburgh Artisans	18	4	2	12	20	52	10

1934-35

Peebles Rovers	21	16	1	4	86	40	33
Chirnside United	21	13	5	3	76	44	31
Vale of Leithen	19	9	6	4	44	35	24
Penicuik Athletic	19	9	5	5	44	40	23
Duns	18	10	2	6	38	33	22
Murrayfield Amateurs	21	6	9	6	44	45	21
Berwick Rangers	21	8	4	9	43	42	20
Selkirk	20	8	3	9	46	40	19
Peebles YMCA	22	8	3	11	52	52	19
Gala Fairydean	15	3	5	7	25	53	11
Coldstream	21	4	0	17	39	68	8
Jedburgh Artisans	19	3	1	15	30	73	7

1935-36

Peebles Rovers	26	19	4	3	97	35	42
Penicuik Athletic	26	19	2	5	71	27	40
Dunfermline Athletic "A"	24	14	4	6	76	35	32
Duns	21	11	5	5	51	24	27
Chirnside United	20	10	5	5	57	39	25
Vale of Leithen	22	11	3	8	51	44	25
Berwick Rangers	22	6	7	9	40	46	19
Coldstream	25	8	3	14	43	60	19
Murrayfield Amateurs	19	9	1	9	31	37	19
Gala Fairydean	23	4	7	12	37	56	15
Leith Amateurs	19	7	1	11	32	60	15
Selkirk	22	6	2	14	36	71	14
Peebles YMCA	24	5	2	17	48	91	12
Jedburgh Artisans	21	3	4	14	35	80	10

1936-37

Jedburgh Artisans	19	13	5	1	51	22	31
Vale of Leithen	22	14	1	7	63	37	29
Peebles Rovers	21	11	2	8	76	48	24
Chirnside United	21	10	4	7	49	44	24
Penicuik Athletic	22	9	4	9	50	50	22
Duns	17	9	3	5	38	23	21
Murrayfield Amateurs	20	6	6	8	52	54	18
Coldstream	20	8	1	11	43	55	17
Berwick Rangers	14	7	2	5	33	38	16
Gala Fairydean	16	4	4	8	38	40	12
Peebles YMCA	17	4	1	12	35	61	9
Edinburgh University	11	2	3	6	15	34	7
Selkirk	16	1	4	11	23	60	6

Berwick Rangers withdrew from the league during January 1937, but their record was included in the final table.

1937-38

Penicuik Athletic	23	23	0	0	112	29	46
Vale of Leithen	24	16	2	6	72	33	34
Berwick Rangers	26	14	2	10	68	53	30
Duns	20	12	4	4	66	39	28
Peebles Rovers	25	11	4	10	80	61	26
Chirnside United	20	7	6	7	46	52	20
Leith Amateurs	21	9	2	10	47	56	20
Dunbar Town	23	7	3	13	41	74	17
Gala Fairydean	18	6	3	9	51	49	15
Murrayfield Amateurs	21	6	3	12	40	48	15
Peebles YMCA	23	6	3	14	50	75	15
Jedburgh Artisans	12	6	1	5	34	24	13
Coldstream	14	6	0	8	27	48	12
Selkirk	16	3	0	13	30	73	6
Edinburgh University	14	1	1	12	20	70	3

Jedburgh Artisans closed down at the end of December, but their record was not expunged.

Several other clubs closed temporarily during the last two months of the season, for financial reasons.

1938-39

Bo'ness	24	18	4	2	94	32	40
Peebles Rovers	23	16	1	6	83	44	33
Chirnside United	19	13	0	6	72	46	26
Berwick Rangers	19	12	1	6	58	40	25
Duns	18	10	1	7	65	40	21
Dunbar Town	18	10	1	7	49	49	21
Selkirk	19	9	1	9	52	57	19
Vale of Leithen	22	7	3	12	65	79	17
Penicuick Athletic	13	8	0	5	39	23	16
Gala Fairydean	14	6	2	6	38	45	14
Coldstream	17	4	1	12	43	77	9
Peebles YMCA	20	2	2	16	42	81	6
Edinburgh University	12	2	0	10	26	49	4
Leith Amateurs	16	1	1	14	21	84	3

An alternate table has also been found which contains clear differences but it is not known which is accurate.

1938-39   Alternative Table

Bo'ness	21	17	2	2	91	29	36
Peebles Rovers	22	15	1	6	76	43	31
Berwick Rangers	17	11	1	5	57	38	23
Selkirk	18	9	1	8	47	51	19
Chirnside United	14	9	0	5	42	36	18
Dunbar Town	15	8	0	7	41	44	16
Duns	15	7	1	7	51	38	15
Gala Fairydean	12	6	1	5	35	36	13
Vale of Leithen	19	5	2	12	51	74	12
Penicuik Athletic	10	5	0	5	26	17	10
Peebles YMCA	17	2	2	13	38	66	6
Coldstream	14	2	1	11	34	66	5
Leith Amateurs	11	2	1	8	21	50	5
Edinburgh University	11	2	0	9	15	23	4

1939-40

Berwick Rangers	2	2	0	0	9	2	4
Chirnside United	2	2	0	0	9	2	4
Bo'ness	2	2	0	0	4	1	4
Duns	2	2	0	0	11	4	4
Peebles Rovers	2	1	0	1	5	8	2
Dunbar Town	1	0	0	1	1	2	0
Selkirk	1	0	0	1	0	2	0
Penicuik Athletic	2	0	0	2	4	8	0
Gala Fairydean	2	0	0	2	3	10	0
Vale of Leithen	2	0	0	2	0	7	0
Coldstream	0	0	0	0	0	0	0

After a small number of matches had been played, the League closed down for the duration of the war.

1945-46

Peebles Rovers	8	7	1	0	35	10	15
Eyemouth United	7	3	2	2	25	22	8
11th Holding Battalion	7	3	1	3	20	20	7
Duns	7	3	0	4	22	20	6
Gala Fairydean	7	0	0	7	14	44	0

1946-47

Berwick Rangers	16	12	1	3	45	27	25
Coldstream	15	9	2	4	41	22	20
Gala Fairydean	16	7	4	5	45	37	18
Duns	15	7	2	6	57	43	16
Eyemouth United	17	5	6	6	60	52	16
Chirnside United	17	5	5	7	40	47	15
Murrayfield Amateurs	15	6	2	7	31	42	14
Selkirk	14	5	2	7	44	58	12
Vale of Leithen	15	3	5	7	32	47	11
Peebles Rovers	14	3	1	10	29	50	7

The last table found for this season was from the *Peebleshire News* dated 31st January 1947. It proved to be a particularly severe winter and it is not known if the fixtures were eventually completed. Two subsequent results have been found and these have been added to the table. These results were as follows:

13th May – Vale of Leithen vs Duns, 3-2
20th May – Gala Fairydean vs Eyemouth United, 3-3

1947-48

Hibernian "B"	24	22	1	1	136	28	45
Eyemouth United	23	16	2	5	85	47	34
Gala Fairydean	20	16	1	3	78	49	33
Berwick Rangers	23	14	0	9	80	65	28
Chirnside United	20	9	3	8	64	61	21
Selkirk	21	7	4	10	55	65	18
Kelso United	23	7	3	13	64	95	17
Edinburgh University	16	6	4	6	55	42	16
Duns	20	7	2	11	47	60	16
Coldstream	21	7	2	12	44	62	16
Peebles Rovers	24	7	2	15	61	97	16
Vale of Leithen	25	5	2	18	42	79	12
Civil Service Strollers	19	4	3	12	50	75	11
Murrayfield Amateurs	15	4	3	8	43	59	11

1948-49

Hibernian "B"	28	22	4	2	122	20	48
Peebles Rovers	28	19	5	4	91	46	43
Gala Fairydean	26	16	5	5	82	47	37
Vale of Leithen	25	15	4	6	79	49	34
Berwick Rangers	25	10	5	10	72	65	25
Penicuik Athletic	26	11	2	13	54	74	24
Murrayfield Amateurs	26	11	2	13	54	58	24
Chirnside United	20	10	3	7	64	54	23
Eyemouth United	23	9	5	9	58	52	23
Selkirk	26	10	2	14	54	59	22
Kelso United	24	9	2	13	57	71	20
Duns	27	6	5	16	56	91	17
Edinburgh University	25	5	4	16	41	75	14
Civil Service Strollers	21	4	4	13	27	70	12
Coldstream	25	4	2	19	33	75	10

1949-50

Heart of Midlothian "B"	30	27	2	1	129	36	56
Hibernian "B"	30	26	1	3	138	30	53
Eyemouth United	30	19	2	9	85	52	40
Chirnside United	29	15	2	12	69	56	32
Gala Fairydean	29	16	0	13	73	61	32
Berwick Rangers	30	14	3	13	76	79	31
Penicuik Athletic	30	13	4	13	59	64	30
Civil Service Strollers	29	13	2	14	67	77	28
Selkirk	29	12	3	14	72	95	27
Peebles Rovers	27	11	4	12	64	58	26
Murrayfield Amateurs	28	11	3	14	62	82	25
Edinburgh University	28	10	2	16	56	72	22
Coldstream	30	9	2	19	46	102	20
Kelso United	30	7	5	18	69	105	19
Duns	29	8	1	20	63	101	17
Vale of Leithen	30	4	2	24	52	110	10

1950-51

Hibernian "B"	30	26	3	1	131	33	55
Heart of Midlothian "B"	30	23	4	3	136	52	50
Peebles Rovers	25	20	2	3	88	33	42
Eyemouth United	29	15	6	8	102	56	36
Civil Service Strollers	28	12	7	9	75	72	31
Berwick Rangers	26	13	4	9	98	47	30
Chirnside United	26	12	4	10	65	69	28
Duns	21	12	1	8	64	50	25
Vale of Leithen	28	10	4	14	79	96	24
Penicuik Athletic	27	9	5	13	70	76	23
Edinburgh University	28	9	5	14	74	96	23
Selkirk	27	7	5	15	43	99	19
Gala Fairydean	27	6	2	19	37	97	14
Murrayfield Amateurs	28	5	3	20	66	131	13
Coldstream	25	3	2	20	44	103	8
Kelso United	23	3	1	19	39	100	7

1951-52

Hibernian "B"	30	24	3	3	129	32	51
Duns	29	21	4	4	94	44	46
Berwick Rangers "A"	30	19	8	3	106	56	46
Eyemouth United	30	21	3	6	104	54	45
Heart of Midlothian "B"	30	20	3	7	93	58	43
Peebles Rovers	30	19	4	7	98	59	42
Vale of Leithen	30	17	1	12	70	73	35
Chirnside United	29	11	3	15	59	73	25
Spartans	30	9	4	17	63	90	22
Coldstream	30	10	2	18	76	109	22
Murrayfield Amateurs	29	9	2	18	53	76	20
Selkirk	30	9	2	19	82	122	20
Kelso United	30	7	3	20	54	91	17
Gala Fairydean	30	6	5	19	56	95	17
Edinburgh University	30	6	3	21	44	91	15
Civil Service Strollers	29	3	4	22	42	100	10

1952-53

Hibernian "B"	26	19	5	2	90	31	43
Peebles Rovers	26	21	0	5	112	38	42
Berwick Rangers "A"	26	20	2	4	91	45	42
Duns	22	14	2	6	82	49	30
Vale of Leithen	25	12	3	10	84	49	27
Eyemouth United	19	11	5	3	79	33	27
Coldstream	24	11	4	9	62	60	26
Spartans	23	11	1	11	55	51	23
Edinburgh University	25	7	6	12	44	58	20
Selkirk	26	7	1	18	39	82	15
Murrayfield Amateurs	24	8	1	15	42	101	15
Civil Service Strollers	24	6	2	16	48	99	14
Gala Fairydean	24	3	4	17	44	98	10
Chirnside United	26	2	0	24	37	98	4

1953-54

Eyemouth United	25	17	3	5	81	38	37
Vale of Leithen	25	16	4	5	93	47	36
Berwick Rangers "A"	22	15	3	4	84	43	33
Gala Fairydean	22	13	6	3	69	50	32
Peebles Rovers	18	14	2	2	93	33	30
Duns	22	13	3	6	81	55	29
Chirnside United	22	10	2	10	67	78	22
Spartans	22	9	3	10	55	55	21
Coldstream	23	6	6	11	37	56	18
Ferranti Thistle	27	7	4	16	59	86	18
Hawick Royal Albert	25	4	6	15	53	93	14
Civil Service Strollers	20	6	1	13	49	68	13
Murrayfield Amateurs	23	4	4	15	31	69	12
Selkirk	23	4	4	15	41	89	12
Edinburgh University	19	2	7	10	15	48	11

The 1953-54 season was declared null & void by the East of Scotland FA due to a large fixture backlog which could not be cleared.

1954-55

Eyemouth United	26	22	1	3	143	41	45
Peebles Rovers	22	17	1	4	105	54	35
Vale of Leithen	22	14	3	5	76	40	31
Gala Fairydean	23	14	2	7	78	53	30
Hawick Royal Albert	26	12	3	11	66	79	27
Murrayfield Amateurs	24	11	2	11	62	70	24
Duns	19	10	4	5	76	42	24
Spartans	21	10	2	9	56	53	22
Civil Service Strollers	26	8	6	12	64	79	22
Chirnside United	26	9	0	17	82	108	18
Selkirk	24	9	2	13	66	87	20
Coldstream	26	7	1	18	59	106	15
Edinburgh University	23	3	5	15	30	81	11
Ferranti Thistle	26	4	2	20	47	117	10

1955-56

Eyemouth United	23	21	2	0	125	41	44
Hawick Royal Albert	26	13	7	6	69	51	33
Duns	25	14	1	10	79	65	29
Vale of Leithen	24	12	3	9	84	76	27
Murrayfield Amateurs	22	11	4	7	58	57	26
Berwick Rangers Reserves	21	12	1	8	69	58	25
Selkirk	25	10	4	11	43	73	24
Civil Service Strollers	23	10	3	10	65	68	23
Spartans	20	9	4	7	53	42	22
Peebles Rovers	21	9	4	8	66	45	22
Chirnside United	22	7	3	12	54	61	17
Gala Fairydean	17	7	2	8	49	54	16
Edinburgh University	22	4	5	13	34	66	13
Ferranti Thistle	25	5	2	18	49	97	12
Coldstream	24	3	3	18	49	106	9

1956-57

Eyemouth United	26	21	2	3	115	54	44
Peebles Rovers	23	16	3	4	91	46	35
Vale of Leithen	24	16	3	5	96	46	35
Hawick Royal Albert	25	13	5	7	58	37	31
Gala Fairydean	25	12	4	9	86	67	28
Duns	21	10	4	7	71	49	24
Chirnside United	26	9	5	12	81	82	23
Murrayfield Amateurs	22	9	4	9	50	56	22
Spartans	24	8	4	12	58	76	20
Selkirk	23	7	5	11	59	89	19
Coldstream	24	6	4	14	52	90	16
Ferranti Thistle	24	6	2	16	60	95	14
Edinburgh University	23	4	4	15	45	76	12
Civil Service Strollers	22	3	3	16	33	92	9

1957-58

Dunfermline Athletic Reserves	28	23	1	4	132	39	47
Duns	26	20	2	4	119	47	42
Peebles Rovers	26	15	4	7	107	63	34
Eyemouth United	20	15	2	3	80	30	32
Hawick Royal Albert	27	11	8	8	57	44	30
Vale of Leithen	22	12	5	5	71	49	29
Gala Fairydean	27	9	3	15	72	118	21
Chirnside United	22	8	4	10	51	72	20
Selkirk	24	8	3	13	58	93	19
Ferranti Thistle	26	8	3	15	47	71	19
Edinburgh University	21	8	1	12	45	60	17
Spartans	22	7	2	13	52	78	16
Murrayfield Amateurs	19	4	6	9	36	42	14
Coldstream	24	5	3	16	50	96	13
Civil Service Strollers	24	1	3	20	29	105	5

1958-59

East Fife Reserves	30	22	4	4	122	44	48
Eyemouth United	22	18	1	3	98	32	37
Hawick Royal Albert	27	16	5	6	62	55	37
Peebles Rovers	29	15	7	7	99	81	37
Duns	27	16	4	7	112	70	36
Edinburgh City Police	29	14	8	7	84	58	36
Vale of Leithen	30	15	4	11	92	86	34
Selkirk	29	11	6	12	82	83	28
Coldstream	24	9	6	9	59	74	24
Edinburgh University	26	9	4	13	72	84	22
Chirnside United	28	8	5	15	64	76	21
Gala Fairydean	26	6	8	12	73	84	20
Ferranti Thistle	27	8	3	16	57	89	19
Spartans	24	5	5	14	58	99	15
Murrayfield Amateurs	27	5	2	20	59	94	12
Civil Service Strollers	29	2	4	23	44	128	8

A number of matches were not played during the 1958/59 season as reflected in the final table shown.

1959-60

Berwick Rangers Reserves	24	23	0	1	108	26	46
Duns	26	22	2	2	90	32	46
Hawick Royal Albert	30	16	8	6	79	47	40
Gala Fairydean	30	15	7	8	87	66	37
Edinburgh City Police	27	14	6	7	66	55	33
Eyemouth United	18	13	2	3	65	18	26
Vale of Leithen	27	11	5	11	77	77	27
Murrayfield Amateurs	25	11	4	10	63	51	26
Peebles Rovers	26	10	3	13	94	73	23
Chirnside United	22	9	1	12	43	71	19
Edinburgh University	21	7	2	12	50	73	16
Civil Service Strollers	26	5	6	15	39	69	16
Ferranti Thistle	26	7	1	18	37	69	15
Spartans	26	6	2	18	49	108	14
Selkirk	28	6	1	21	47	102	13
Coldstream	25	3	3	19	49	109	9

A number of matches were not played during the 1959/60 season as reflected in the final table shown above.

1960-61

Berwick Rangers Reserves	27	20	4	3	101	42	44
Gala Fairydean	27	19	5	3	99	40	43
Eyemouth United	30	16	9	5	78	57	41
Duns	26	17	6	3	91	46	40
Vale of Leithen	30	13	6	11	104	81	32
Peebles Rovers	25	14	3	8	88	59	31
Hawick Royal Albert	29	15	3	11	92	78	33
Chirnside United	28	12	4	12	73	75	28
Murrayfield Amateurs	26	13	1	12	78	83	27
Coldstream	27	11	4	12	75	84	26
Selkirk	30	9	5	16	66	102	23
Edinburgh University	23	6	6	11	61	70	18
Edinburgh City Police	28	7	4	17	72	83	18
Civil Service Strollers	29	4	7	18	43	81	15
Ferranti Thistle	27	3	4	20	34	114	10
Spartans	26	2	5	19	30	90	9

Gala Fairydean were named champions.

1961-62

Gala Fairydean	29	25	3	1	130	30	53
Peebles Rovers	28	20	5	3	110	42	45
Duns	27	19	4	4	88	44	42
Eyemouth United	26	19	2	5	80	40	40
Vale of Leithen	29	15	7	7	77	42	37
Chirnside United	27	11	8	8	67	57	30
Hawick Royal Albert	25	12	5	8	82	57	29
Edinburgh City Police	28	11	3	14	65	58	25
Berwick Rangers Reserves	27	10	3	14	51	64	23
Edinburgh University	27	9	3	15	53	94	21
Ferranti Thistle	30	9	3	18	57	80	21
Murrayfield Amateurs	26	6	7	13	52	92	19
Coldstream	30	8	3	19	51	98	19
Civil Service Strollers	29	7	3	19	46	96	17
Selkirk	25	4	4	17	43	66	12
Spartans	27	3	1	23	23	111	7

1962-63

Gala Fairydean	23	20	2	1	89	26	42
Edinburgh City Police	26	16	4	6	74	58	36
Peebles Rovers	20	16	3	1	78	30	35
Selkirk	23	17	1	5	69	37	35
Vale of Leithen	27	12	7	8	74	55	31
Hawick Royal Albert	24	12	4	8	56	45	28
Chirnside United	23	11	5	7	59	37	27
Duns	21	11	2	8	60	44	24
Ferranti Thistle	26	9	3	14	54	63	21
Eyemouth United	20	7	5	8	48	40	19
Coldstream	22	8	2	12	45	63	18
Berwick Rangers Reserves	24	6	5	13	50	73	17
Spartans	22	6	3	13	43	65	15
Edinburgh University	21	3	2	16	38	77	8
Murrayfield Amateurs	21	2	4	15	35	82	8
Civil Service Strollers	23	2	0	21	24	99	4

A number of matches were not played during the 1962/63 season as reflected in the final table shown above.

1963-64

Gala Fairydean	30	23	1	6	118	41	47
Peebles Rovers	30	20	2	8	107	46	42
Eyemouth United	29	18	5	6	80	44	41
Vale of Leithen	28	16	6	6	83	55	38
Selkirk	27	16	3	8	76	50	35
Ferranti Thistle	30	15	4	11	79	72	34
Edinburgh City Police	29	16	1	12	91	76	33
Chirnside United	27	15	2	10	87	66	32
Duns	21	13	2	6	82	54	28
Berwick Rangers Reserves	29	12	4	13	69	69	28
Hawick Royal Albert	26	14	1	11	87	48	29
Edinburgh University	26	7	1	18	49	95	15
Spartans	29	6	2	21	43	111	14
Coldstream	29	4	5	20	57	137	13
Murrayfield Amateurs	28	3	4	21	48	115	10
Civil Service Strollers	27	2	3	22	21	98	7

1964-65

Gala Fairydean	27	22	4	1	95	22	48
Duns	25	18	2	5	105	45	38
Vale of Leithen	26	16	2	8	79	46	34
Peebles Rovers	25	14	4	7	56	33	32
Hawick Royal Albert	22	13	3	6	68	48	29
Eyemouth United	26	14	1	11	59	45	29
Edinburgh City Police	24	13	2	9	78	64	28
Coldstream	24	11	3	10	46	56	25
Berwick Rangers Reserves	25	9	5	11	49	61	23
Ferranti Thistle	27	10	0	17	61	68	20
Selkirk	25	8	4	13	57	73	20
Edinburgh University	23	7	2	14	28	61	16
Chirnside United	26	6	1	19	33	81	13
Spartans	23	3	6	14	20	56	12
Civil Service Strollers	28	4	1	23	19	101	9

1965-66

Gala Fairydean	25	22	2	1	81	20	46
Vale of Leithen	25	16	3	6	58	41	35
Eyemouth United	24	15	3	6	50	41	33
Hawick Royal Albert	21	12	5	4	56	32	29
Berwick Rangers Reserves	24	10	7	7	64	45	27
Duns	20	11	3	6	49	38	25
Edinburgh City Police	21	9	3	9	52	42	21
Ferranti Thistle	24	9	3	12	50	56	21
Peebles Rovers	21	9	2	10	47	52	20
Edinburgh University	19	8	1	10	39	44	17
Selkirk	25	7	3	15	49	85	17
Coldstream	22	6	2	14	41	61	14
Civil Service Strollers	25	4	2	19	34	84	10
Spartans	25	2	1	22	33	77	5

1966-67

Border Section

Berwick Rangers Reserves	15	11	0	4	52	26	22
Hawick Royal Albert	11	10	1	0	35	12	21
Eyemouth United	14	10	1	3	41	22	21
Gala Fairydean	16	9	1	6	44	28	19
Coldstream	15	6	2	7	44	40	14
Duns	14	6	2	6	34	38	14
Vale of Leithen	12	3	2	7	26	33	8
Chirnside United	13	2	0	11	25	52	4
Selkirk	14	0	1	13	17	67	1

Edinburgh Section

East Fife Reserves	14	10	3	1	39	19	23
Raith Rovers Reserves	14	10	2	2	47	26	22
Postal United	14	8	2	4	34	30	18
Spartans	14	5	5	4	28	21	15
Edinburgh City Police	14	6	2	6	33	33	14
Civil Service Strollers	14	3	2	9	17	31	8
Ferranti Thistle	14	3	1	10	29	43	7
Edinburgh University	14	2	1	11	22	46	5

The league was split into two sections – the Borders and Edinburgh – the top 4 clubs from each section then progressed into two further sections – A and B – with the winners of "Section A" being declared league champions.

Section "A"

Hawick Royal Albert	6	5	1	0	8	1	11
Berwick Rangers Reserves	6	5	0	1	23	12	10
Gala Fairydean	6	4	1	1	13	11	9
Eyemouth United	6	3	2	1	15	8	8
East Fife Reserves	8	3	1	4	13	16	7
Spartans	8	0	2	6	8	24	2
Postal United	8	0	1	7	9	19	1
Raith Rovers Reserves	?	?	?	?	?	?	?

Section "B"

Duns	8	7	0	1	27	5	14
Vale of Leithen	8	5	3	0	22	13	13
Edinburgh City Police	9	4	4	1	31	22	12
Civil Service Strollers	10	5	0	5	23	20	10
Coldstream	7	2	3	2	17	17	7
Selkirk	8	3	1	4	17	22	7
Edinburgh University	10	2	2	6	21	32	6
Ferranti Thistle	9	1	2	6	12	23	4
Chirnside United	7	1	1	5	14	30	3

1967-68

Border Section

Hawick Royal Albert	10	9	0	1	36	10	18
Gala Fairydean	12	8	1	3	54	22	17
Coldstream	12	5	3	4	35	32	13
Berwick Rangers Reserves	12	5	3	4	39	32	13
Kelso United	12	4	3	5	34	32	11
Duns	11	3	1	7	27	44	7
Chirnside United	11	0	1	10	9	62	1

Edinburgh Section

Vale of Leithen	12	9	0	3	46	14	18
Ferranti Thistle	12	8	2	2	36	14	18
Postal United	12	5	3	4	27	26	13
Spartans	12	2	6	4	17	32	10
Edinburgh University	10	3	4	3	17	19	10
Edinburgh City Police	12	2	3	7	22	39	7
Civil Service Strollers	12	2	2	8	19	40	6

Championship Play-off

Hawick Royal Albert vs Vale of Leithen		4-1, 3-0

Hawick Royal Albert won 7-1 on aggregate to become Champions.

1968-69

Gala Fairydean	20	14	5	2	64	23	33
Coldstream	21	14	3	4	56	35	31
Kelso United	18	11	3	4	49	37	25
Vale of Leithen	16	8	4	4	41	23	20
Hawick Royal Albert	15	9	2	4	49	29	20
Civil Service Strollers	20	7	3	10	51	68	17
Eyemouth United	17	6	4	7	30	35	16
Edinburgh City Police	20	6	3	11	43	51	15
Edinburgh University	17	6	3	8	31	46	15
Spartans	17	4	2	11	34	46	10
Postal United	19	3	3	13	27	60	9
Ferranti Thistle	16	3	3	10	27	50	9

1969-70

Cowdenbeath Reserves	28	20	6	2	83	29	46
Arbroath Reserves	27	19	2	6	68	25	40
Hawick Royal Albert	28	16	6	6	70	33	38
Gala Fairydean	26	16	4	6	59	32	36
Heart of Midlothian "A"	28	16	4	8	66	46	36
Eyemouth United	27	13	7	7	62	45	33
Vale of Leithen	26	12	8	6	63	45	32
Kelso United	28	12	7	9	57	48	31
Edinburgh City Police	28	7	5	16	44	59	19
Civil Service Strollers	28	8	3	17	55	79	19
Postal United	28	8	3	17	41	76	19
Edinburgh University	27	6	6	15	40	65	18
Spartans	27	6	4	17	36	68	16
Coldstream	27	6	2	19	57	95	14
Ferranti Thistle	27	4	6	17	20	72	14

1970-71

Eyemouth United	32	26	2	4	89	25	56
Arbroath Reserves	32	23	6	3	80	37	49
Queen of the South Reserves	32	21	6	5	97	37	47
Raith Rovers Reserves	32	19	9	8	82	33	47
Heart of Midlothian "A"	32	21	7	4	73	50	46
Edinburgh City Police	32	12	9	11	64	52	35
Ferranti Thistle	32	14	12	6	62	51	34
Gala Fairydean	32	14	14	4	56	47	32
Hawick Royal Albert	32	11	12	9	67	56	31
Spartans	32	14	15	3	60	67	31
Postal United	32	9	16	7	44	59	25
Duns	32	8	17	7	56	73	23
Civil Service Strollers	32	7	16	9	39	66	23
Vale of Leithen	32	8	18	6	48	77	22
Edinburgh University	32	9	21	2	30	84	20
Kelso United	32	5	21	6	40	80	16
Coldstream	32	3	26	3	26	115	9

1971-72

Spartans	27	20	2	5	75	36	42
Hibernian "A"	33	17	8	8	70	46	42
Gala Fairydean	31	19	3	9	78	56	41
Eyemouth United	32	17	6	9	85	53	40
Cowdenbeath Reserves	28	17	2	9	82	42	36
Ferranti Thistle	32	15	6	11	68	52	36
Vale of Leithen	31	16	3	12	61	51	35
Postal United	31	13	8	10	70	65	34
Civil Service Strollers	30	14	5	11	69	49	33
Heart of Midlothian "A"	28	15	2	11	61	46	32
Kelso United	32	11	9	12	62	66	31
Hawick Royal Albert	31	12	4	15	65	64	28
Selkirk	33	10	5	18	55	90	25
Edinburgh City Police	26	7	6	13	43	64	20
Coldstream	28	7	6	15	31	58	20
Heriot-Watt University	28	5	4	19	42	94	14
Edinburgh University	26	5	4	17	34	64	14
Duns	29	5	3	21	36	93	13

1972-73

Civil Service Strollers	27	17	5	5	78	53	39
Selkirk	28	16	7	5	59	36	39
Hawick Royal Albert	28	15	6	7	71	49	36
Hibernian "A"	26	13	5	8	68	38	31
Spartans	26	11	8	7	52	40	30
Ferranti Thistle	24	11	5	8	54	41	27
Eyemouth United	27	11	3	13	59	59	25
Gala Fairydean	28	10	4	14	61	66	24
Vale of Leithen	25	7	10	8	33	39	24
Heart of Midlothian "A"	26	7	7	12	45	50	21
Heriot-Watt University	23	8	5	10	41	52	21
Postal United	27	8	5	14	42	67	21
Duns	27	6	5	16	45	66	17
Coldstream	28	4	6	18	37	84	14
Edinburgh University	?	?	?	?	?	?	?

1973-74

Hawick Royal Albert	26	20	1	5	66	30	41
Hibernian "A"	26	17	6	3	56	17	40
Selkirk	26	14	5	7	63	40	33
Spartans	26	14	5	7	52	33	33
Ferranti Thistle	25	12	7	6	54	20	31
Gala Fairydean	26	13	4	9	50	52	30
Civil Service Strollers	26	10	6	10	38	41	26
Eyemouth United	26	9	6	11	45	57	24
Postal United	26	9	5	12	51	59	23
Duns	24	6	6	12	37	63	18
Coldstream	26	8	2	16	33	59	18
Edinburgh University	25	4	9	12	24	35	17
Vale of Leithen	26	5	6	15	37	69	16
Heriot-Watt University	24	2	4	18	27	58	8

1974-75

Selkirk	23	17	5	1	85	19	39
Edinburgh University	23	17	4	2	72	31	38
Spartans	23	11	8	4	46	27	30
Gala Fairydean	23	11	8	4	57	33	30
Hawick Royal Albert	23	10	8	5	61	38	28
Eyemouth United	24	9	6	9	33	34	24
Postal United	24	9	5	10	40	51	23
Kelso United	24	9	3	12	41	57	21
Civil Service Strollers	23	7	4	12	39	55	18
Vale of Leithen	23	4	6	13	29	58	14
Coldstream	23	2	7	14	27	69	11
Heriot-Watt University	23	5	1	17	28	76	11
Hibernian "A"	15	3	2	10	13	19	8

1975-76

Selkirk	22	17	5	0	73	30	39
Hawick Royal Albert	22	11	5	6	42	31	27
Vale of Leithen	22	11	4	7	49	31	26
Edinburgh University	21	9	7	5	50	31	25
Postal United	19	9	4	6	37	28	22
Spartans	20	10	2	8	43	36	22
Civil Service Strollers	18	8	3	7	38	34	19
Eyemouth United	21	6	6	9	32	37	18
Gala Fairydean	22	6	4	12	38	51	16
Coldstream	22	4	4	14	26	52	12
Kelso United	21	3	6	12	34	69	12
Heriot-Watt University	20	5	2	13	27	64	12

The table shown is taken from a press report with some
subsequent results found elsewhere added.

1976-77

Selkirk	26	20	4	2	80	28	44
Vale of Leithen	26	18	4	4	74	20	40
Edinburgh University	24	18	3	3	83	27	39
Civil Service Strollers	26	16	3	7	71	36	35
Craigroyston	26	13	5	8	58	46	31
Spartans	26	12	3	11	68	44	27
Kelso United	26	11	6	9	47	48	26
Gala Fairydean	26	10	4	12	39	36	24
Postal United	25	10	4	11	42	44	24
Hawick Royal Albert	25	10	3	12	43	37	23
Chirnside United	25	6	4	15	53	78	16
Heriot-Watt University	26	5	2	19	28	91	12
Eyemouth United	25	3	2	20	24	122	8
Coldstream	26	3	1	22	16	81	7

1977-78

Vale of Leithen	26	18	5	3	70	27	41
Spartans	26	18	3	5	76	31	39
Selkirk	26	17	4	5	64	29	38
Hawick Royal Albert	26	16	6	4	65	31	38
Civil Service Strollers	26	12	6	8	43	28	30
Postal United	26	11	6	9	56	43	28
Kelso United	26	11	6	9	59	46	28
Edinburgh University	26	11	6	9	72	47	28
Gala Fairydean	26	9	8	9	42	33	26
Craigroyston	26	8	6	12	42	47	22
Eyemouth United	26	8	4	14	47	56	20
Coldstream	26	5	2	19	26	85	12
Heriot-Watt University	26	3	1	22	36	122	7
Chirnside United	26	2	2	22	30	114	6

1978-79

Selkirk	28	17	8	3	64	30	42
Vale of Leithen	27	17	6	4	70	36	40
Spartans	28	12	10	6	73	37	34
Hawick Royal Albert	28	11	10	7	55	43	32
Postal United	28	11	10	7	53	42	32
Civil Service Strollers	28	14	4	10	57	45	32
Berwick Rangers Reserves	28	12	7	9	63	36	31
Gala Fairydean	28	13	5	10	52	36	31
Edinburgh University	28	13	5	10	52	48	31
Kelso United	28	9	9	10	48	53	27
Coldstream	27	7	10	10	34	37	24
Craigroyston	28	9	6	13	46	55	24
Eyemouth United	28	7	7	14	44	66	21
Heriot-Watt University	28	3	3	22	35	88	9
Chirnside United	28	3	2	23	31	115	8

1979-80

Whitehill Welfare	32	21	5	6	73	30	47
Vale of Leithen	32	20	6	6	62	37	46
Selkirk	32	18	9	5	69	45	45
Berwick Rangers Reserves	31	16	11	4	82	52	43
Hawick Royal Albert	29	18	4	7	71	38	40
Gala Fairydean	32	14	9	9	56	42	37
Coldstream	32	12	12	8	49	55	36
Spartans	31	12	10	9	66	57	34
Craigroyston	31	14	6	11	68	60	34
Dunbar Blue Circle	32	10	10	12	52	53	30
Edinburgh University	32	11	5	16	50	54	27
Eyemouth United	32	8	11	13	51	60	27
Postal United	32	10	7	15	45	57	27
Civil Service Strollers	32	8	7	17	50	55	23
Kelso United	32	6	6	20	40	58	18
Heriot-Watt University	32	3	8	21	35	95	14
Peebles Rovers	30	3	2	25	22	93	8

1980-81

	P	W	D	L	F	A	Pts
Whitehill Welfare	32	24	5	3	81	24	53
Civil Service Strollers	32	21	7	4	59	26	49
Spartans	31	20	2	9	76	54	42
Berwick Rangers Reserves	32	16	7	9	65	40	39
Gala Fairydean	31	16	6	9	72	48	38
Hawick Royal Albert	28	16	4	8	60	38	36
Coldstream	32	15	4	13	57	56	34
Eyemouth United	32	11	11	10	45	42	33
Kelso United	32	12	7	13	53	65	31
Vale of Leithen	32	12	6	14	80	60	30
Edinburgh University	31	11	8	12	45	54	30
Selkirk	31	10	5	16	47	60	25
Dunbar Blue Circle	32	5	12	15	39	36	22
Postal United	31	8	5	18	31	53	21
Heriot-Watt University	31	6	7	18	36	65	19
Craigroyston	32	7	5	20	43	83	19
Peebles Rovers	32	4	7	21	32	96	15

1983-84

	P	W	D	L	F	A	Pts
Spartans	30	22	4	4	103	37	48
Gala Fairydean	30	21	6	3	89	30	48
Selkirk	30	19	5	6	84	43	43
Hawick Royal Albert	30	19	4	7	81	48	42
Craigroyston	30	16	7	7	62	32	39
Postal United	30	16	6	8	76	38	38
Vale of Leithen	30	15	8	7	72	41	38
Civil Service Strollers	30	16	3	11	63	43	35
Whitehill Welfare	30	13	7	10	57	41	33
Kelso United	30	11	4	15	51	49	26
Eyemouth United	30	9	6	15	51	59	24
Easthouses Miners Welfare	30	7	9	14	45	59	23
Heriot-Watt University	30	6	4	20	46	99	16
Edinburgh University	30	6	2	22	27	78	14
Peebles Rovers	30	2	4	24	26	133	8
Coldstream	30	2	1	27	18	121	5

1981-82

	P	W	D	L	F	A	Pts
Whitehill Welfare	34	20	9	5	68	35	49
Gala Fairydean	34	20	7	7	106	56	47
Hawick Royal Albert	34	19	8	7	75	47	46
Craigroyston	34	19	7	6	66	44	46
Postal United	34	17	9	8	59	33	43
Vale of Leithen	34	17	8	9	64	41	42
Berwick Rangers Reserves	34	15	11	8	71	45	41
Spartans	34	15	10	9	78	57	40
Coldstream	34	16	8	10	53	52	40
Civil Service Strollers	34	14	9	11	62	47	37
Edinburgh University	34	13	9	12	71	64	35
Kelso United	34	13	8	13	59	69	34
Eyemouth United	34	11	11	12	63	60	33
Easthouses Miners Welfare	34	5	10	19	43	63	20
Dunbar Blue Circle	34	6	6	22	45	87	18
Heriot-Watt University	34	7	4	23	45	88	18
Peebles Rovers	34	6	4	24	56	135	16
Selkirk	34	3	2	29	39	103	8

1984-85

	P	W	D	L	F	A	Pts
Whitehill Welfare	28	21	7	0	75	17	49
Spartans	28	21	4	3	70	24	46
Gala Fairydean	28	21	1	6	84	37	43
Vale of Leithen	28	18	6	4	67	27	42
Postal United	28	16	5	7	64	25	37
Hawick Royal Albert	27	15	4	8	74	48	34
Civil Service Strollers	28	12	5	11	48	41	29
Craigroyston	28	11	4	13	56	56	26
Kelso United	28	7	8	13	44	52	22
Easthouses Miners Welfare	28	9	3	16	41	54	21
Peebles Rovers	28	7	4	17	40	73	18
Coldstream	28	6	6	16	27	62	18
Edinburgh University	28	4	7	17	35	75	15
Heriot-Watt University	27	2	5	20	19	74	9
Eyemouth United	28	3	3	22	30	104	9

Hawick Royal Albert vs Heriot-Watt University was not played

1982-83

	P	W	D	L	F	A	Pts
Whitehill Welfare	32	22	7	3	98	31	51
Gala Fairydean	32	22	5	5	117	42	49
Spartans	31	23	3	5	92	41	49
Postal United	32	16	10	6	62	39	42
Craigroyston	32	16	6	10	78	50	38
Easthouses Miners Welfare	32	15	8	9	67	51	38
Hawick Royal Albert	31	14	9	8	75	44	37
Coldstream	32	14	9	9	59	49	37
Berwick Rangers Reserves	32	15	3	14	53	39	33
Vale of Leithen	32	11	11	10	72	65	33
Selkirk	32	11	8	13	50	58	30
Kelso United	32	9	8	15	62	77	26
Eyemouth United	32	9	3	20	54	76	21
Civil Service Strollers	32	8	5	19	55	84	21
Heriot-Watt University	32	6	7	19	44	76	19
Edinburgh University	32	7	2	23	41	85	16
Peebles Rovers	32	0	2	30	20	197	2

1985-86

	P	W	D	L	F	A	Pts
Whitehill Welfare	28	21	5	2	85	23	47
Gala Fairydean	28	20	5	3	59	28	45
Postal United	28	17	6	5	56	30	40
Vale of Leithen	28	18	3	7	97	44	39
Kelso United	28	15	9	4	55	30	39
Peebles Rovers	28	11	8	9	43	36	30
Spartans	28	10	8	10	54	53	28
Hawick Royal Albert	28	10	5	13	44	52	22
Eyemouth United	28	7	9	12	56	71	23
Easthouses Miners Welfare	28	8	6	14	34	43	22
Craigroyston	28	9	4	15	47	58	22
Civil Service Strollers	28	6	8	14	39	60	20
Coldstream	28	6	6	16	41	59	18
Heriot-Watt University	28	5	1	22	32	95	11
Edinburgh University	28	4	3	21	39	87	11

1986-87

Vale of Leithen	34	24	7	3	114	38	55
Kelso United	34	23	5	6	84	38	51
Gala Fairydean	34	23	4	7	104	38	50
Whitehill Welfare	34	21	8	5	70	28	50
Spartans	34	21	6	7	75	31	48
Edinburgh City	34	19	7	8	85	35	45
Civil Service Strollers	34	18	7	9	77	38	43
Hawick Royal Albert	34	16	4	14	57	54	36
Pencaitland	34	13	7	14	55	49	33
Craigroyston	34	16	1	17	62	61	33
Berwick Rangers Reserves	34	13	7	14	45	47	33
Selkirk	34	8	11	15	57	85	27
Eyemouth United	34	10	6	18	57	68	26
Peebles Rovers	34	10	6	18	51	78	26
Easthouses Miners Welfare	34	8	7	19	41	67	23
Heriot-Watt University	34	6	5	23	33	101	17
Edinburgh University	34	6	3	25	39	95	15
Coldstream	34	0	1	33	17	172	1

1987-88

Premier Division

Whitehill Welfare	18	9	7	2	41	17	25
Vale of Leithen	18	8	6	4	43	32	22
Gala Fairydean	18	8	6	4	26	15	22
Civil Service Strollers	18	10	2	6	27	21	22
Kelso United	18	6	8	4	32	25	20
Edinburgh City	18	6	6	6	25	32	18
Craigroyston	18	6	4	8	25	31	16
Spartans	18	5	5	8	23	22	15
Hawick Royal Albert	18	4	4	10	17	43	12
Pencaitland	18	3	2	13	18	39	8

First Division

Annan Athletic	18	12	5	1	57	33	29
Eyemouth United	18	11	3	4	46	22	25
Peebles Rovers	18	10	4	4	39	27	24
Coldstream	18	8	6	4	36	24	22
Berwick Rangers Reserves	18	7	6	5	27	23	20
Easthouses Miners Welfare	18	6	6	6	28	32	18
Tollcross United	18	7	3	8	32	34	17
Edinburgh University	18	4	2	12	18	42	10
Selkirk	18	2	5	11	23	44	9
Heriot-Watt University	18	2	2	14	19	44	6

1988-89

Premier Division

Gala Fairydean	18	10	5	3	39	23	25
Civil Service Strollers	18	7	8	3	35	26	22
Whitehill Welfare	18	7	7	4	34	31	21
Eyemouth United	18	9	2	7	35	43	20
Spartans	18	7	5	6	32	27	19
Craigroyston	18	7	4	7	29	32	18
Kelso United	18	5	6	7	20	22	16
Annan Athletic	18	5	4	9	29	35	14
Edinburgh City	18	3	7	8	25	36	13
Vale of Leithen	18	4	4	10	21	24	12

First Division

Peebles Rovers	18	10	5	3	31	16	25
Berwick Rangers Reserves	18	10	5	3	35	21	25
Pencaitland	18	10	2	6	45	39	22
Hawick Royal Albert	18	8	5	5	39	25	21
Easthouses Miners Welfare	18	8	4	6	30	29	20
Coldstream	18	6	5	7	25	27	17
Tollcross United	18	7	3	8	33	38	17
Selkirk	18	5	6	7	27	32	16
Edinburgh University	18	5	2	11	24	31	12
Heriot-Watt University	18	1	3	14	13	44	5

Easthouses Miners Welfare were renamed Easthouses Lily before the start of the next season.

1989-90

Premier Division

Annan Athletic	18	11	5	2	38	24	27
Civil Service Strollers	18	12	2	4	37	19	26
Gala Fairydean	18	9	3	6	31	28	21
Whitehill Welfare	18	7	7	4	29	30	21
Spartans	18	8	3	7	25	20	19
Peebles Rovers	18	3	11	4	24	25	17
Berwick Rangers Reserves	18	6	2	10	22	26	14
Craigroyston	18	4	5	9	19	23	13
Kelso United	18	3	7	8	18	30	13
Eyemouth United	18	3	3	12	18	36	9

First Division

Coldstream	18	12	3	3	36	18	27
Edinburgh City	18	11	4	3	43	17	26
Vale of Leithen	18	11	3	4	54	27	25
Easthouses Lily	18	10	5	3	43	27	25
Selkirk	18	8	4	6	35	31	20
Tollcross United	18	7	4	7	33	29	18
Hawick Royal Albert	18	5	5	8	28	38	15
Pencaitland	18	5	3	10	26	32	13
Edinburgh University	18	4	3	11	27	48	11
Heriot-Watt University	18	0	0	18	6	64	0

1990-91

Premier Division

Gala Fairydean	18	12	5	1	43	26	29
Whitehill Welfare	18	11	3	4	44	27	25
Edinburgh City	18	9	5	4	34	21	23
Spartans	18	6	6	6	23	19	18
Berwick Rangers Reserves	18	6	6	6	32	31	18
Coldstream	18	7	2	9	32	26	16
Annan Athletic	18	5	5	8	35	45	15
Craigroyston	18	5	5	8	29	43	15
Civil Service Strollers	18	5	4	9	24	25	14
Peebles Rovers	18	2	3	13	20	53	7

First Division

Easthouses Lily	18	12	6	0	48	18	30
Vale of Leithen	18	11	2	5	50	28	24
Eyemouth United	18	9	6	3	37	26	24
Hawick Royal Albert	18	9	5	4	42	35	23
Pencaitland	18	8	6	4	31	20	22
Selkirk	18	9	4	5	36	34	22
Kelso United	18	5	2	11	18	45	12
Tollcross United	18	5	1	12	33	34	11
Edinburgh University	18	5	1	12	27	39	11
Heriot-Watt University	18	0	1	17	7	50	1

1991-92

Premier Division

Team							
Easthouses Lily	16	13	1	2	44	25	27
Whitehill Welfare	16	11	2	3	50	22	24
Vale of Leithen	16	9	3	4	34	23	21
Gala Fairydean	16	8	1	7	34	30	17
Craigroyston	16	6	4	6	27	23	16
Edinburgh City	16	4	4	8	24	32	12
Coldstream	16	4	4	8	21	45	12
Spartans	16	3	4	9	18	26	10
Annan Athletic	16	1	3	12	17	43	5

First Division

Team							
Manor Thistle	20	16	2	2	39	9	34
Tollcross United	20	15	1	4	49	23	31
Selkirk	20	12	2	6	50	36	26
Kelso United	20	8	5	7	37	28	21
Hawick Royal Albert	20	8	5	7	45	40	21
Pencaitland	20	7	5	8	26	31	19
Civil Service Strollers	20	7	4	9	42	38	18
Peebles Rovers	20	7	3	10	29	47	17
Eyemouth United	20	5	2	13	26	56	12
Heriot-Watt University	20	4	3	13	22	44	11
Edinburgh University	20	3	4	13	31	44	10

1992-93

Premier Division

Team							
Whitehill Welfare	18	10	7	1	46	23	27
Spartans	18	9	5	4	27	20	23
Gala Fairydean	18	9	4	5	27	20	22
Vale of Leithen	18	9	3	6	35	25	21
Edinburgh City	18	7	7	4	31	29	21
Easthouses Lily	18	4	9	5	27	33	17
Craigroyston	18	6	4	8	30	27	16
Manor Thistle	18	4	7	7	29	33	15
Tollcross United	18	3	7	8	27	34	13
Coldstream	18	0	5	13	17	52	5

First Division

Team							
Civil Service Strollers	18	11	4	3	46	21	26
Annan Athletic	18	12	2	4	38	27	26
Hawick Royal Albert	18	11	3	4	53	29	25
Kelso United	18	9	5	4	43	26	23
Edinburgh University	18	8	6	4	37	20	22
Pencaitland	18	7	7	4	29	20	21
Peebles Rovers	18	5	3	10	16	45	13
Selkirk	18	3	4	11	31	49	10
Heriot-Watt University	18	3	3	12	26	44	9
Eyemouth United	18	1	3	14	25	63	5

1993-94

Premier Division

Team							
Whitehill Welfare	18	13	4	1	58	17	30
Vale of Leithen	18	9	3	6	36	29	21
Gala Fairydean	18	7	5	6	28	18	19
Craigroyston	18	7	5	6	23	22	19
Annan Athletic	18	7	5	6	31	34	19
Spartans	18	6	6	6	30	30	18
Civil Service Strollers	18	7	3	8	29	35	17
Easthouses Lily	17	5	5	7	19	29	15
Manor Thistle	17	4	4	9	21	39	12
Edinburgh City	18	4	0	14	22	44	8

First Division

Team							
Tollcross United	18	14	3	1	80	17	31
Edinburgh University	18	11	5	2	54	21	27
Kelso United	18	9	4	5	37	23	22
Selkirk	18	9	4	5	35	25	22
Heriot-Watt University	18	7	5	6	28	34	19
Pencaitland	18	6	6	6	20	16	18
Coldstream	18	6	4	8	30	36	16
Peebles Rovers	18	3	4	11	17	35	10
Hawick Royal Albert	18	4	1	13	34	63	9
Eyemouth United	18	1	4	13	16	51	6

1994-95

Premier Division

Team							
Whitehill Welfare	18	13	4	1	55	18	30
Gala Fairydean	18	10	8	0	31	12	28
Annan Athletic	18	10	1	7	34	29	21
Civil Service Strollers	18	10	1	7	33	30	21
Craigroyston	18	7	5	6	35	35	19
Vale of Leithen	18	7	3	8	36	30	17
Spartans	18	5	7	6	22	21	17
Edinburgh University	18	5	6	7	33	35	16
Easthouses Lily	18	4	2	12	26	52	10
Tollcross United	18	0	1	17	12	55	1

First Division

Team							
Pencaitland	20	12	4	4	39	24	28
Preston Athletic	20	11	5	4	41	26	27
Hawick Royal Albert	20	10	4	6	38	29	24
Heriot-Watt University	20	8	7	5	34	31	23
Coldstream	20	9	4	7	44	41	22
Selkirk	20	9	1	10	61	56	19
Manor Thistle	20	7	3	10	35	32	17
Edinburgh City	20	7	3	10	34	41	17
Kelso United	20	6	4	10	35	43	16
Peebles Rovers	20	5	4	11	31	54	14
Eyemouth United	20	4	5	11	28	43	13

1995-96

Premier Division

Team							
Whitehill Welfare	18	16	0	2	71	14	48
Gala Fairydean	18	10	4	4	37	25	34
Annan Athletic	18	9	6	3	41	30	33
Spartans	18	8	2	8	24	32	26
Craigroyston	18	6	4	8	33	37	22
Pencaitland	18	5	6	7	25	28	21
Preston Athletic	18	4	7	7	29	42	19
Edinburgh University	18	3	6	9	18	31	15
Vale of Leithen	18	3	6	9	28	50	15
Civil Service Strollers	18	3	5	10	24	41	14

First Division

Team							
Edinburgh City	22	14	5	3	67	33	47
Manor Thistle	22	14	4	4	58	29	46
Lothian Thistle	22	12	3	7	46	34	39
Peebles Rovers	22	11	3	8	46	38	36
Easthouses Lily	22	11	3	8	58	51	36
Selkirk	22	10	4	8	44	42	34
Tollcross United	22	9	4	9	41	40	31
Eyemouth United	22	8	3	11	40	55	27
Hawick Royal Albert	22	7	5	10	45	50	26
Kelso United	22	7	2	13	31	50	23
Coldstream	22	3	8	11	30	47	17
Heriot-Watt University	22	3	2	17	32	69	11

Manor Thistle were renamed Edinburgh Athletic.

1996-97

Premier Division

Spartans	18	11	5	2	36	17	38
Whitehill Welfare	18	10	6	2	44	18	36
Gala Fairydean	18	10	2	6	31	27	32
Edinburgh Athletic	18	7	5	6	29	26	26
Annan Athletic	18	7	4	7	31	29	25
Edinburgh City	18	7	4	7	40	39	25
Pencaitland	18	6	4	8	21	26	22
Craigroyston	18	6	4	8	23	31	22
Preston Athletic	18	5	6	7	21	23	21
Edinburgh University	18	0	2	16	10	50	2

First Division

Lothian Thistle	22	17	3	2	68	21	54
Civil Service Strollers	22	15	5	2	46	22	50
Selkirk	22	11	5	6	49	36	38
Hawick Royal Albert	22	11	3	8	57	59	36
Peebles Rovers	22	10	4	8	50	35	34
Vale of Leithen	22	10	4	8	54	45	34
Coldstream	22	10	3	9	42	35	33
Tollcross United	22	8	7	7	41	34	31
Kelso United	22	9	3	10	38	50	30
Easthouses Lily	22	5	3	14	27	47	18
Eyemouth United	22	1	6	15	30	63	6
Heriot-Watt University	22	1	2	19	28	83	5

Eyemouth United had 3 points deducted.

1997-98

Premier Division

Whitehill Welfare	18	13	3	2	48	19	42
Spartans	18	8	5	5	37	26	29
Craigroyston	18	8	5	5	27	28	29
Annan Athletic	18	8	4	6	44	28	28
Edinburgh City	18	8	4	6	31	23	28
Civil Service Strollers	18	8	3	7	30	31	27
Lothian Thistle	18	5	7	6	25	36	22
Pencaitland	18	5	6	7	27	28	21
Gala Fairydean	18	6	3	9	24	39	21
Edinburgh Athletic	18	0	2	16	19	54	2

First Division

Peebles Rovers	22	14	4	4	44	22	46
Tollcross United	22	13	7	2	40	20	46
Coldstream	22	12	5	5	46	25	41
Preston Athletic	22	12	4	6	43	25	40
Edinburgh University	22	9	8	5	31	25	35
Kelso United	22	8	6	8	44	41	30
Vale of Leithen	22	8	5	9	46	37	29
Easthouses Lily	22	7	6	9	27	29	27
Hawick Royal Albert	22	6	7	9	38	42	25
Selkirk	22	5	8	9	33	49	23
Heriot-Watt University	22	4	2	16	25	56	14
Eyemouth United	22	2	2	18	18	64	8

1998-99

Premier Division

Whitehill Welfare	18	14	3	1	43	15	45
Spartans	18	13	4	1	42	16	43
Annan Athletic	18	11	4	3	39	26	37
Civil Service Strollers	18	9	2	7	31	34	29
Edinburgh City	18	6	5	7	23	26	23
Lothian Thistle	18	5	7	6	32	28	22
Craigroyston	18	5	3	10	29	39	18
Peebles Rovers	18	3	6	9	28	38	15
Tollcross United	18	2	3	13	14	32	9
Pencaitland	18	2	3	13	14	41	9

First Division

Easthouses Lily	24	16	7	1	45	20	55
Vale of Leithen	24	15	5	4	65	34	50
Coldstream	24	13	7	4	54	29	46
Threave Rovers	24	14	3	7	73	39	45
Preston Athletic	24	12	8	4	51	29	44
Hawick Royal Albert	24	9	6	9	49	52	33
Edinburgh University	24	8	8	8	38	39	32
Gala Fairydean	24	9	4	11	37	33	31
Selkirk	24	7	4	13	45	65	25
Edinburgh Athletic	24	6	6	12	31	52	24
Heriot-Watt University	24	5	5	14	31	50	20
Kelso United	24	4	4	16	33	62	16

1999-2000

Premier Division

Annan Athletic	22	15	6	1	62	21	51
Whitehill Welfare	22	15	5	2	59	13	50
Spartans	22	14	5	3	62	31	47
Lothian Thistle	22	11	4	7	45	32	37
Vale of Leithen	22	11	3	8	50	42	36
Edinburgh City	22	9	5	8	42	39	32
Civil Service Strollers	22	9	3	10	42	47	30
Coldstream	22	7	4	11	34	40	25
Craigroyston	22	8	1	13	29	53	25
Easthouses Lily	22	6	2	14	27	50	20
Peebles Rovers	22	6	1	15	29	56	19
Tollcross United	22	1	1	20	19	76	4

First Division

Threave Rovers	20	15	3	2	55	26	48
Gala Fairydean	20	13	3	4	41	21	42
Kelso United	20	10	3	7	30	31	33
Preston Athletic	20	12	2	6	58	29	32
Edinburgh University	20	11	2	7	39	22	32
Eyemouth United	20	8	3	9	27	44	27
Pencaitland & Ormiston	20	7	4	9	24	29	25
Hawick Royal Albert	20	6	4	10	32	38	22
Heriot-Watt University	20	4	4	12	26	42	16
Edinburgh Athletic	20	5	1	14	20	44	16
Selkirk	20	3	3	14	29	55	12

Preston Athletic had 6 points deducted after fielding an ineligible player.

Edinburgh City had 3 points deducted for failing to produce medical certificates for a game which they called off.

Pencaitland merged with Ormiston Primrose during 1999 to become Pencaitland & Ormiston

2000-01

Premier Division

Annan Athletic	22	13	6	3	48	26	45
Whitehill Welfare	22	13	5	4	47	18	44
Threave Rovers	22	11	6	5	39	28	39
Spartans	22	10	8	4	45	31	38
Craigroyston	22	9	5	8	30	28	32
Edinburgh City	22	8	6	8	37	40	30
Lothian Thistle	22	7	6	9	30	30	27
Vale of Leithen	22	7	3	12	34	42	24
Coldstream	22	7	3	12	28	42	24
Gala Fairydean	22	7	3	12	29	45	24
Civil Service Strollers	22	7	2	13	35	43	23
Easthouses Lily	22	5	3	14	21	50	18

First Division

Pencaitland & Ormiston	20	13	4	3	43	16	43
Edinburgh University	20	12	6	2	35	11	42
Peebles Rovers	20	9	7	4	44	26	34
Hawick Royal Albert	20	8	5	7	41	40	29
Edinburgh Athletic	20	9	2	9	28	33	29
Preston Athletic	20	8	4	8	33	29	28
Eyemouth United	20	8	3	9	30	47	27
Tollcross United	20	5	7	8	25	28	22
Kelso United	20	6	3	11	32	38	21
Selkirk	20	5	2	13	30	49	17
Heriot-Watt University	20	3	5	12	23	47	14

2001-02

Premier Division

Spartans	22	18	3	1	61	16	57
Whitehill Welfare	22	16	4	2	49	16	52
Annan Athletic	22	11	3	8	53	40	36
Threave Rovers	22	10	3	9	40	36	33
Vale of Leithen	22	9	6	7	32	33	33
Edinburgh City	22	8	4	10	35	36	28
Lothian Thistle	22	8	3	11	38	43	27
Craigroyston	22	7	5	10	38	35	26
Coldstream	22	6	7	9	42	52	25
Gala Fairydean	22	6	5	11	24	48	23
Pencaitland & Ormiston	22	4	5	13	28	52	17
Edinburgh University	22	4	2	16	22	55	14

First Division

Preston Athletic	22	17	2	3	63	27	53
Peebles Rovers	22	15	5	2	58	23	50
Easthouses Lily	22	12	3	7	45	38	39
Kelso United	22	11	3	8	50	42	36
Dalbeattie Star	22	10	6	6	42	39	36
Eyemouth United	22	11	2	9	40	39	35
Civil Service Strollers	22	11	0	11	49	34	33
Edinburgh Athletic	22	8	5	9	39	44	29
Tollcross United	22	6	3	13	35	48	21
Selkirk	22	4	6	12	35	47	18
Heriot-Watt University	22	6	0	16	26	54	18
Hawick Royal Albert	22	2	3	17	21	68	9

2002-03

Premier Division

Whitehill Welfare	22	14	6	2	55	18	48
Annan Athletic	22	14	2	6	59	32	44
Spartans	22	13	4	5	71	38	43
Gala Fairydean	22	12	5	5	55	42	41
Threave Rovers	22	11	4	7	51	37	37
Craigroyston	22	10	3	9	47	49	33
Lothian Thistle	22	8	5	9	32	41	29
Edinburgh City	22	8	4	10	36	40	28
Preston Athletic	22	8	3	11	37	46	27
Vale of Leithen	22	5	4	13	38	57	19
Coldstream	22	5	4	13	36	65	19
Peebles Rovers	22	1	2	19	23	75	5

First Division

Edinburgh University	22	17	0	5	56	27	51
Civil Service Strollers	22	13	3	6	52	26	42
Dalbeattie Star	22	11	7	4	53	32	40
Kelso United	22	11	5	6	48	33	38
Edinburgh Athletic	22	10	7	5	37	23	37
Heriot-Watt University	22	10	5	7	46	42	35
Pencaitland & Ormiston	22	7	5	10	27	33	26
Selkirk	22	7	5	10	44	52	26
Hawick Royal Albert	22	6	7	9	36	40	25
Easthouses Lily	22	5	7	10	32	44	22
Tollcross United	22	4	5	13	28	46	17
Eyemouth United	22	1	4	17	22	83	7

Pencaitland & Ormiston were renamed Ormiston before the start of the next season.

2003-04

Premier Division

Spartans	22	15	6	1	60	25	51
Edinburgh City	22	14	4	4	56	29	46
Threave Rovers	22	10	7	5	44	28	37
Annan Athletic	22	11	4	7	49	45	37
Gala Fairydean	22	9	4	9	34	38	31
Edinburgh University	22	8	6	8	32	30	30
Civil Service Strollers	22	9	2	11	43	38	29
Preston Athletic	22	8	4	10	34	36	28
Lothian Thistle	22	6	3	13	24	45	21
Whitehill Welfare	22	5	5	12	38	51	20
Vale of Leithen	22	4	7	11	35	56	19
Craigroyston	22	5	4	13	29	57	19

First Division

Kelso United	22	15	3	4	52	29	48
Dalbeattie Star	22	14	4	4	76	35	46
Ormiston	22	14	4	4	49	27	46
Heriot-Watt University	22	12	3	7	56	34	39
Easthouses Lily	22	11	5	6	49	28	38
Peebles Rovers	22	10	6	6	53	44	36
Edinburgh Athletic	22	9	6	7	42	34	33
Selkirk	22	9	5	8	40	35	32
Coldstream	22	4	5	13	33	58	17
Hawick Royal Albert	22	4	4	14	24	61	16
Tollcross United	22	3	2	17	24	55	11
Eyemouth United	22	2	3	17	21	79	9

2004-05

Premier Division

Spartans	20	18	1	1	74	17	55
Annan Athletic	20	15	1	4	66	29	46
Edinburgh University	20	10	5	5	37	26	35
Whitehill Welfare	20	8	7	5	37	35	31
Lothian Thistle	20	6	5	9	36	44	23
Preston Athletic	20	6	5	9	25	36	23
Edinburgh City	20	5	7	8	35	40	22
Dalbeattie Star	20	4	8	8	24	41	20
Civil Service Strollers	20	6	2	12	27	46	20
Kelso United	20	3	6	11	27	49	15
Gala Fairydean	20	3	5	12	25	50	13

Gala Fairydean had 1 point deducted.

First Division

Easthouses Lily	22	15	3	4	55	15	48
Heriot-Watt University	22	13	5	4	64	31	44
Selkirk	22	13	5	4	48	28	44
Edinburgh Athletic	22	11	7	4	48	15	40
Vale of Leithen	22	11	5	6	53	32	38
Craigroyston	22	11	4	7	57	38	37
Ormiston	22	8	10	4	50	21	34
Peebles Rovers	22	10	4	8	37	42	34
Hawick Royal Albert	22	5	4	13	31	66	19
Coldstream	22	5	3	14	39	70	18
Tollcross United	22	2	4	16	22	67	10
Eyemouth United	22	0	2	20	9	88	-1

Eyemouth United had 3 points deducted.

Tollcross United and Tynecastle merged and continued to play under the Tynecastle name.

2005-06

Premier Division

Edinburgh City	22	12	7	3	44	27	43
Heriot-Watt University	22	13	2	7	54	35	41
Lothian Thistle	22	11	6	5	49	30	39
Spartans	22	10	7	5	39	19	37
Whitehill Welfare	22	10	7	5	40	24	37
Annan Athletic	22	11	4	7	37	31	37
Preston Athletic	22	9	5	8	30	32	32
Edinburgh University	22	6	5	11	25	28	23
Easthouses Lily	22	7	4	11	24	37	19
Civil Service Strollers	22	4	7	11	23	44	19
Dalbeattie Star	22	4	5	13	28	51	17
Kelso United	22	4	3	15	18	53	15

Easthouses Lily had 6 points deducted

First Division

Craigroyston	20	14	5	1	42	18	47
Selkirk	20	10	7	3	38	21	37
Edinburgh Athletic	20	8	7	5	36	30	31
Vale of Leithen	20	7	8	5	41	35	29
Ormiston	20	8	3	9	34	41	27
Coldstream	20	8	3	9	31	40	27
Peebles Rovers	20	6	7	7	38	39	25
Eyemouth United	20	7	3	10	34	37	24
Tynecastle	20	7	3	10	31	40	24
Gala Fairydean	20	4	5	11	32	41	17
Hawick Royal Albert	20	3	5	12	38	53	14

Peebles Rovers merged with local amateur teams to form Peebles FC, who continued to play in the league.

2006-07

Premier Division

Annan Athletic	22	17	3	2	64	18	54
Spartans	22	16	4	2	63	19	52
Whitehill Welfare	22	12	5	5	43	28	41
Edinburgh University	22	11	4	7	41	32	37
Edinburgh City	22	9	8	5	33	20	35
Preston Athletic	22	9	6	7	30	30	33
Easthouses Lily	22	9	2	11	38	40	29
Lothian Thistle	22	8	3	11	38	55	27
Craigroyston	22	6	4	12	34	52	22
Selkirk	22	3	7	12	30	40	16
Heriot-Watt University	22	4	3	15	28	62	15
Civil Service Strollers	22	2	3	17	24	70	9

First Division

Dalbeattie Star	20	16	3	1	62	18	51
Coldstream	20	12	4	4	53	29	40
Vale of Leithen	20	10	4	6	64	28	34
Gala Fairydean	20	9	4	7	43	33	31
Tynecastle	20	8	6	6	35	31	30
Edinburgh Athletic	20	8	3	9	28	37	27
Peebles	20	6	7	7	30	30	25
Kelso United	20	7	3	10	28	24	24
Eyemouth United	20	7	2	11	28	59	23
Ormiston	20	5	5	10	26	36	20
Hawick Royal Albert	20	1	1	18	17	89	4

2007-08

Premier Division

Whitehill Welfare	22	15	2	4	59	23	50
Edinburgh University	22	15	4	3	41	14	49
Spartans	22	14	5	3	57	23	47
Edinburgh City	22	12	4	6	50	34	40
Preston Athletic	22	11	7	4	41	28	40
Dalbeattie Star	22	11	2	9	45	37	35
Annan Athletic	22	7	7	8	40	33	28
Lothian Thistle	22	7	5	10	30	44	26
Easthouses Lily	22	6	2	14	31	50	20
Coldstream	22	5	4	13	28	65	19
Selkirk	22	3	3	16	22	44	12
Craigroyston	22	2	1	19	21	70	7

First Division

Heriot-Watt University	22	16	2	4	53	21	50
Peebles	22	15	2	5	53	17	47
Tynecastle	22	13	5	4	46	20	44
Civil Service Strollers	22	14	2	6	47	31	44
Gala Fairydean	22	11	4	7	51	40	37
Vale of Leithen	22	10	4	8	39	34	34
Kelso United	22	10	1	11	39	42	31
Berwick Rangers Reserves	22	7	2	13	29	37	23
Eyemouth United	22	7	2	13	28	56	20
Hawick Royal Albert	22	5	3	14	26	71	18
Ormiston	22	3	5	14	19	43	14
Edinburgh Athletic	22	3	4	15	27	45	13

Edinburgh Athletic faced the prospect of having to re-apply for admission to the League due to maladministration. However, they merged with amateur club Leith Athletic, and were allowed to retain their place, taking the name of the latter, whilst still playing at their own ground.

2008-09

Premier Division

Spartans	22	16	4	2	73	26	52
Dalbeattie Star	22	14	4	4	61	26	46
Lothian Thistle	22	11	3	8	46	26	36
Edinburgh University	22	8	8	6	37	19	32
Whitehill Welfare	22	8	8	6	38	28	32
Preston Athletic	22	9	5	8	36	31	32
Heriot-Watt University	22	9	3	10	33	31	30
Edinburgh City	22	8	5	9	45	34	29
Coldstream	22	8	5	9	30	30	29
Selkirk	22	8	3	11	19	55	27
Easthouses Lily	22	7	2	13	40	40	23
Peebles	22	1	0	21	12	124	3

First Division

Tynecastle	22	17	3	2	58	22	54
Civil Service Strollers	22	15	1	6	48	29	46
Stirling University	22	13	5	4	50	21	44
Gretna 2008	22	13	5	4	50	22	44
Craigroyston	22	12	3	7	47	34	39
Gala Fairydean	22	10	4	8	45	37	31
Vale of Leithen	22	9	4	9	41	37	31
Leith Athletic	22	8	4	10	44	34	28
Ormiston	22	6	2	14	30	61	20
Eyemouth United	22	5	2	15	33	47	17
Kelso United	22	4	5	13	28	48	17
Hawick Royal Albert	22	0	2	20	15	97	2

2009-10

Premier Division

Spartans	20	17	1	2	63	18	52
Whitehill Welfare	20	12	1	7	30	22	37
Lothian Thistle	20	11	3	6	46	25	36
Tynecastle	20	9	6	5	40	32	33
Civil Service Strollers	20	9	6	5	27	26	33
Heriot Watt University	20	10	0	10	42	45	30
Edinburgh City	20	9	1	10	37	39	28
Edinburgh University	20	6	5	9	21	25	23
Preston Athletic	20	5	2	13	27	39	17
Selkirk	20	4	3	13	28	56	15
Coldstream	20	3	2	15	28	62	11

First Division

Stirling University	22	19	2	1	75	16	59
Vale of Leithen	22	19	2	1	63	18	59
Craigroyston	22	14	3	5	57	23	45
Gretna 2008	22	13	4	5	53	20	43
Leith Athletic	22	11	5	6	68	33	38
Easthouses Lily	22	7	6	9	41	38	27
Gala Fairydean	22	8	2	12	42	44	26
Kelso United	22	6	5	11	32	44	23
Ormiston	22	7	0	15	28	54	21
Eyemouth United	22	4	7	11	37	51	19
Peebles	22	3	1	18	23	107	10
Hawick Royal Albert	22	1	3	18	20	91	6

2010-11

Premier Division

Spartans	22	17	4	1	62	18	55
Stirling University	22	12	5	5	58	28	41
Lothian Thistle	22	10	4	8	40	36	34
Whitehill Welfare	22	9	5	8	32	29	32
Edinburgh University	22	8	8	6	27	26	32
Edinburgh City	22	6	13	3	32	30	31
Vale of Leithen	22	7	9	6	30	29	30
Civil Service Strollers	22	8	5	9	29	37	29
Tynecastle	22	6	6	10	32	35	24
Selkirk	22	4	5	13	31	54	17
Preston Athletic	22	4	5	13	30	61	17
Heriot-Watt University	22	3	7	12	27	47	16

First Division

Gretna 2008	22	19	1	2	85	18	58
Leith Athletic	22	18	2	2	79	24	56
Eyemouth United	22	12	4	6	62	49	40
Gala Fairydean	22	11	4	7	54	49	37
Easthouses Lily	22	10	5	7	45	33	32
Craigroyston	22	8	6	8	42	36	30
Peebles Rovers	22	9	3	10	36	58	30
Berwick Rangers Reserves	22	8	2	12	43	50	26
Coldstream	22	7	2	13	34	48	23
Kelso United	22	4	8	10	40	52	23
Ormiston	22	2	7	13	25	49	13
Hawick Royal Albert	22	1	2	19	17	96	5

2011-12

Premier Division

Stirling University	22	16	3	3	74	32	51
Spartans	22	16	3	3	66	28	51
Whitehill Welfare	22	12	3	7	45	34	39
Edinburgh University	22	10	3	9	38	26	33
Edinburgh City	22	10	3	9	41	39	33
Gretna 2008	22	9	6	7	40	46	33
Civil Service Strollers	22	10	1	11	38	46	31
Vale of Leithen	22	9	1	12	49	47	28
Tynecastle	22	8	3	11	33	52	27
Lothian Thistle Hutchison Vale	22	6	3	13	36	50	21
Leith Athletic	22	5	4	13	32	59	19
Selkirk	22	3	3	16	24	57	12

First Division

Heriot-Watt University	24	17	4	3	61	25	55
Preston Athletic	24	14	6	4	73	35	48
Gala Fairydean	24	15	3	6	55	31	48
Eyemouth United	24	14	5	5	63	42	47
Craigroyston	24	10	8	6	37	33	38
Duns	24	10	6	8	48	39	36
Coldstream	24	11	3	10	51	53	36
Kelso United	24	8	4	12	43	54	28
Ormiston	24	8	2	14	27	56	26
Berwick Rangers	24	5	8	11	53	64	23
Peebles	24	3	9	12	28	48	18
Easthouses Lily	24	3	8	13	37	59	17
Hawick Royal Albert	24	3	4	17	24	61	13

2012-13

Premier Division

Whitehill Welfare	22	18	1	3	53	21	55
Stirling University	22	15	2	5	54	22	47
Spartans	22	14	4	4	44	23	46
Gretna 2008	22	9	7	6	34	25	34
Edinburgh City	22	9	3	10	31	32	30
Lothian Thistle Hutchison Vale	22	8	3	11	35	38	27
Preston Athletic	22	7	3	12	41	55	24
Civil Service Strollers	22	7	3	12	30	56	24
Vale of Leithen	22	5	8	9	41	49	23
Heriot-Watt University	22	6	5	11	21	37	23
Edinburgh University	22	4	8	10	26	40	20
Tynecastle	22	5	3	14	41	53	18

At the end of the season, Whitehill Welfare and Spartans both left to join the newly-formed Lowland Football League.

First Division

Craigroyston	26	21	2	3	77	29	65
Coldstream	26	18	5	3	80	25	59
Leith Athletic	26	18	3	5	88	38	57
Berwick Rangers	26	15	4	7	74	46	49
Eyemouth United	26	15	3	8	70	59	48
Easthouses Lily	26	14	3	9	69	63	45
Gala Fairydean	26	12	3	11	56	69	39
Kelso United	26	9	6	11	59	62	33
Selkirk	26	8	4	14	34	49	28
Duns	26	6	6	14	43	56	24
Ormiston	26	6	5	15	46	53	23
Peebles	26	6	5	15	36	76	23
Burntisland Shipyard	26	3	5	18	34	84	14
Hawick Royal Albert	26	2	4	20	32	89	10

At the end of the season, Edinburgh City, Gretna 2008, Preston Athletic, Stirling University and Vale of Leithen all left to join the newly-formed Lowland Football League.

2013-14

Premier Division

Lothian Thistle Hutchison Vale	18	15	1	2	46	16	46
Stirling University Reserves	18	10	2	6	35	34	32
Craigroyston	18	9	4	5	36	22	31
Tynecastle	18	9	1	8	45	40	28
Edinburgh University	18	5	8	5	30	25	23
Spartans Reserves	18	6	5	7	30	28	23
Leith Athletic	18	6	5	7	35	36	23
Coldstream	18	6	2	10	23	35	20
Civil Service Strollers	18	5	1	12	25	51	16
Heriot-Watt University	18	3	3	12	19	37	12

At the end of the season, Edinburgh University left to join the Lowland Football League.

First Division

Hibernian Colts	18	15	1	2	72	16	46
Easthouses Lily	18	13	3	2	54	19	42
Berwick Rangers Reserves	18	11	0	7	42	27	33
Peebles	18	7	4	7	35	37	25
Kelso United	18	6	4	8	28	38	22
Burntisland Shipyard	18	6	3	9	24	43	21
Hawick Royal Albert	18	6	1	11	29	44	19
Duns	18	5	3	10	29	46	18
Ormiston	18	6	0	12	27	48	18
Eyemouth United	18	4	3	11	31	53	15

2014-15

Premier Division

Lothian Thistle Hutchison Vale	24	16	4	4	70	36	52
Easthouses Lily	24	16	4	4	65	42	52
Leith Athletic	24	14	5	5	62	33	47
Tynecastle	24	9	7	8	48	41	34
Civil Service Strollers	24	9	6	9	45	42	33
Spartans Reserves	24	9	5	10	44	46	32
Stirling University Reserves	24	5	4	15	36	59	19
Craigroyston	24	4	6	14	29	59	18
Coldstream	24	2	7	15	35	76	13

First Division

Peebles Rovers	28	22	4	2	85	29	70
Heriot-Watt University	28	17	5	6	74	34	56
Duns	28	17	4	7	84	54	55
Ormiston	28	16	1	11	63	60	49
Burntisland Shipyard	28	12	7	9	64	47	43
Eyemouth United	28	7	0	21	46	90	21
Kelso United	28	4	3	21	27	73	15
Hawick Royal Albert	28	4	2	22	30	86	14

At the end of the season, the league was merged into a single division.

2015-16

Leith Athletic	28	24	0	4	103	23	72
Lothian Thistle Hutchison Vale	28	20	3	5	99	42	63
Civil Service Strollers	28	18	1	9	74	49	55
Tynecastle	28	16	4	8	72	71	52
Hawick Royal Albert	28	15	3	10	70	50	48
Peebles Rovers	28	13	4	11	57	60	43
Spartans	28	14	2	12	67	61	41
Ormiston	28	12	5	11	70	70	41
Stirling University	28	10	5	13	65	55	35
Heriot Watt University	28	9	6	13	61	65	33
Coldstream	28	10	2	16	63	87	32
Craigroyston	28	10	2	16	48	74	32
Burntisland Shipyard	28	8	3	17	43	67	27
Duns	28	4	2	22	46	88	14
Eyemouth United	28	5	2	21	39	115	11

Eyemouth had 6 points deducted.
Spartans had 3 points deducted.
Kelso United resigned from the league after just three games and their record was expunged.

2016-17

Lothian Thistle Hutchison Vale	20	17	2	1	85	16	53
Leith Athletic	20	15	2	3	80	18	47
Tynecastle	20	14	1	5	56	26	43
Heriot-Watt University	20	12	3	5	61	30	39
Coldstream	20	9	4	7	39	51	31
Stirling University Reserves	20	9	3	8	55	36	30
Eyemouth United	20	7	2	11	34	53	23
Peebles Rovers	20	6	1	13	28	45	19
Ormiston	20	4	0	16	25	57	12
Tweedmouth Rangers	20	3	3	14	28	77	12
Burntisland Shipyard	20	3	1	16	12	94	10

Duns resigned their membership of the league and their results were expunged.

2017-18

Kelty Hearts	24	23	0	1	143	12	69
Lothian Thistle Hutchison Vale	24	22	1	1	97	20	67
Preston Athletic	24	16	3	5	74	36	51
Leith Athletic	24	15	4	5	80	41	49
Tynecastle	24	13	0	11	79	48	39
Heriot-Watt University	24	11	6	7	59	53	39
Peebles Rovers	24	12	2	10	59	73	38
Burntisland Shipyard	24	8	1	15	52	69	25
Stirling University Reserves	24	6	6	12	48	73	24
Coldstream	24	5	3	16	52	79	18
Eyemouth United	24	6	0	18	44	114	18
Ormiston	24	3	3	18	17	68	12
Tweedmouth Rangers	24	1	1	22	21	139	4

The league was increased from 13 to 39 teams for the next season, split into three parallel conferences, each containing 13 teams. The additional teams consisted of 24 clubs who applied to switch from the SJFA East Region, one from the SJFA West Region, one new team and Hawick Royal Albert who were relegated from the Lowland League.

2018-19

Conference A

Penicuik Athletic (Q)	24	20	3	1	92	15	63
Hill of Beath Hawthorn (Q)	24	20	2	2	99	17	62
Musselburgh Athletic (Q)	24	17	3	4	74	31	54
Newtongrange Star (Q)	24	14	5	5	79	32	47
Dunbar United (Q)	24	13	4	7	62	34	43
Leith Athletic	24	10	4	10	41	51	34
Coldstream	24	10	3	11	56	51	30
Easthouses Lily Miners Welfare	24	9	1	14	41	67	28
Oakley United	24	6	5	13	34	50	23
Arniston Rangers	24	7	2	15	34	71	23
Peebles Rovers	24	6	4	14	40	73	22
Hawick Royal Albert	24	4	1	19	21	86	13
Tweedmouth Rangers	24	1	1	22	20	115	4

Coldstream had 3points deducted for fielding an ineligible player.

Conference B

Bonnyrigg Rose Athletic (Q)	24	22	1	1	105	17	67
Bo'ness United (Q)	24	18	4	2	81	27	58
Tranent Juniors (Q)	24	16	2	6	81	37	50
Dundonald Bluebell (Q)	24	15	4	5	79	42	49
Crossgates Primrose (Q)	24	13	2	9	65	42	41
Sauchie Juniors (Q)	24	12	4	8	50	39	40
Lothian Thistle Hutchison Vale	24	10	3	11	43	47	33
Dalkeith Thistle	24	9	5	10	41	45	32
Haddington Athletic	24	9	4	11	72	54	31
Tynecastle	24	5	3	16	37	80	18
Burntisland Shipyard	24	5	1	18	39	87	16
Dunipace	24	4	3	17	32	66	15
Eyemouth United	24	0	0	24	21	163	-3

Eyemouth United had 3 points deducted for fielding an ineligible player.

Conference C

Broxburn Athletic (Q)	24	22	0	2	83	21	66
Linlithgow Rose (Q)	24	20	1	3	106	24	61
Jeanfield Swifts (Q)	24	17	4	3	91	30	55
Camelon Juniors (Q)	24	17	3	4	87	33	54
Blackburn United (Q)	24	10	2	12	61	59	32
Preston Athletic	24	9	5	10	50	57	32
Heriot-Watt University	24	9	3	12	42	53	30
St Andrews United	24	8	5	11	41	46	29
Stirling University Reserves	24	7	4	13	46	78	25
Craigroyston	24	7	1	16	28	79	22
Edinburgh United	24	5	2	17	34	69	17
Inverkeithing Hillfield Swifts	24	5	1	18	35	85	16
Ormiston	24	3	3	18	32	102	12

At the end of the season, the three conference winners took part in a three match round-robin competition to determine the league champion, and subject to meeting the required licensing criteria, promotion to the Lowland League.

Championship play-off

Penicuik Athletic vs Broxburn Athletic	3-2
Bonnyrigg Rose Athletic vs Penicuik Athletic	2-1
Broxburn Athletic vs Bonnyrigg Rose Athletic	2-3

Bonnyrigg Rose Athletic	2	2	0	0	5	3	6
Penicuik Athletic	2	1	0	1	4	4	3
Broxburn Athletic	2	0	0	2	4	6	0

Bonnyrigg Rose Athletic were crowned champions after winning both of their play-off matches. However, after their application for full Scottish FA membership was rejected as their ground did not meet grading requirements, it initially appeared that they would not be allowed promotion. However, floodlights were quickly built following an appeal and SFA Membership was granted so the club were duly promoted to the Lowland Football League for the next season.

The top 5 clubs in each conference, along with the best 6th placed team formed a new 16-team Premier Division for the next season. The remaining clubs were split between two 12-team First Division conferences.

2019-20

Premier Division

Bo'ness United	**21**	**14**	**5**	**2**	**42**	**22**	**47**	**2.24**
Hill of Beath Hawthorn	18	10	5	3	45	20	37	2.06
Broxburn Athletic	19	11	5	3	40	29	38	2.00
Tranent Juniors	20	10	4	6	37	25	34	1.70
Camelon Juniors	20	10	4	6	38	33	34	1.70
Jeanfield Swifts	16	8	2	6	36	28	26	1.63
Dundonald Bluebell	18	8	3	7	46	35	27	1.50
Penicuik Athletic	18	8	3	7	37	32	27	1.50
Linlithgow Rose	17	7	3	7	41	37	24	1.41
Musselburgh Athletic	21	8	3	10	42	42	27	1.29
Dunbar United	21	6	5	10	32	39	23	1.10
Crossgates Primrose	21	6	5	10	37	55	23	1.10
Sauchie Juniors	22	6	5	11	33	44	20	0.91
Blackburn United	20	5	3	12	22	44	18	0.90
Whitehill Welfare	18	4	4	10	20	35	16	0.89
Newtongrange Star	22	4	3	15	32	60	15	0.68

Hill of Beath Hawthorn were awarded 2 points and Sauchie Juniors deducted 3 points after Sauchie fielded a suspended player in their match on 27th July 2019.
Play was suspended during March 2020 due to the Covid-19 pandemic. With the season not being fully completed, a points per game formula was subsequently used to determine the final standings, with Bo'ness United declared champions and winning promotion to the Lowland League.
No teams were relegated from the Premier Division.

First Division – Conference A

Lothian Thistle Hutch. V.	**24**	**16**	**6**	**2**	**66**	**29**	**54**	**2.25**
Leith Athletic	25	16	5	4	67	29	53	2.12
Kinnoull	17	12	2	3	44	11	35	2.06
Dunipace	24	15	3	6	67	27	48	2.00
Heriot-Watt University	25	14	1	10	60	37	43	1.72
Haddington Athletic	24	13	2	9	65	35	41	1.71
St Andrews United	22	11	2	9	61	37	35	1.59
Oakley United	20	10	1	9	38	36	31	1.55
Burntisland Shipyard	20	8	5	7	59	43	29	1.45
Ormiston	19	3	4	12	24	68	13	0.68
Peebles Rovers	20	2	2	16	12	81	8	0.40
Craigroyston	25	0	3	22	24	122	3	0.12

Kinnoull had 3 points deducted for fielding a suspended player.

First Division – Conference B

Tynecastle	**23**	**21**	**2**	**0**	**125**	**22**	**65**	**2.83**
Inverkeithing Hill. Swifts	**20**	**15**	**0**	**5**	**56**	**30**	**45**	**2.25**
Glenrothes	21	13	2	6	56	39	41	1.95
Edinburgh United	20	11	2	7	59	39	35	1.75
Preston Athletic	21	10	4	7	50	34	34	1.62
Dalkeith Thistle	22	10	3	9	46	43	33	1.50
Coldstream	22	10	1	11	42	51	31	1.41
Stirling University Res.	25	7	2	16	44	83	23	0.92
Easthouses Lily M.W.	18	4	0	14	35	59	12	0.67
Tweedmouth Rangers	24	4	4	16	47	94	16	0.67
Hawick Royal Albert U.	25	4	3	18	37	90	15	0.60
Arniston Rangers	22	4	3	15	21	66	9	0.41

Arniston Rangers had 6 ponts deducted after fielding ineligible players.

The runners-up of First Division Conferences A and B would have played-off for a place in the Premier Division, or both have been promoted automatically if the Premier Division would otherwise have been short of 16 clubs. However, after the season was curtailed due to the COVID-19 pandemic, Lothian Thistle Hutchison Vale from Conference A and Tynecastle and Inverkeithing Hillfield Swifts from Conference B were all promoted.